Published by The Witte Museum
San Antonio, Texas

Distributed by Maverick Books, an imprint of Trinity University Press
San Antonio, Texas

Photography by Al Rendón, San Antonio, Texas.
Book design by Arturo Guzman, San Antonio, Texas.

Cover photo: *Tía Lupe* (1986)
Back photo: *Al Rendón* (2022) Abraham Aguillon Orsagh

ISBN 978-1-59534-286-7 [hardcover or paperback]

The Witte Museum and Trinity University Press strive to produce books using methods
and materials in an environmentally sensitive manner. We favor working with manufacturers
that practice sustainable management of all natural resources, produce paper using recycled
stock, and manage forests with the best possible practices for people, biodiversity, and
sustainability. The press is a member of the Green Press Initiative, a nonprofit program
dedicated to supporting publishers in their efforts to reduce their impacts on endangered
forests, climate change, and forest-dependent communities.

The paper used in this publication meets the minimum requirements of the American
National Standard for Information Sciences—Permanence of Paper for Printed Library
Materials, ANSI 39.48-1992.

Printing line

27 26 25 24 23 | 5 4 3 2 1

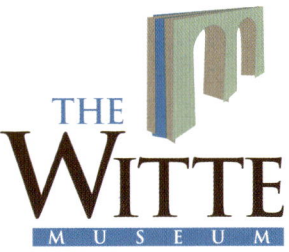

CONTENTS

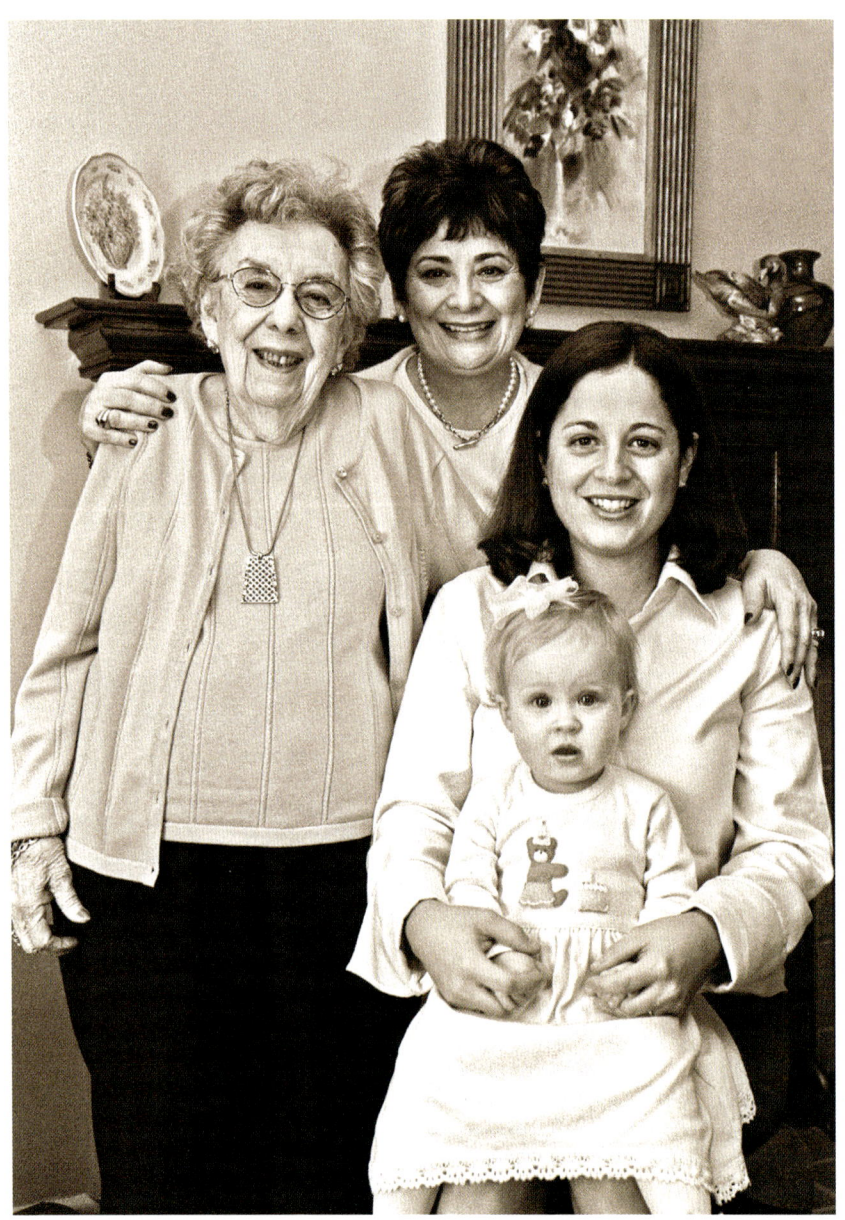

Maria de Jesus Rendón Showing Four Generations (2004)
San Antonio, Texas

DEDICATION

This book is dedicated to a few of the most important people in my life. To my Mom, Maria de Jesus Rendón, whose dedication to photographing all aspects of our family life as we grew up inspired me to document *Mi Cultura.*

To my Father, Enrique L. Rendón, who taught me the value of hard work and perseverance, encouraged me to pursue my dreams of being a photographic artist. He collaborated with me on several exhibits by producing hand carved wood frames for all my artwork.

To my Tía, Guadalupe Martinez Torres, in whose eyes I could do no wrong and who helped to raise me with her love and patience.

Finally to my wonderful wife and partner in life, Elizabeth Rendón, whose love and support has sustained me and given me the freedom to pursue my artwork.

I would also like to recognize and thank Billy Joe "Red" McCombs and his family for their generous support of my artistic endeavors over the years. Red was an inspiration to me and a mentor beginning with our first photographic session over forty years ago.

FOREWORD

by Marise McDermott
President and CEO, Witte Museum

It is with great joy and pride that in 2023, the Witte Museum presents the 50-year retrospective exhibition of Al Rendón's work: *Mi Cultura: Bringing Shadows into the Light: The Photography of Al Rendón* and produces this accompanying book of the same name. Al Rendón has been the visual narrator for the Witte Museum for decades. His photographs illustrating five Witte books, his photographic documentation of hundreds of artifacts, and his capture of Texas landscapes are part of the exhibitions, collections, and archives of the Witte. In 2002, the Witte hosted *Squeezebox: Accordion Communities in the United States,* featuring Al's photographs, and in 2008, *La Cultura Transciende Fronteras: A Personal Portrait of Tejanos and Mexicanos* featured photographs in frames hand-carved by Al's father, Enrique Rendón.

The Witte Museum welcomes hundreds of thousands of school children from throughout San Antonio and multi-generational families from throughout Texas. We are honored to provide access to all those who will experience the photographic grace and grit of Al Rendón's photographs. They will see themselves in his photographs, in the food and dress and work and culture. They will remember the scenes he's captured and be entranced by those they see for the first time.

The book and exhibition provide a comprehensive offering of Al's photographic work, from his focus on Tejano life in San Antonio: conjunto, charreada, injustice, tragedy, celebration, and Selena. To provide context to the enormity and complexity of Al's photographic prowess are essays by renowned cultural leaders: Eduardo Díaz, Deputy Director of the National Museum of the American Latino, Smithsonian Institution; Tomás Ybarra Frausto, formerly of the Rockefeller Foundation and Stanford University; Juan Tejeda, Founding Director of the Tejano Conjunto Festival en San Antonio; and Bruce Shackelford, Witte Museum Curator of Texas History.

Each essayist offers a glimpse of their relationship and admiration for Al, as I must do as well. Witte Curator of Archaeology Harry Shafer and I asked Al to photograph the museum's artifacts for the book *Painters in Prehistory: Archaeology and Art of the Lower Pecos Canyonlands* (Trinity University Press, 2013). Al arranged fragile 4000-year-old basketry, all shades of brown, on dark yellow paper. I walked into the Witte Museum's storage gallery and noted that there wasn't much contrast. Al glanced at me and went back to work, saying only "trust me." As the photo on this page illustrates, Al Rendón is a skillful artist, in this case, capturing the artistry of the first people of what we now call Texas with respect, allure, intensity and subtlety. As nuanced is the photograph where Al sensitively placed children's toys on a timeless playground, providing a view of an ancient past.

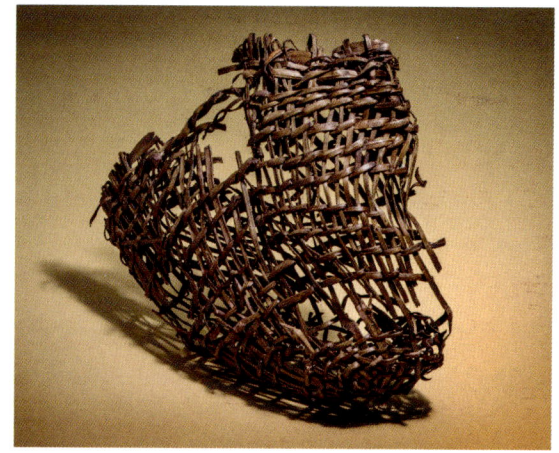

Photo by Al Rendón (2009)
Witte Museum Collection

It is not surprising that Al Rendón's work is at the Smithsonian's National Portrait Gallery, National Museum of American History, and National Museum of the American Latino, the Wittliff Collections at Texas State University, and the Witte Museum.

Mi Cultura: Bringing Shadows into the Light: The Photography of Al Rendón, the book, is registered at the Library of Congress, and the exhibition is cemented in the history and archives of the Witte Museum.

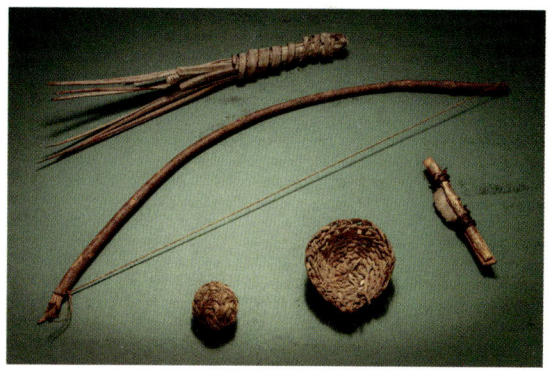

Photo by Al Rendón (2009)
Witte Museum Collection

We are grateful to Marsha Shields and the McCombs Family Foundation for enlightened early support and generous underwriting of the book. We thank Jean Cheever of the Cheever Family Foundation for being the Presenting Sponsor of the 50-year retrospective exhibition of Al Rendón's photography at the Witte Museum. We also thank the WellMed Charitable Foundation for supporting both the book and the exhibition.

INTRODUCTION

by Eduardo Díaz
Deputy Director, National Museum of the American Latino
Smithsonian Institution

Photography is an austere and blazing poetry of the real.

-Ansel Adams

Three months after the horrific massacre at Robb Elementary in Uvalde on May 24, 2022, I got wind of a mural project intended to help heal that community from a communal loss too horrific for most of us to contemplate. I happened to be in Austin at the time and established contact with the project leaders. I let them know that I would be driving to Uvalde the next morning. My next call was to Al Rendón. I asked Al if he would accompany me to Uvalde to check things out and take a few photographs of the mural project in process; that we at the Smithsonian Institution's National Museum of the American Latino might be able to respond in some way utilizing visual documentation of the murals. I told him I could not commit to paying him for his services at this time. Al said that payment was the furthest thing from his mind. He wanted to go because this was about his community.

During our first visit last July, Al was able to photograph three of the completed murals and the locations of the 18 murals that remained to be completed. We met with the project's organizers, Mónica Maldonado and Abel Ortiz. Mónica heads MÁS Cultura in Austin. Abel lives in Uvalde where he teaches art at Southwest Texas Junior College and manages his own gallery. He is also one of the muralists. Informed of the production schedule, Al returned numerous times to Uvalde on his own to complete the photo documentation of the completed 21 murals. He also took pictures of the muralists and impacted family members. His photos allowed us at the National Museum of the American Latino to produce a virtual exhibition of the Uvalde mural project on our website and at the Museum's Molina Family Latino Gallery, located in the Smithsonian's National Museum of American History on the National Mall.

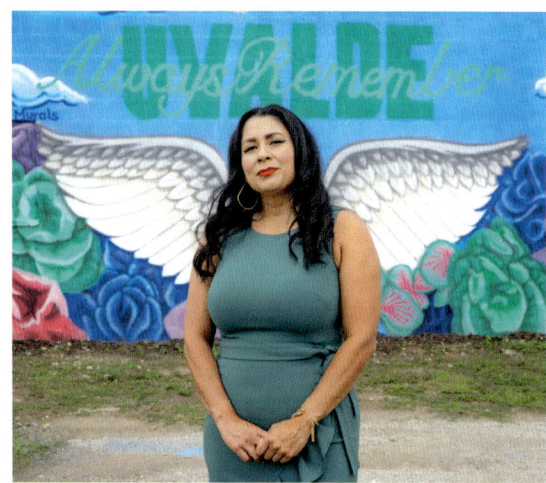

Mónica Maldonado (2022)
Uvalde, Texas
In the collection of the National
Museum of the American Latino

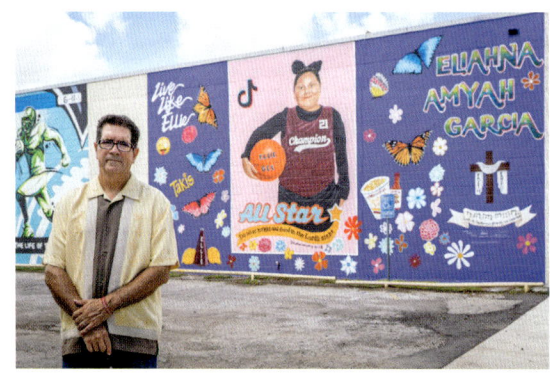

Abel Ortiz (2022)
Uvalde, Texas
In the collection of the National
Museum of the American Latino

The day after our first Uvalde visit, Al and I went out to Quintana Road in San Antonio's deep Southside to see the gripping memorial that had been erected to the honor the 53 migrants who suffocated to death in the back of a tractor-trailer in late June. To see the 53 crosses with scrolled names, the flags of Mexico, El Salvador, Honduras and Guatemala, and the makeshift *ofrendas* was as stunningly tragic as it was emblematic of the danger that too many in our diverse communities continue to confront—and yes, these migrants are part of us. There are an estimated 5.3 million Salvadorans, Hondurans and Guatemalans living in the United States. Most of the dead were ready to join their families already here and become part of needed workforces in this country, and part of the larger Latino community. Instead, they met a death of unspeakable horror. Al took photos and video with the aplomb of a caring police investigator.

For obvious reasons, documenting the Uvalde healing mural project and the migrant memorial was extraordinarily important to do, but it was simply ordinary for Al to be in the right place at the right time to document an important community project and to pay homage. It is a matter of secondary nature.

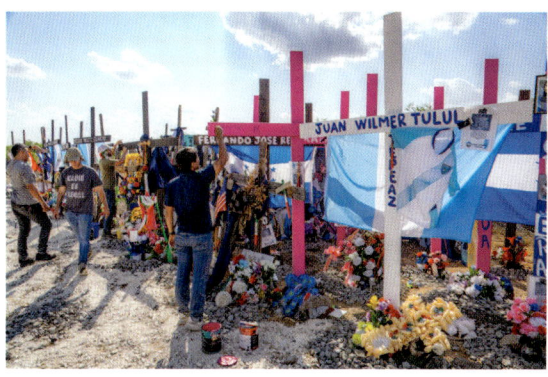

Immigrant Memorial (2022)
San Antonio, Texas
In the collection of the National
Museum of the American Latino

There is one thing the photo must contain—the humanity of the moment.

-Robert Frank

Over the course of his long and distinguished career, photographer extraordinaire Al Rendón has always been about community. He has borne witness, he has interpreted, he has contextualized, and he has honored and beautified all that is our wonderful and diverse Tejano community. I would imagine there are not too many San Antonians who, at one point in their lives, have not laid eyes on an image that bears his mark. You know those images that graced the construction fences around the Convention Center awhile back? Yup, those too were Al's.

I came to work at the Guadalupe Cultural Arts Center in 1983 to manage the newly renovated Guadalupe Theater and direct San Antonio CineFestival. I arrived in the run-up to the Tejano Conjunto Festival and, like all Guadalupe staff, my presence was required at Rosedale Park and other venues to help out. It was not too long before I noticed this lanky guy running and wandering about with cameras slung over his shoulder snapping all manner of photos. He always seemed to be in the right position. Two of Al's iconic photos from the Festival hang in my Washington, DC condo—one of the incomparable accordionist Steve Jordan and one of sets of dancers *taquachando* under the Rosedale Park pavilion.

Another photo, undoubtedly more well known, also comprises part of my modest collection—that of Selena Quintanilla. A similar, stunning photo of our dear Selena is in the permanent collection of the Smithsonian's National Portrait Gallery. It is the national portrait of Selena. In the Portrait Gallery's collection you will also find Al's photos of the legendary accordionist Flaco Jiménez and the award-winning author Sandra Cisneros. When Taína Caragol, the Portrait Gallery's Curator of Painting, Sculpture and Latino Art and History, is looking for a portrait having to do with Texas, she knows who to call. Another former Smithsonian Latino art curator also knew who to call. E. Carmen Ramos is now the Chief Curatorial and Conservation Officer at the National Gallery of Art. Before accepting this position, Carmen was the Curator of Latinx Art at the Smithsonian American Art Museum who, over the span of a few years, built the largest collection of Latina and Latino art of any major art museum in the country. Within this prestigious collection you will find 10 of Al's images capturing San Antonio's emblematic charreada culture.

Understandably and deservedly so, Al Rendón is proud to have his work in these prestigious national collections. I've taken note of that on the several occasions when I've welcomed Al and his beloved Liz into my home in DC. But Al is the kind of guy who really does not need the national acclaim to validate his work. Why? Because he is so solidly rooted in San Antonio and Tejano culture, and that is what really matters at the end of the day—to capture and share the essence of the people and culture that we all cherish so deeply. I will hasten to add, however, that Al understands the full, intrinsic value of establishing Tejano culture as quintessential American culture and is proud to play a role in making that point obvious to all whose eyes gaze at this striking and heartfelt work.

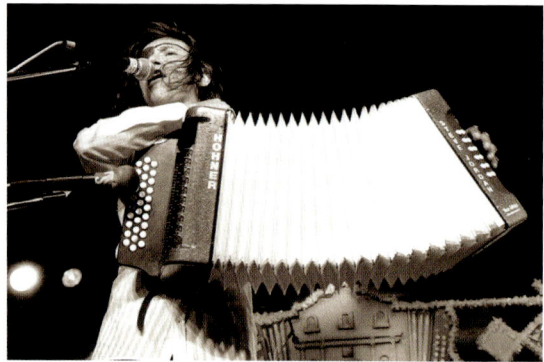

Esteban Jordan (1990)
San Antonio, Texas

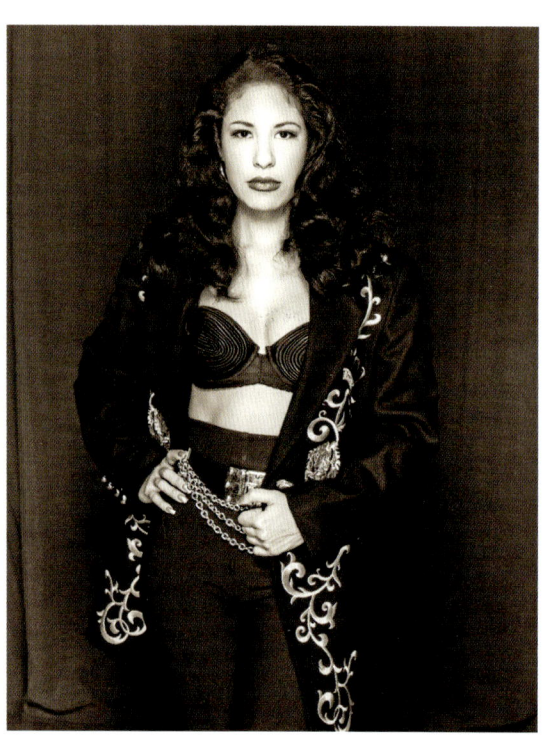

Selena (1993)
San Antonio, Texas
In the collection of the National Portrait Gallery

Al likes people. But he also adores the natural world, especially plants—both edible and romantic. His portfolio of fruits and vegetables that define the Tejano kitchen and palate, and the flowers and succulents that convey a sensual essence are stunning in their simplicity and sheer beauty. Take it from me, they make for excellent and treasured gifts to special people in your life.

This book and exhibition, *Mi Cultura: Bringing Shadows into the Light,* are overdue, particularly when you consider the breadth and scope of Al's prodigious portfolio, and the ambassadorial function of his work in capturing and promoting the Tejano experience. Some cities and states have their official historians and poets. If the City of San Antonio were ever to name an official photographer, it would most certainly be Al Rendón. The Witte Museum symbolizes a lot of what San Antonio and South Texas are about. I am very thankful to the Museum's leadership and curatorial and installation staff for bringing Al's remarkable body of work forward for all to see and lavish in.

One of the founding fathers of photography, George Eastman, once said, "Light makes photography. Embrace light. Admire it. Love it. But above all, know light. Know if for all you are worth, and you will know the key to photography." Photographer Ted Grant remarked, "Always shoot from the shadow side." The subtitle of this exhibition is *Bringing Shadows into the Light.* For nearly six decades Al Rendón has lived between the worlds of shadow and light, using the camera as an instrument that, as Dorothea Lange insisted, "teaches people how to see without a camera." In a world where the mobile phone has enabled all of us to fancy ourselves as photographers, it is the touching and inspiring craftsmanship of Al Rendón that I hope will compel us to put away our devices and take in his world, unfiltered and in submission.

If you can't feel what you're looking at, then you're never going to get others to feel anything when they look at your pictures.

-Don McCullin

ESSAYS

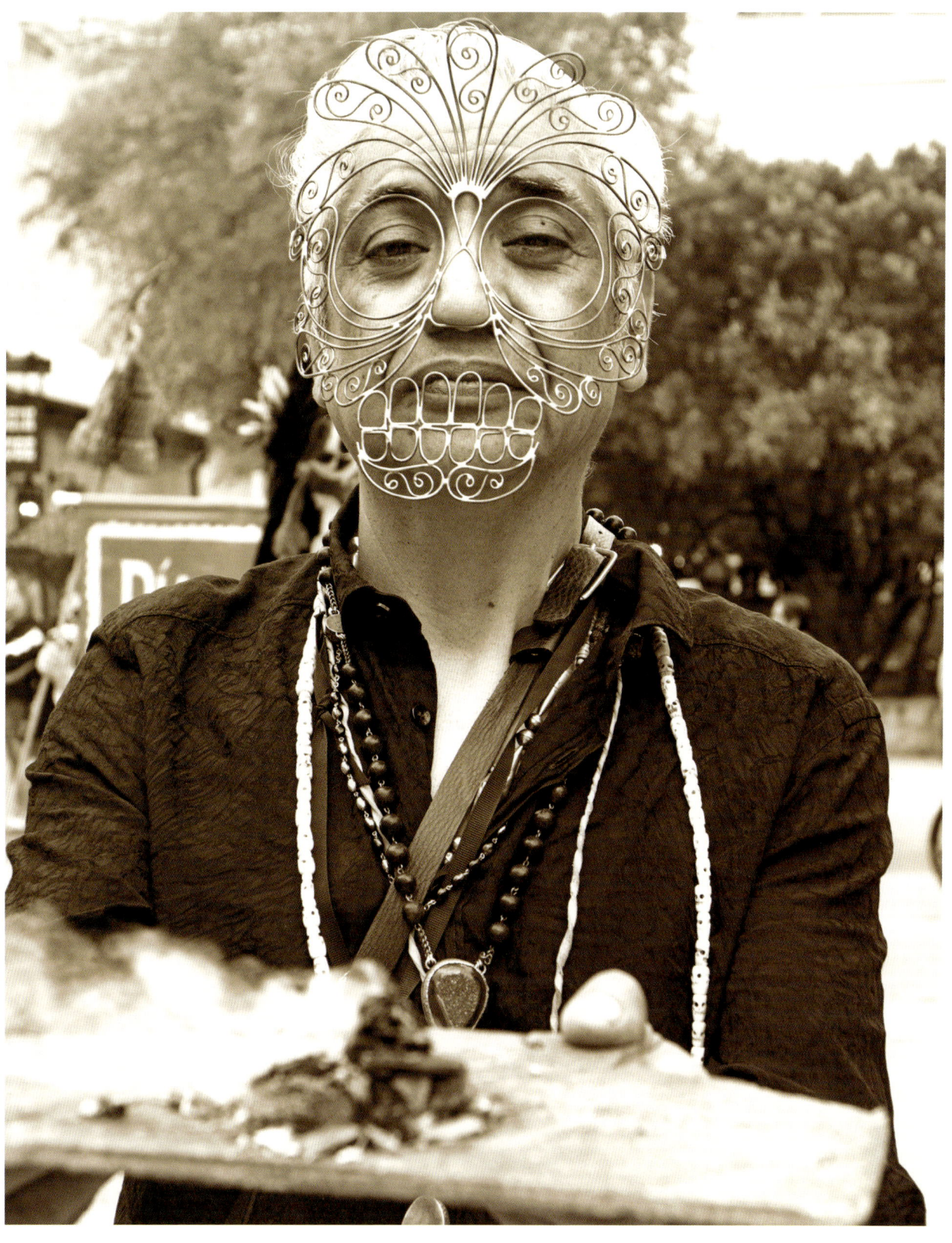

Alejandro Sifuentes (2014)
San Antonio, Texas

BRINGING SHADOWS INTO THE LIGHT: THE PHOTOGRAPHY OF AL RENDÓN

by Tomás Ybarra Frausto

San Antonio selects a yearly poet laureate. If the category of photographer laureate were created, Al Rendón would be a strong contender for the honor. His photographs capture the special *ambiente* of the city as a multicultural metropolis with historical and contemporary roots in an amalgam of European and New World peoples and their customs and traditions.

Rendón's discerning eye is turned inward to his Mexican American heritage and outward to the multiple cultures of San Antonio. He creates images that capture and convey the complexity of the Mexican American experience in the borderlands. As an independent photographer, Rendón earns a living and makes a life making commercial and studio photography. His images are human documents visualizing the way of life of ordinary people doing ordinary things.

His studio photographs are in museum collections across the nation including the National Portrait Gallery at the Smithsonian Institution in Washington D.C., The Houston Museum of Fine Arts, The Witte Museum in San Antonio, and many private collections.

Rendón has been taking photographs for more than fifty years. In the beginning Rendón learned about photography by watching his mother who was always taking pictures of special family celebrations like Thanksgiving, Christmas, and Easter and photos of family trips. As she grew older, Mrs. Rendón's eyesight worsened. When she could no longer focus, Al, her youngest son, took over as family photographer.

Viva Max

In 1969, Rendón was twelve years old and a sixth grader at St. Mary's Parochial School in downtown San Antonio. Sixth grade boys at St.

Mary's came to school on Saturday, either for Boy Scout meetings or to serve Mass as an altar boy. Rendón was both.

When he heard that a Hollywood film crew helicopter and film stars Jonathan Winters and Peter Ustinov would be filming "Viva Max" a film based on Jim Lehrer's imaginative story about Mexican troops coming to reclaim the Alamo, Rendón grabbed his Kodak Diana camera loaded with a 120 roll of Black and White film, left school, and walked to the film's Alamo location.

As he arrived at the Alamo, Jonathan Winters as an American officer and Peter Ustinov as a Mexican officer were rehearsing a scene and the media were allowed to move into the rehearsal space to take pictures.

Rendón figured that no one would pay attention to a boy with a camera, and he was able to take two photographs before being removed by security. The two photographs became the first documentary photos in his collection. Today many years later, Rendón still gets a thrill from shooting performing artists at work.

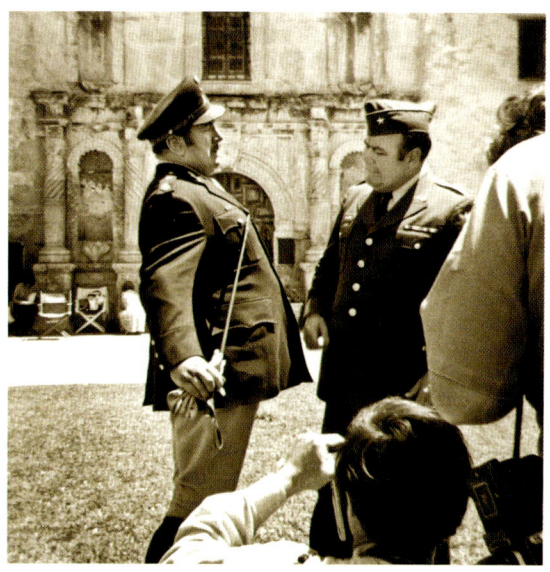

Viva Max (1969)
San Antonio, Texas

The Apprenticeship Years

While attending St. Mary's Parochial School and Central Catholic High School, students were encouraged to join extra curricular activities. Rendón chose to join the photography department and after several efforts, he was allowed in, where he learned the rudimentary rules and photographic techniques such as lighting and formal composition from classwork and from books in the school library. He remembers looking and learning from illustrated books like the many volumes of the Time/Life Library of Photography that featured biographies and photographs by famous photographers like Henri Cartier-Bresson, Manuel Alvarez Bravo, Edward Weston, Tina Modotti, Paul Strand, and other photographers.

Still a freshman at Central, Rendón persisted and was finally admitted as a member of the Photography Club. He dropped by the darkroom nearly every day. Still, the competition for photo assignments was fierce and freshman rarely got to touch one of the school cameras. 1972 was an election year and Democratic candidate George McGovern came to

San Antonio to speak at the Alamo. The evening of McGovern's speech coincided with a major Central football game and none of the senior members of the Photography Club were able to attend the speech.

Rendón volunteered and was trusted with a Nikkormat loaded with Tri-x black and white film and a 200mm telephoto lens. So, Rendón went to join the media crowd at the Alamo. The only spot to get a clear shot was from on top of one of the old O.P. Schnable's Beautify San Antonio litter boxes that was strapped to light poles all over downtown San Antonio.

On top of the litter box, Rendón was just above the crowd. A spotlight dominated the frame, throwing off the light meter resulting in under exposed film. In the darkroom, it took additional manipulation to get a stable image. Rendón was lucky when looking at the contact sheet from the session; the only workable image was the 36th frame, the last frame on the roll.

This image was Rendón's first published image at the front of the 1973 Central Catholic Yearbook, "The Rattler." It shows McGovern speaking at the campaign stop at the Alamo just before the 1972 Presidential election that he lost to Republican Richard Nixon.

In the mid 70s and 80s San Antonio was an obligatory stop for rock and roll musicians performing in the old Hemisphere arena. Rendón became friends with many of the local and national promoters and the announcers of KISS FM, the rock and roll radio station.

After the demise of the rock and roll era, Rendón continued to photograph musicians. He became the photographer of the Conjunto Festival at the Guadalupe Theater and at Rosedale Park. His portfolio contains photographs of all the greats of borderland Mexican American music. He photographed musicians and singers of diverse genres like, Rosita Fernández, Lydia Mendoza, Selena, and others. Music continues to be a major strand of the Mexican American cultural fabric of San Antonio.

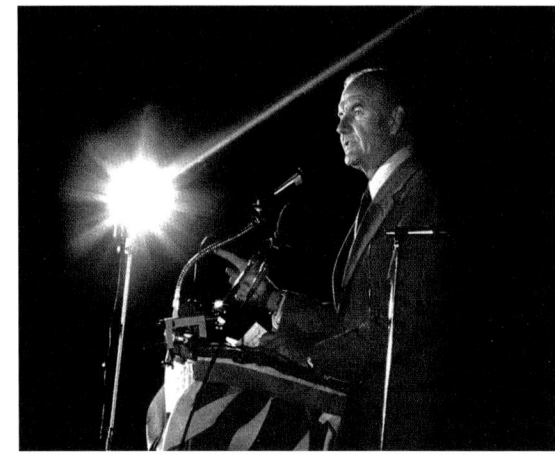

George McGovern (1972)
San Antonio, Texas

Costumbrista Photography

Rendón's photographs have affinities to diverse photographic traditions. One significant historical antecedent is 19th century Costumbrista photography in Mexico, focused on representation of Mexican everyday life, customs and traditions. Similarly in the United States, Rendón's photographs depict Mexican Americans engaged in everyday life and activities. Rendón's images are at heart realistic and documentary.

Al Rendón: A Mexican American Flâneur

Rendón is a Mexican American *flâneur*, an urban wanderer who observes and carefully documents the ebb and flow of the daily life swirling around him. As a flâneur Rendón walks leisurely about the urban streets, people watching, ready to capture on film any unpredictable or spontaneous happening. He favors the side streets or places where crowds congregate.

One of Rendón's favorite places to linger for a while is San Antonio's Mercado or Market Square, the old farmer's market—now a tourist center with shops, restaurants, an art center, and places to sit amidst plants, fountains, and strolling musicians.

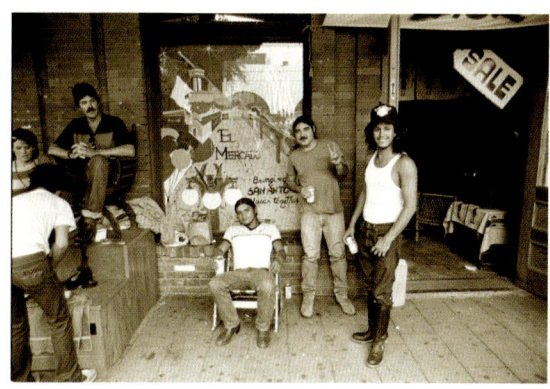

Mercado (1980)
San Antonio, Texas

Rendón might sit in a café hoping that an interesting thing might occur at any moment like the arrival of a wedding party with the bride and groom posing for photographs in the garden like atmosphere or young people erupting in a spontaneous dance to the music of the strolling musicians. Rendón's photographic portfolio has many photographs that capture the city streets and the epiphanies of urban lives and urban lifestyles. The traditions of Costumbrista photography and flâneur iconography are the two linchpins of Rendón's image making.

In summation, the multiple genres of Al Rendón's photographs are an immense reservoir of Mexican American cultural information. They function as constellations of memory functioning as visual texts that implore us to honor our lineage, remember our histories, and reclaim our heritage.

AL RENDÓN AND CHARRERÍA

by Bruce Shackelford
Texas History Curator, Witte Museum

Since the Spanish brought horses and cattle to North America in the 1500s there have been contests and demonstrations of horsemanship and ranching skills. Paintings done in San Antonio by Theodore Gentilz and other 19th century artists show horseback competitions held on holidays and feast days, from races to vaqueros grabbing watermelons and chickens from the ground. The contests evolved to include roping, bull riding and wild horse riding to dangerous passes between running horses.

A precursor to American rodeo, the public performance of Charreada has been documented extensively with books and articles written and published in Mexico and the United States, detailing the events, the requirements to participate and the skills required. The complexities of scoring and the historic sources of events and styles have been described in print and can be seen in historic paintings, prints and illustrations. In the 19th century, Emperor Maximilian of Mexico was regularly photographed wearing charro dress, or *traje*, as were his courtiers. But no images depict charrería and the public performance of 20th century charreada like the photographs of Al Rendón.

In 1981, Al Rendón, then in his early 20s, received an assignment that changed the content of much of his photography over the next 30 years. The San Antonio Fiesta Commission sent Al to the San Antonio Charro Association's *lienzo*, or arena, at Mission County Park to photograph the events of the charreada as one of the events of the Annual April Fiesta Celebration. Rendón, a native San Antonian, had never attended a charreada. In fact, he thought the participants in the event were from Mexico. Al quickly discovered the riders were local and members of the San Antonio Charro Association. Rendón documented all aspects of Charreria from formal dinners to preparing for events at the lienzo.

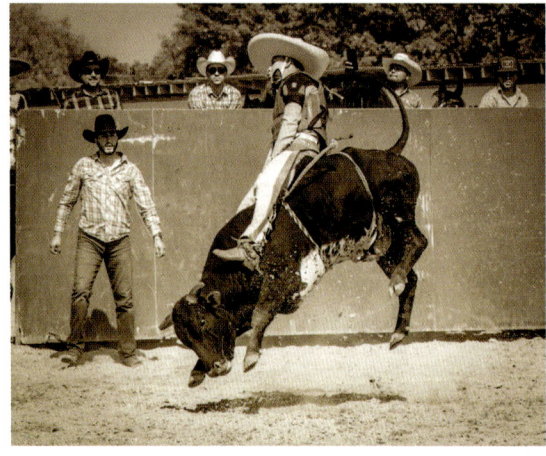

Bull Riding (2022)
San Antonio, Texas

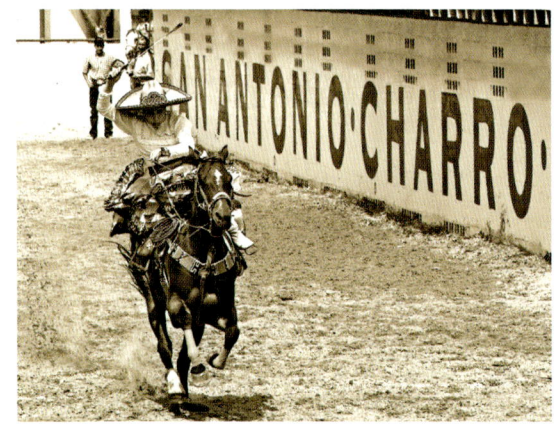

Escaramuza Reining Event (2018)
San Antonio, Texas

Founded in 1947, the San Antonio Charro Association was the first chapter in the United States licensed by the Federacíon Nacional de Charros in Mexico. The goals of the San Antonio Charros are stated as "Upholding the authenticity and pageantry of Charrería; Celebrating its tradition, Art, Culture, and History; Honoring its enduring customs of attire, culture, horsemanship and commitment to Family."

Rendón photographed events held by the San Antonio Charro Association on a regular basis after 1981 and was befriended by the members. Photographing the charreadas became Al's personal interest and no longer an assignment. He made photographs of the installation of officers, of the presentation of Charro Queens during Fiesta and the crowds at the colorful gatherings; but his main interest continued to be the horseback events. Al is known and accepted at the Charro Lienzo by Association members to document this historic part of the community of Texas and the Southwest.

Unlike American rodeo where a timing clock often determines a winner, charro judges' scores are based on style, dress and details of skills to determine scores more than timing. Most of the events go back centuries with some like the *calas*, or reining, originating in Spain and the Middle East. Other events like the *escaramuza*, or skirmish, date to the 20th century. Al's images capture the details of the performances, documenting details of garments, the participants, and especially the action of the events.

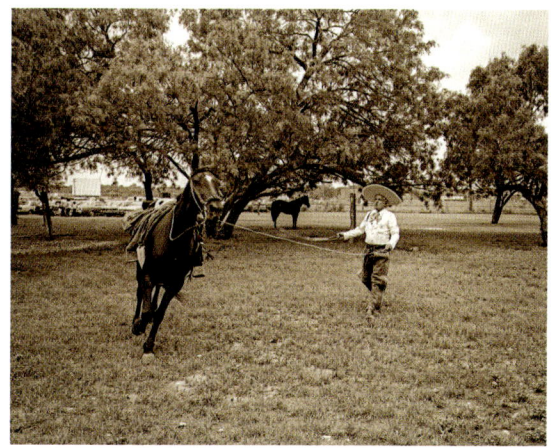

Poncho N. Lopez (1981)
San Antonio, Texas
In the collection of the
Smithsonian American Art Museum

The charro's roping and the dangerous horseback maneuvers were some of his favorite subjects, but a particular interest in the riders of the escaramuza captured Al's lens. Starting in the 1950s, escaramuzas are young women in the most feminine of dresses making dangerous passes on horseback at a full gallop. The teams ride sidesaddle performing complex synchronized patterns often to music. The demonstration commemorates the Mexican Revolution of 1910 to 1920 and the mounted *adelitas* who fought as revolutionaries. The women riding in the escaramuza often attended local high schools and were organized and trained by an older horsewoman handing down the traditions. They practiced on the weekends and evenings to perfect their skills.

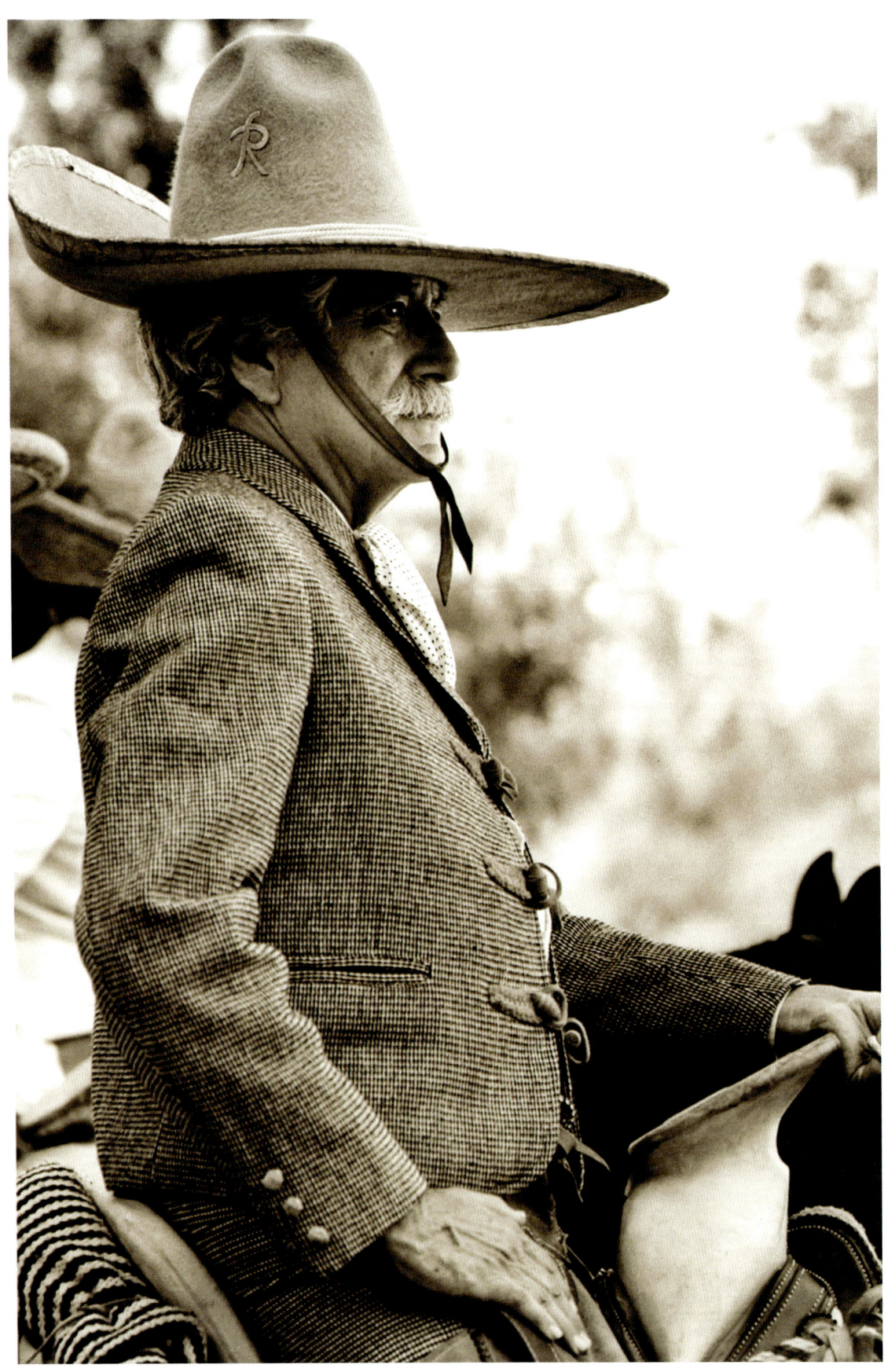

Don Socrates (1998)
San Antonio, Texas
In the collection of the
Smithsonian American Art Museum

Al learned the performers in Charreada are very different than rodeo riders or those in professional equestrian events. They are from the community where he lived. The riders are not professionals but inspired amateurs performing to continue their love of the riding traditions and ranching skills of Mexico and the American southwest. Participation in charrería is living history with centuries old origins. Al photographed Socrates Ramírez in his *traje*, or charro dress. An Eagle Scout and former Marine from Laredo, Texas, Socrates was a scholar of the history of Charrería and was active throughout his life with the San Antonio Charros. He was often the subject of Al's photographs.

As works of art Al Rendón's images speak for themselves. The photographs document decades of the San Antonio Charro Association's activities with a sensibility to composition, tone and subject as the best fine art does. Many of the subjects in the photographs have married, grown older, and some have passed from the charro life. The San Antonio Charro Association has worked diligently to maintain the traditions and skills documented by Rendón's photographs. As an added challenge to the photographer, on the days of a charreada, the arena was often dust dry or wet and muddy from the unpredictable spring weather. The difficulty of capturing the exact second a rider changes horses in the *paso de la muerte* is almost an impossibility, but it was that second that Al burned onto film, and not a computer chip. The moment of action in many of the photographs took hundreds of discarded film negatives and hundreds of attempts by the photographer.

Dodging moving horses, cattle, ropes, and excited crowds for over twenty years, Al Rendón has artfully captured the beauty, action and excitement of the charraría life for the rest of the world to see: the lives of Al's neighbors and community for the world.

AL RENDÓN: FOTÓGRAFO DEL PUEBLO/ PHOTOGRAPHER OF THE PEOPLE AND A CITY

by Juan Tejeda
Consultant, Guadalupe Cultural Arts Center

I don't remember when or where I first met Al Rendón. We both went to, and graduated from, Central Catholic High School in San Antonio, Texas back in the early 70s, but he was a couple of years behind me so I don't think I met him then.

It must've been around 1984. I had been working as the Xicano Music Program Director for the Guadalupe Cultural Arts Center for the last four years and we had just completed producing the 3rd Annual Tejano Conjunto Festival en San Antonio. Begun in 1982, the Tejano Conjunto Festival (TCF) is dedicated to Conjunto music, that original ensemble and style of Tejano, or Texas Mexican, music that uses the button accordion and the 12-string bajo sexto guitar as its principal instruments.

The oldest and largest festival of its kind, the TCF is a five-day event that annually features the best in Conjunto Music (about 30 bands), honors the pioneers of the genre, hosts educational workshops on the music, produces a city-wide poster contest to get the official poster, publishes a program magazine with articles and interviews on Conjunto Music and its musicians, has food and craft vendors, and presents a whole slew of related activities. It definitely is the largest single event, and money-generator, that the Guadalupe Cultural Arts Center produces. The TCF had been successful from the beginning, and it was growing. And so was the Guadalupe.

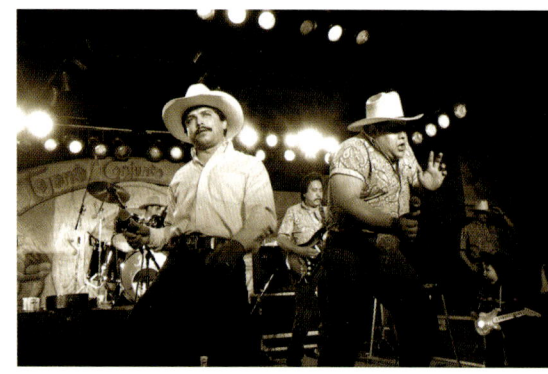

Emilio y Raulito Navaira (1990)
San Antonio, Texas

At that time in 1984, we had programs and directors in various arts disciplines: Visual Arts, Literature, Theatre Arts, Video/Film, which produced the annual CineFestival at the newly renovated Teatro Guadalupe, and the Xicano Music program that I directed. I think all of us at the Guadalupe were aware that we were making history and that it was important for us to document our cultural, artistic and educational programs for history's sake, and for our people. And by documenting we meant collecting and keeping and storing all the posters, flyers, files, press releases, newspaper and magazine articles, photos, etc., that were created and generated; as well as videotaping and audio recording, where applicable and affordable, and photographing all of these events and classes. For instance, we videotaped and audio recorded, in different formats, all of the bands that performed during the first three years of the TCF, which was extended to 17 years until 1998 when I left the Guadalupe.

There were a combination of factors that brought Al Rendón to my attention. The first photographer for TCF received a scholarship to study photography, so we needed a professional photographer to document the festival and the music classes that we offered in the community. Robert Sosa, owner of an ad agency in San Antonio and Guadalupe Cultural Arts Center board member, had worked with Al and recommended him. Al was a young Chicano rock music photographer who was gaining notoriety freelancing for the Express-News and different local and national publications.

I still don't remember when, where or how I met Al for the first time. We probably met in my office at the Guadalupe. What I know is that Al and I hit it off from the start and the Xicano Music Program hired him to photograph the entire TCF the following year in 1985. Pedro Rodríguez, Executive Director of the Guadalupe Cultural Arts Center, subsequently contracted him to photograph and document all of the events, activities and classes that the Guadalupe produced and presented throughout the year. In effect, Al became the Guadalupe's official photographer. He would work with us for the next ten years, from 1985 to 1994, and beyond.

Al brought a greater degree of professionalism, credibility and artistic sensibility to his role as photographer/chronicler of the Guadalupe Cultural Arts Center's many events and classes. This article focuses on the important work Al did in photographing and documenting the Conjunto musicians at the Tejano Conjunto Festival en San Antonio. What immediately struck me about Al's photos of musicians and music performances, were that they were primarily in black and white and very intimate and dramatic. I mean, he did give us some color photos and slides, but you could tell that he really liked to shoot in black and white. He would send me contact sheets from which I would choose the photos that we wanted to make prints of for our documentation of the TCF, or to use in our publications or for the media.

During this ten-year period, from 1985-1994, Al photographed pretty much all of the early Conjunto legends who pioneered this original American musical ensemble and style of music, as well as those popular Conjunto musicians and bands of the day, and their performances at the annual TCF.

He shot two iconic photos of one of the "fathers" of Conjunto music and Conjunto Music Hall of Famer, Narciso Martínez "El Huracán del Valle." One is where he's performing at the TCF in 1987. He's wearing a dark fedora-type hat, coat and tie, with his accordion strapped on his chest as he executes a four-finger chord on the buttons next to a microphone. Narciso, serious and intent, looks to his right, away from the camera, as he plays. Behind him is the word Conjunto, partially obscured by Narciso, which is painted on the official festival stage banner. The second photograph is Narciso sitting at a picnic table at Rosedale Park playing his accordion, and Hall of Famer Fred Zimmerle is sitting next to him accompanying him on a Macías bajo sexto guitar as they warm up for their performance on stage. What's iconic about this photo, besides there being two icons of Conjunto music in the photo, is that Narciso is smiling. I don't think that there has ever been, before or since, a photo of Narciso Martínez smiling while he is playing the accordion. This photo was used on the back cover of the book *Puro Conjunto: An Album in Words & Pictures/Writings, Posters and Photographs from the Tejano Conjunto Festival en San Antonio, 1982-1998*, that I edited along with Avelardo Valdez (University of Texas Press, 2001). Included in this book are 23 classic black and white photos at the TCF by Al Rendón. These photos captured some of the all-time Conjunto greats at the TCF, including Valerio Longoria, Lydia Mendoza, Rubén Vela, Juan Viesca, Flaco Jiménez,

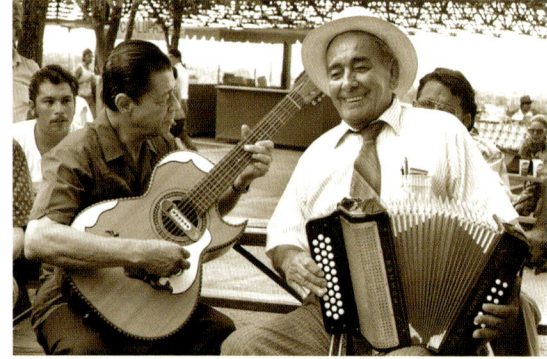

Fred Zimmerle y Narciso Martínez (1991)
San Antonio, Texas

Los Alegres de Terán, Tony De la Rosa, Paulino Bernal, Esteban Jordán, Toby Torres, Mingo Saldívar, Santiago Jiménez, Jr., Eva Ybarra, Lupita Rodela, and Roberto Pulido.

A few of these photos are worthy of special mention. One is where Juan Viesca, "El Rey del Tololoche," put lighter fluid on his stand-up bass and set it on fire while performing with Narciso Martínez on stage at the Guadalupe Theater in 1988. Al captured this moment with Juan's bass fully engulfed in flames. Juan Viesca had been lighting his bass on fire since at least 1951, way before Jimmy Hendrix did the same to his guitar. In 1986, Al also photographed the classic jam session at the end of our first "New Directions in Conjunto Music" night at Rosedale Park that featured Esteban Jordán jamming with Los Lobos and Doug Sahm, Augie Meyers and the Westside Horns (Rocky Morales, Charlie McBirney and Al Gómez). In 1989, Al photographed Queen Ida and the Bon Temps Zydeco Band jamming with Esteban Jordan at the first "Conjunto Meets Cajun/Zydeco" night at the TCF. Billed as "Where the Bayou Meets the Barrio," they performed a joyous rendition of "Jambalaya" that we included, and closes out, the first live recording of the Best of the 9th Annual Tejano Conjunto Festival en San Antonio 1989 cassette tape.

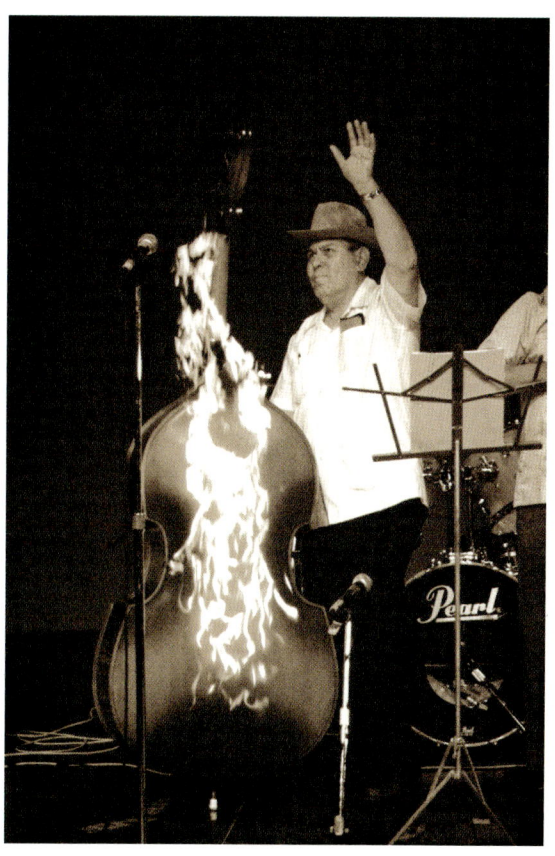

Juan Vescia (1988)
San Antonio, Texas

Conjunto music is dance music: the polkas, waltzes, cumbias and boleros. Al took some great photos of people dancing at the festival. One photo in *Puro Conjunto* depicts a young couple dancing to what looks like a polka Tejana beat, or maybe a ranchera sung in polka time. The male Chicano is wearing a black *tandito* (*pachuco*-style hat), black short-sleeve shirt, black pants and black Stacey Adams shoes, and the Chicana is wearing jeans and a short-sleeve white blouse with hushpuppy-type shoes. Her right hand is at a ninety-degree angle from her arm next to her right shoulder, and the Chicano's left arm is fully extended and his hand and fingers are interlaced with her right hand. His right arm is wrapped around her shoulders in a dancing embrace. And though Al has stopped time in this photo, you can almost see the couple's arms and hands going back and forth in the classic *serruchito* (little saw) and *taquachito* (little opossum) styles of polka dancing that has become popular in Conjunto music. Behind this couple there are various other couples that dance around the pavilion, including two young girls, about 7 or 8 years old, who are dancing together.

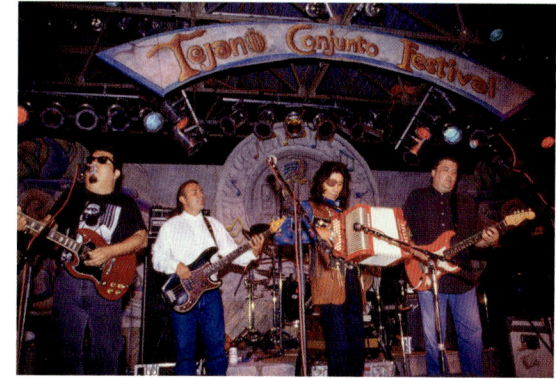

Los Lobos with Steve Jordan (1993)
San Antonio, Texas

There's also a beautiful photo of legendary singer and guitarist, Lydia Mendoza, all glittered out in one of her Mexican folkloric dresses that she used for performances, accepting her award as she was inducted into the Conjunto Music Hall of Fame in 1991; two photos of the Conjunto classes that were offered in the community: the button accordion class with instructor/maestro Valerio Longoria, and the bajo sexto guitar class with Toby Torres; and finally, a picture of "The Dancing Cowboy," Mingo Saldívar, as he slings that accordion across his chest and kicks up his left leg in his inimitable style of playing that squeezebox while performing intricate and energetic dance moves.

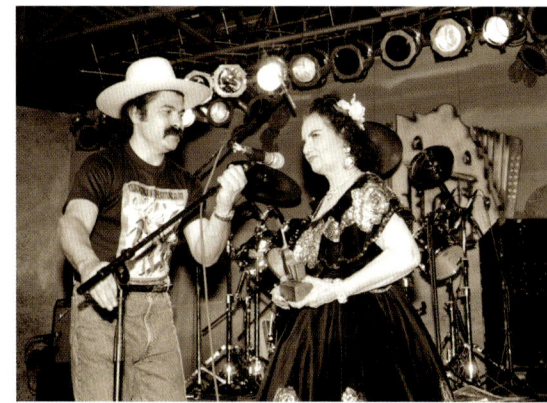

Lydia Mendoza y Juan Tejeda (1991)
San Antonio, Texas

It is hard to describe music without hearing it played; just as it's hard to describe a photo of a couple dancing without seeing them in the moment, when the music is playing and you're witnessing the stylized dance moves and steps that they execute. Al Rendón's photos can make you hear the music, see the dancers glide as they circle the concrete dance floor pavilion out at Rosedale Park, and feel like you are at the TCF itself. *Qué más quieres de un fotógrafo?* These photos are our history. These photos are us. And Al's photos are there and archived for all of history.

Al Rendón must've photographed over 300 different Conjuntos at the TCF, including some of the most popular bands in the history of Conjunto Music, such as Los Dos Gilbertos, Los Aguilares, Oscar Hernández, Ramón Ayala, Ángel Flores, Los Pavos Reales, Chacha Jiménez, Laura Canales, Emilio Navaira, David Lee Garza y Los Musicales, Bernardo y sus Compadres, Gilberto Pérez, and so many others. He also photographed the young up-and-coming bands that performed at the festival, student recitals, the poster contest judging and posters, and workshops that were offered. He was photographing the festival during the peak years of 1991 and 1992 when we had a seven-day festival, Monday through Sunday, and 42 and 46 Conjuntos performing, respectively.

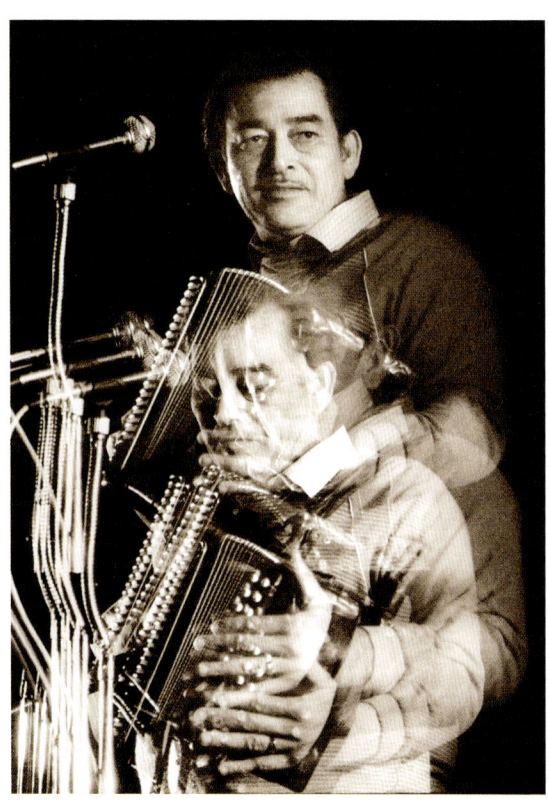

Flaco Jiménez (1987)
San Antonio, Texas
In the collection of the National Portrait Gallery
Artist insight on page 123

Many of the photos that Al took of these Conjunto musicians and their performances at the TCF are portraits, really. Al's double exposure black and white photo of Flaco Jiménez performing at the TCF in 1986 (after he had won his first Grammy for his recording of his father's, Santiago Sr.'s, song "Ay Te Dejo en San Antonio"), now hangs at the Smithsonian National Portrait Gallery in Washington DC. In fact, Al Rendón is one of only a handful of Latino artists and photographers whose work has been collected by three

Smithsonian Museums: the Smithsonian National Portrait Gallery, the Smithsonian National Museum of American History, and the Smithsonian American Art Museum.

Even after Al stopped working as the Guadalupe Cultural Arts Center's photographer in 1994, he continued to photograph certain performers and aspects of the TCF. I would say that Al has one of the best, if not the best, photo collections of Conjunto musicians and performers at the TCF, in the world. He, himself, credits the Tejano Conjunto Festival and the Guadalupe Cultural Arts Center with reintroducing him to his Mexican American roots. He said that he was excited about taking photos of the people who created the music that his father listened to on the radio as he worked at his home wood workshop. This led Al to a newfound awakening, appreciation and love for his own Mexican American people, history and culture, and the realization that he had to document it.

And document it he has. From the Conjunto musicians and dancers at the Tejano Conjunto Festival, to his iconic photos of Selena that graced the covers of People and Newsweek magazines. From the five historic San Antonio missions, including the Alamo/Misión San Antonio de Valero, to the complex revelry of the 10-day Fiesta San Antonio celebration. From the San Antonio Riverwalk, to Mexican Charreadas and the Charro Ranch. He's documented San Antonio places and landmarks, as well as the movers, shakers and cultural creatives who call San Antonio home. In the process, Al, himself, has become a beloved *hijo del pueblo* (native Yanawana/San Antonio son) and artist who has captured and documented the soul of this city.

Gracias, Al, for your beautiful photos. Gracias for documenting the Tejano Conjunto Festival en San Antonio and all of those Conjunto Music giants who created this genre, many who have now passed on into the spirit world. Tlazokamati for documenting our Indigenous/Mexicano/Mexican American/Tejano/Xicanx/Latinx history and culture in photos. Gracias for all of your dedicated years of work. This is a grand gift and legacy that you leave all future generations.

And there's more to come. Looking forward to it.

Pa'lante/Tiahui.
To all our relations/Tewahayo nah'o k'tu,

ROCK & ROLL

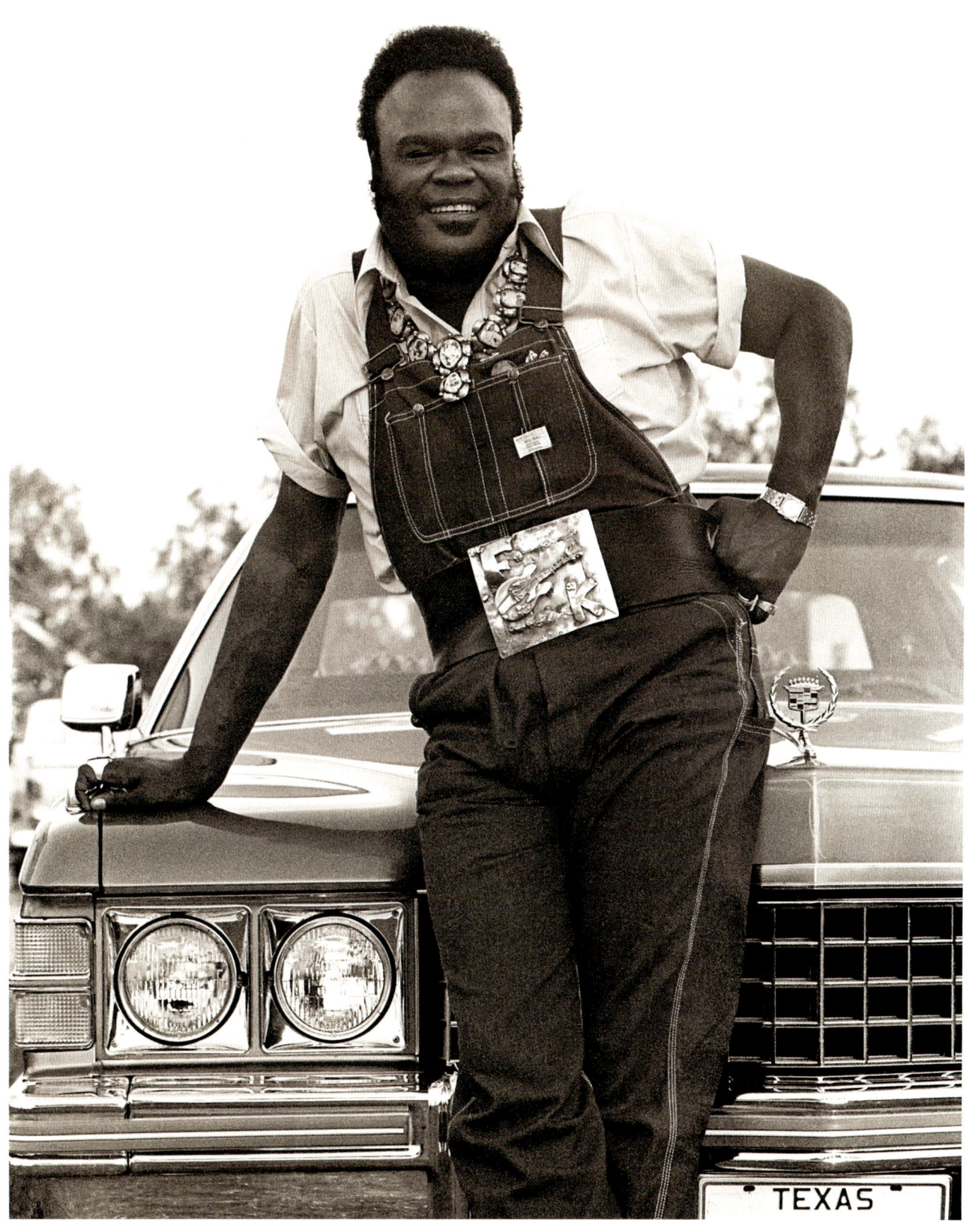

Freddy King (1974)
San Antonio, Texas

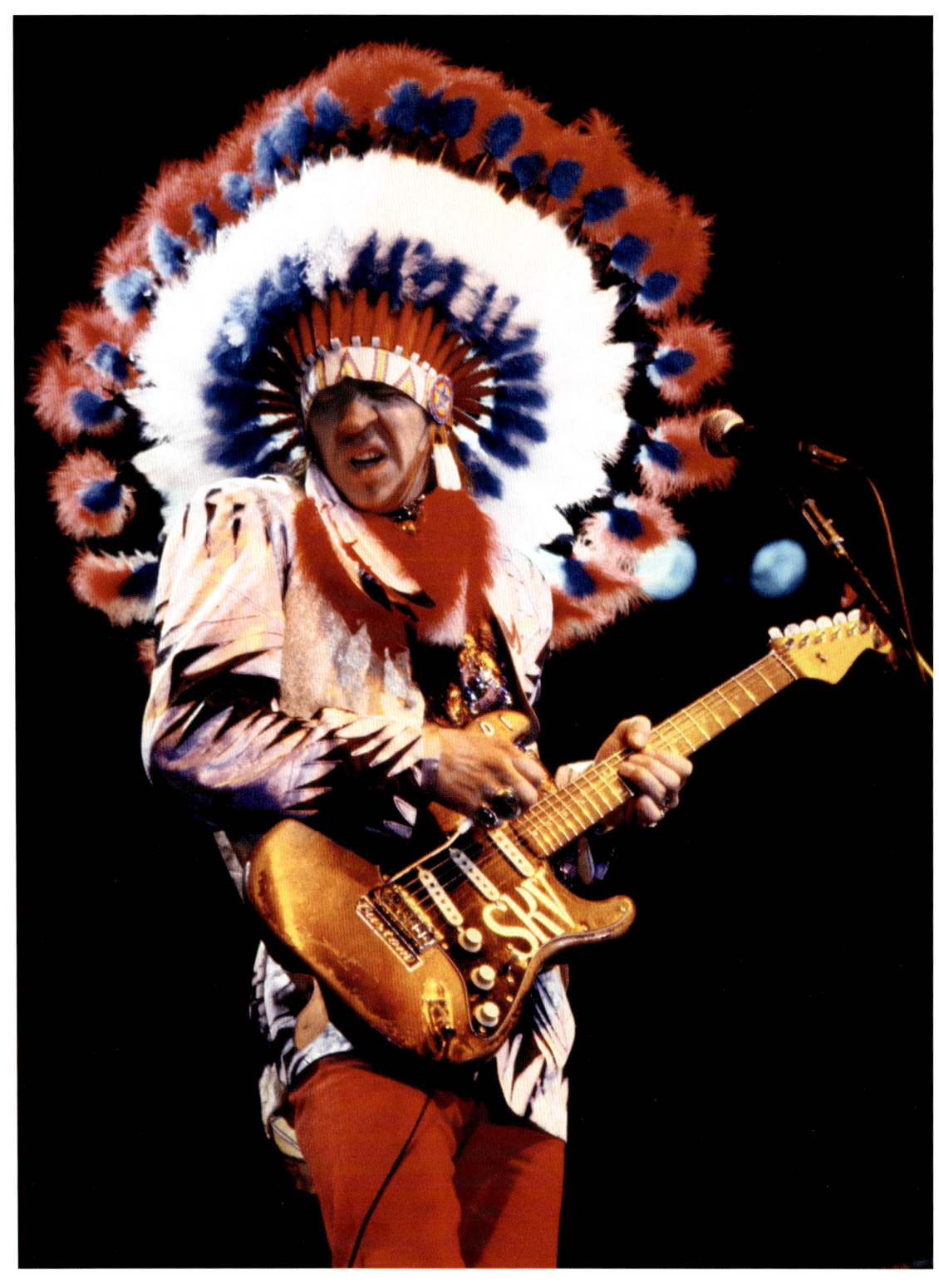

Stevie Ray Vaughn (1985)
San Antonio, Texas

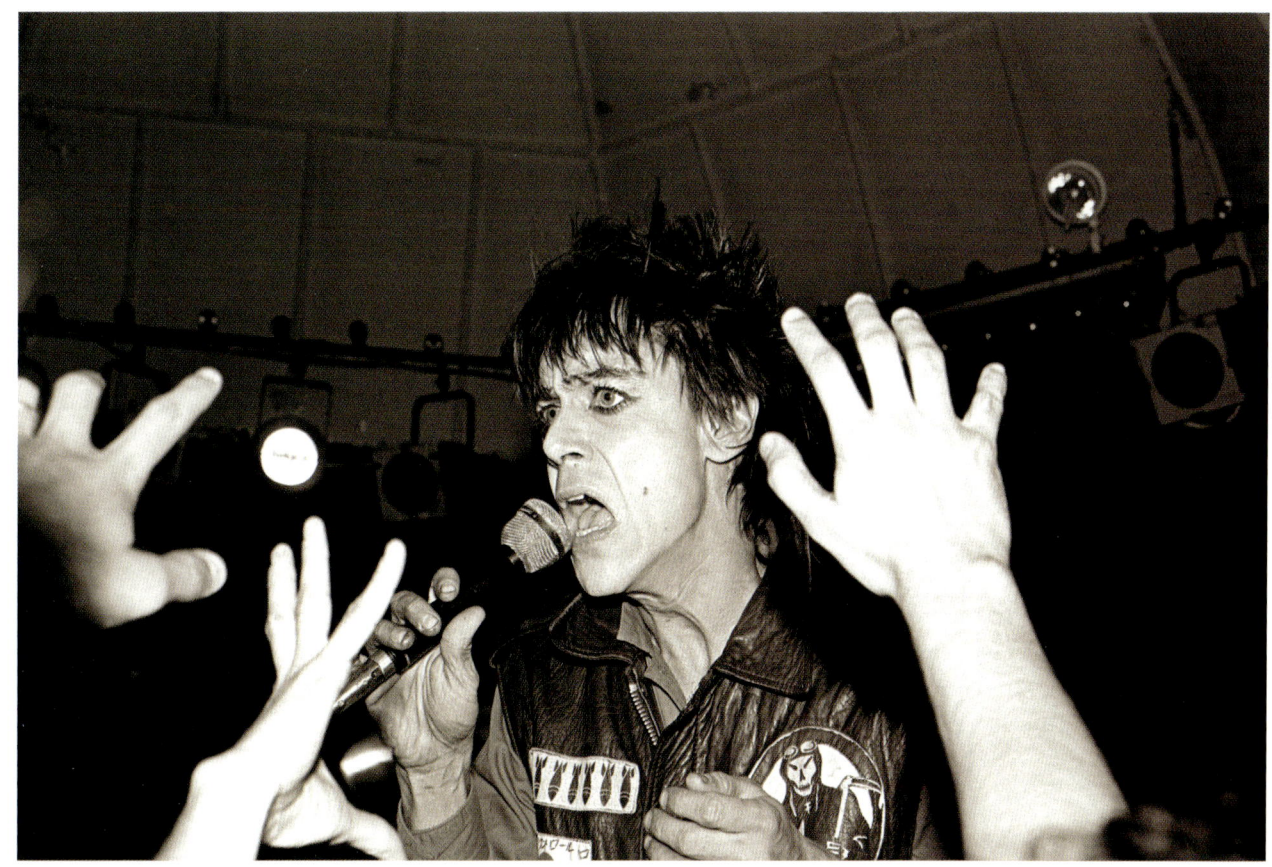

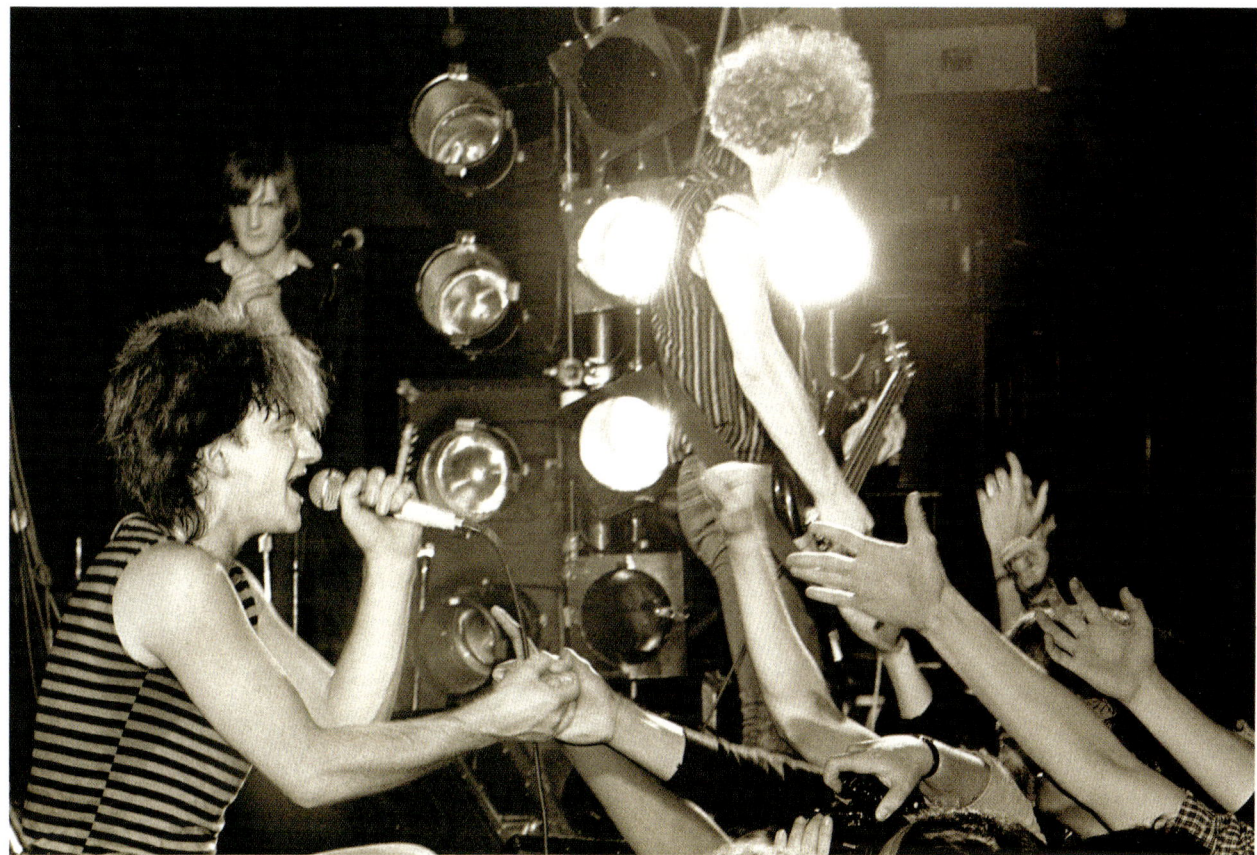

Top: *Iggy Pop, Bonham Exchange* (1983)
San Antonio, Texas
In the collection of the Smithsonian
National Portrait Gallery

Bottom: *U2, Cardi's* (1982)
San Antonio, Texas

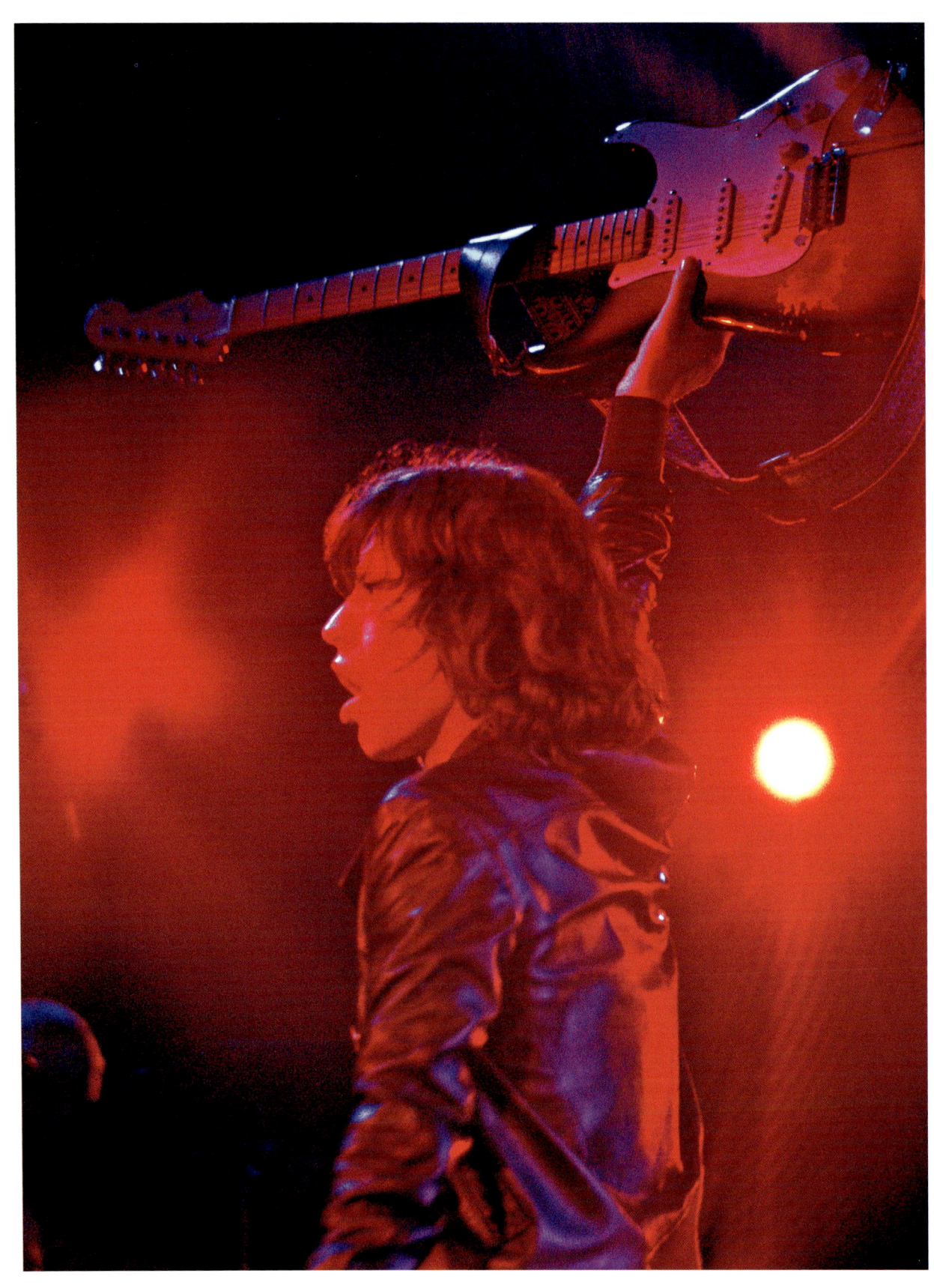

Mick Jagger (1975)
San Antonio, Texas

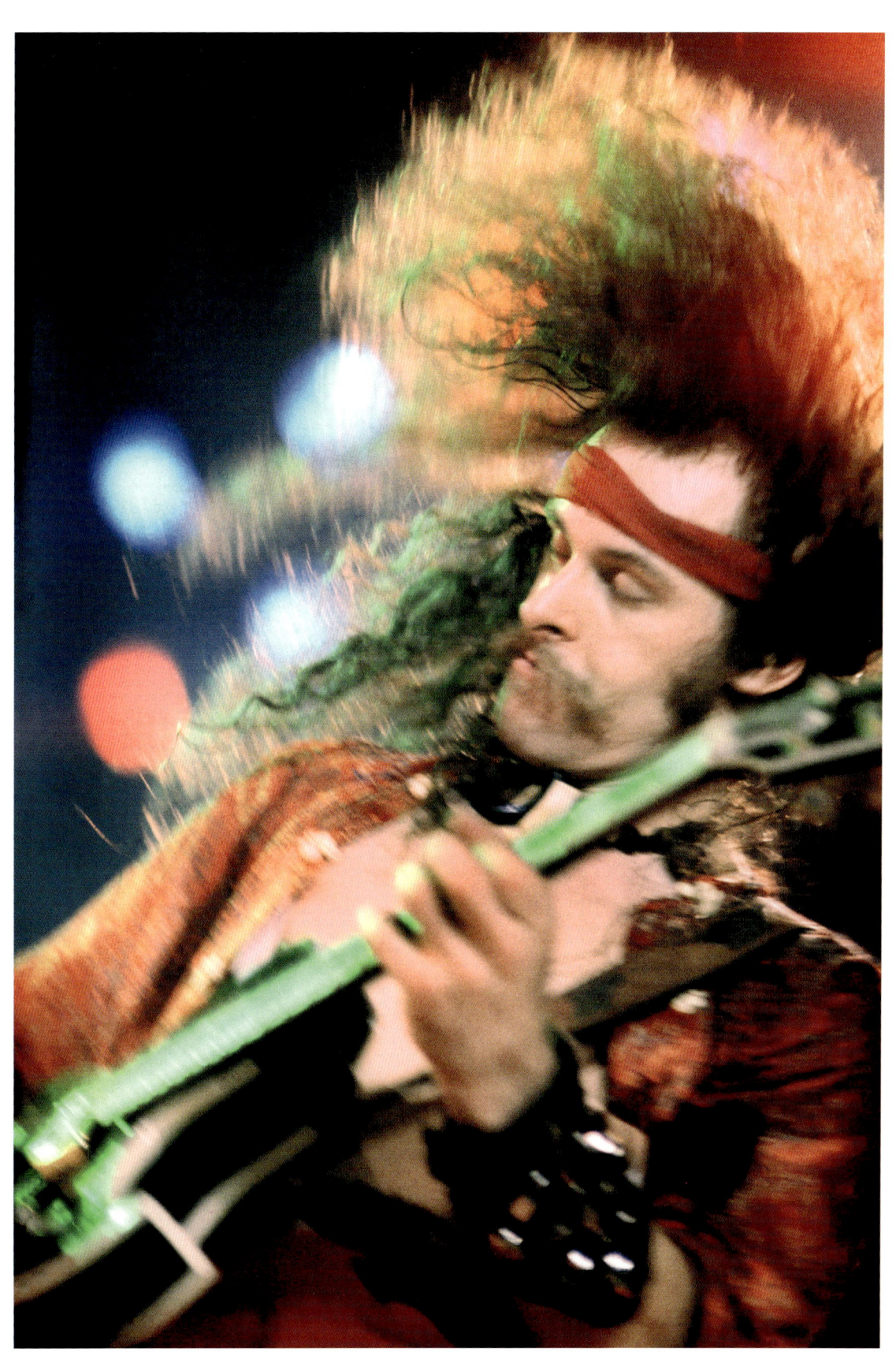

Ted Nugent (1975)
San Antonio, Texas
In the collection of the National Portrait Gallery

MI CULTURA

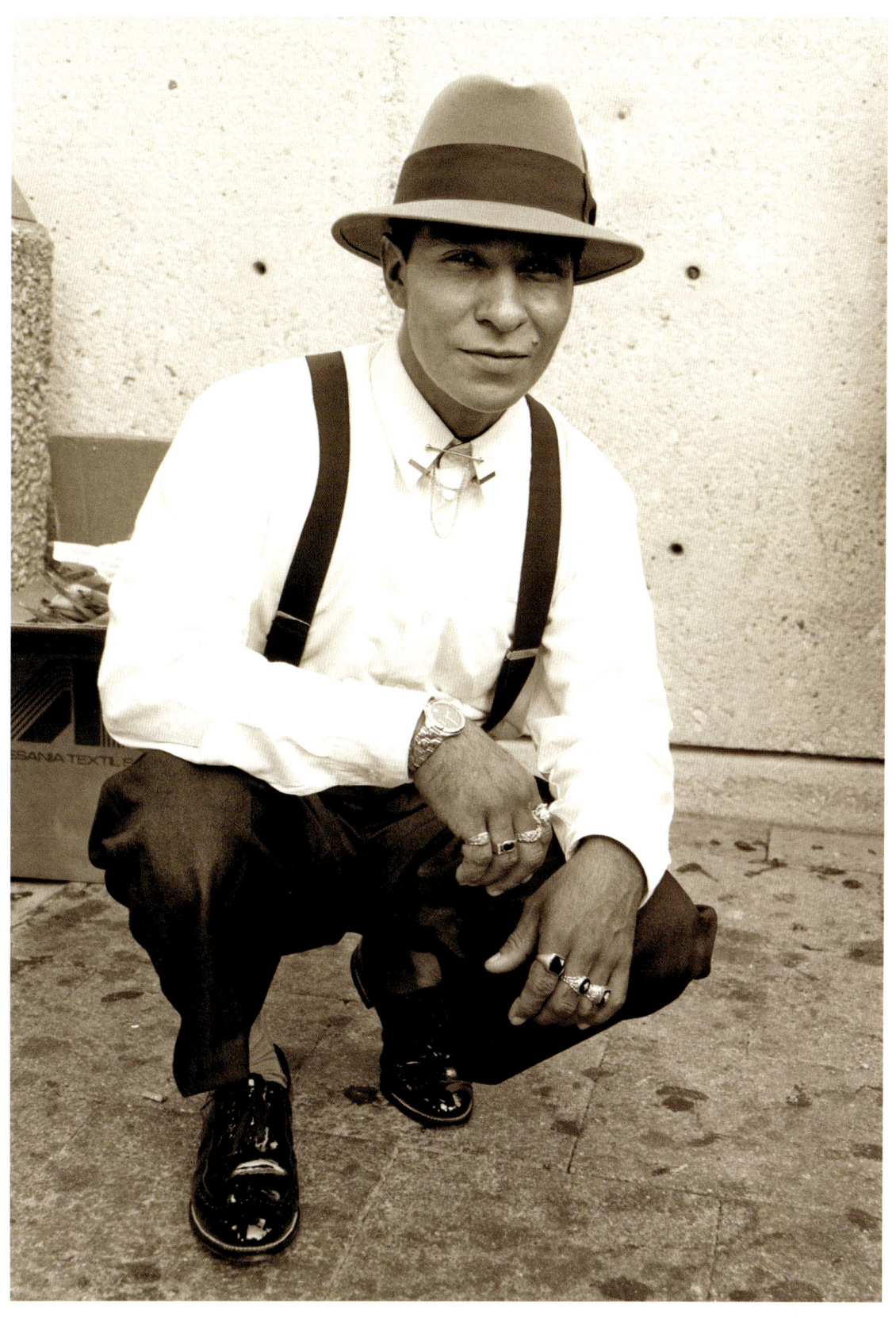

Vato (1990's)
San Antonio, Texas

Artist insight on page 114

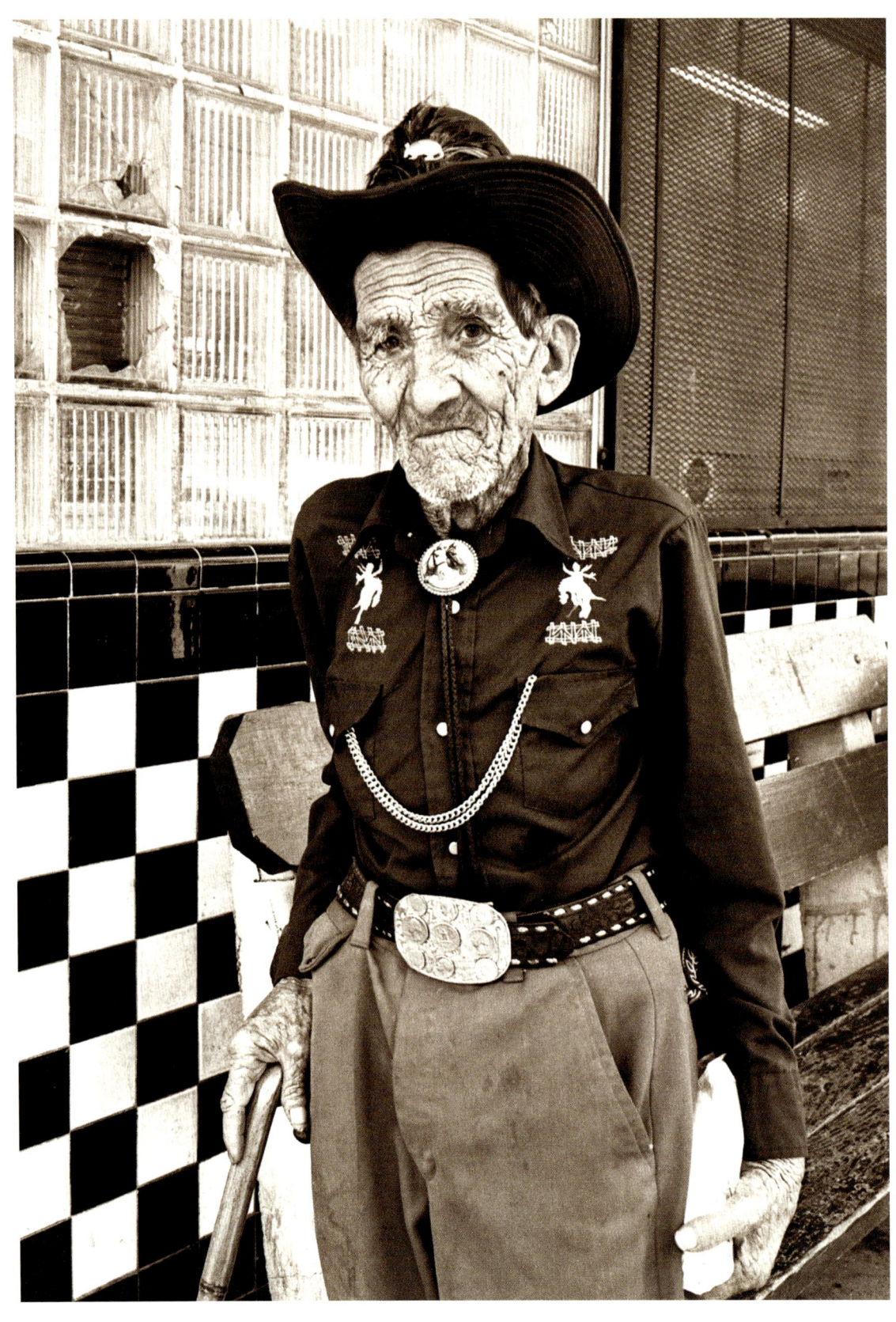

Cisco Kid (1989)
San Antonio, Texas

Artist insight on page 115

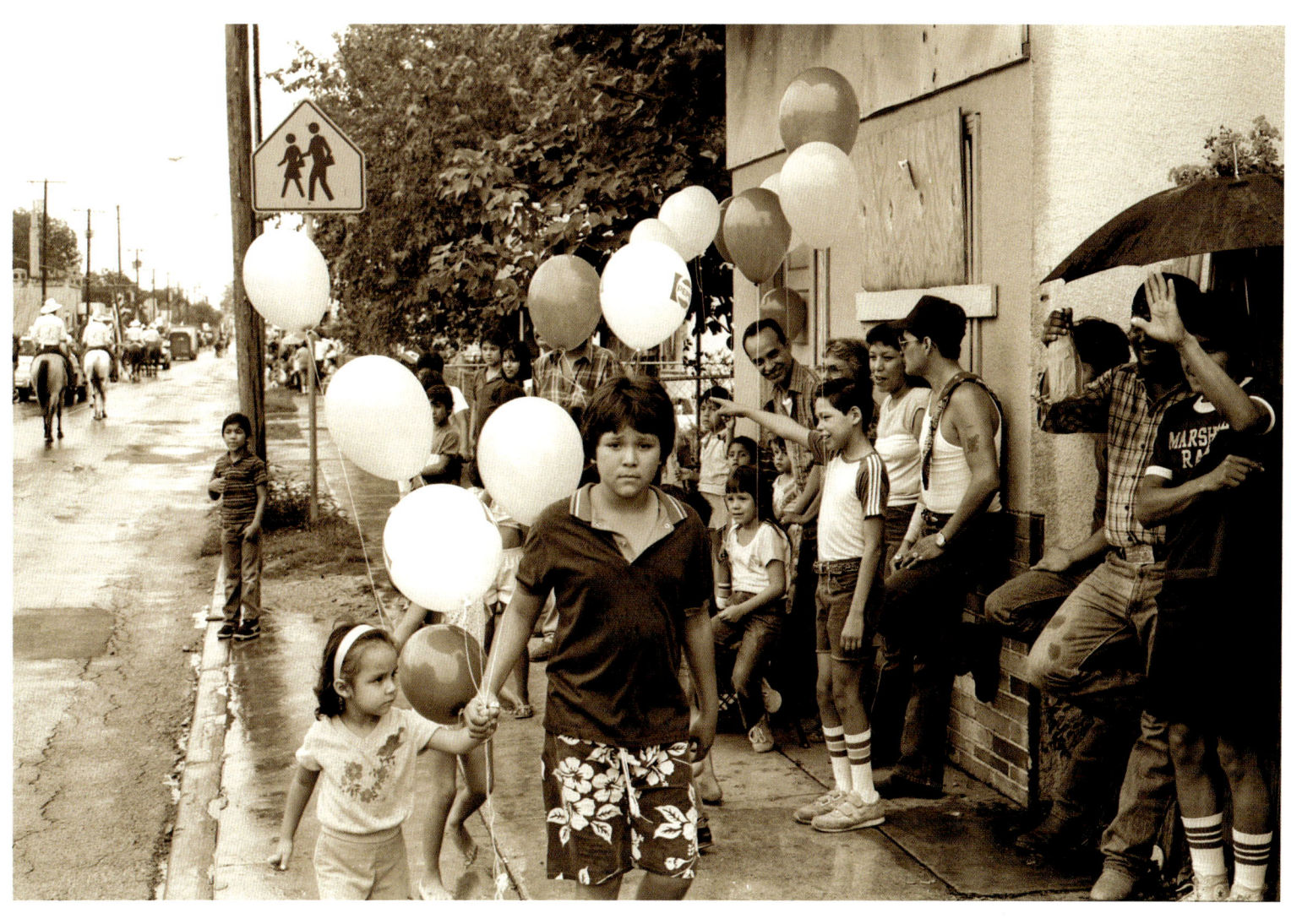

Balloons (1985)
San Antonio, Texas

Artist insight on page 115

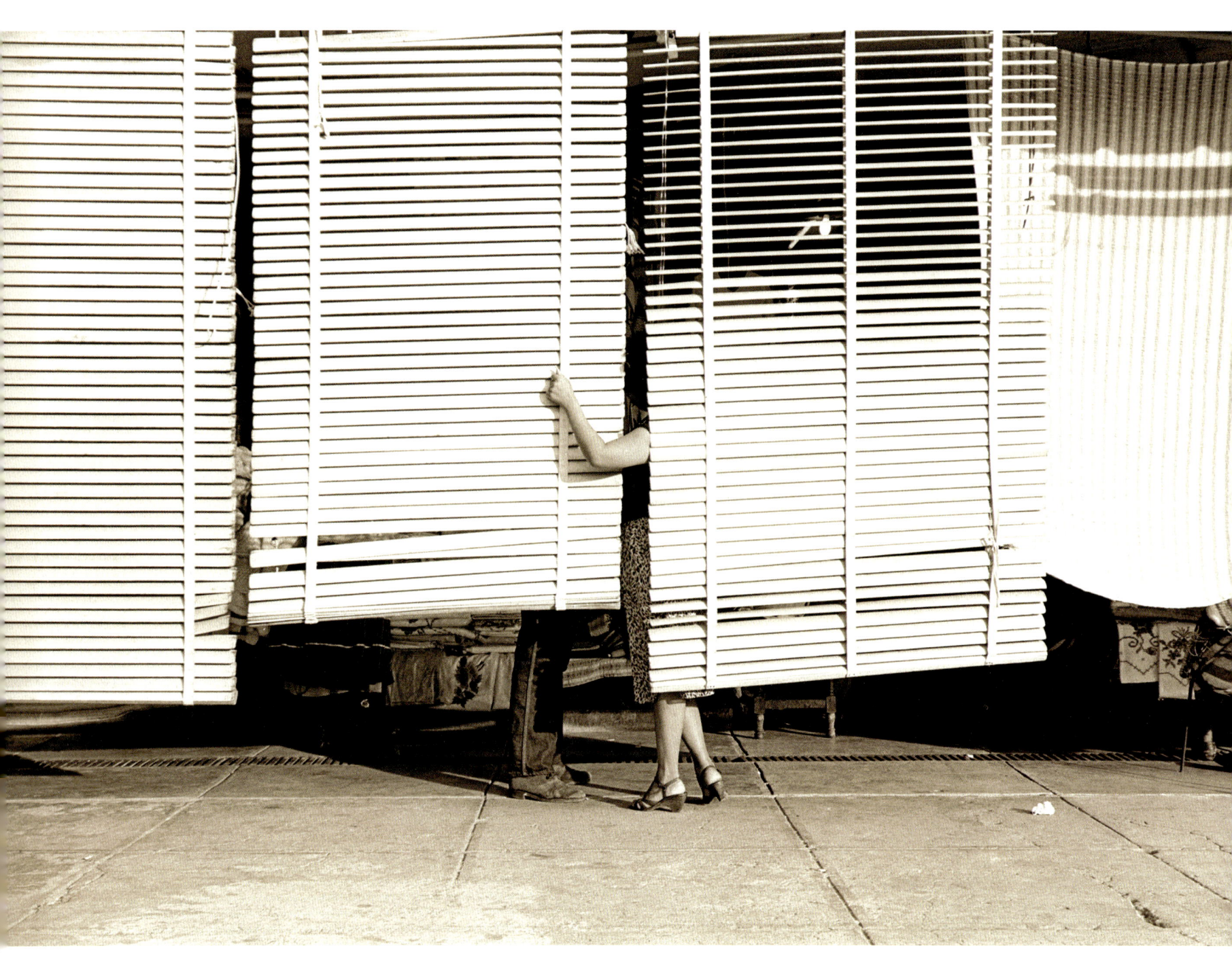

Shades of Guadalajara (1984)
Guadalajara, Mexico
Artist insight on page 116

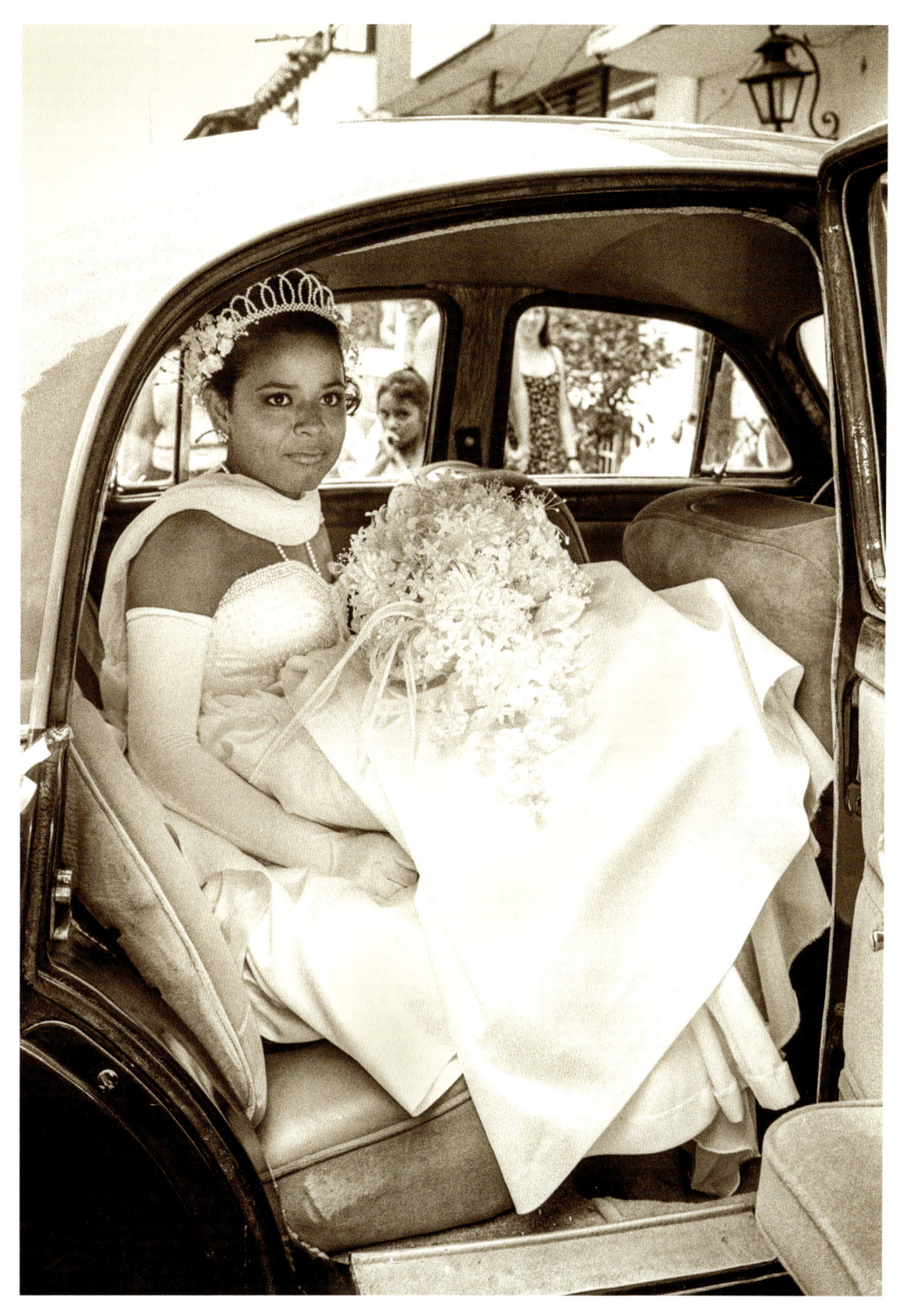

La Reina (1986)
Puerto Vallarta, Mexico

Artist insight on page 116

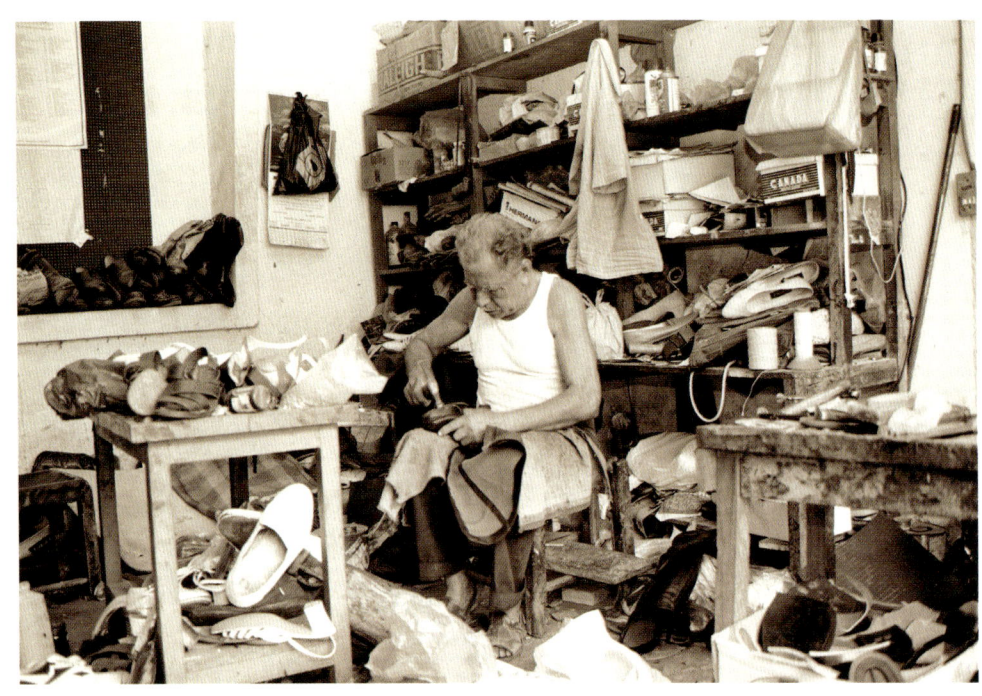

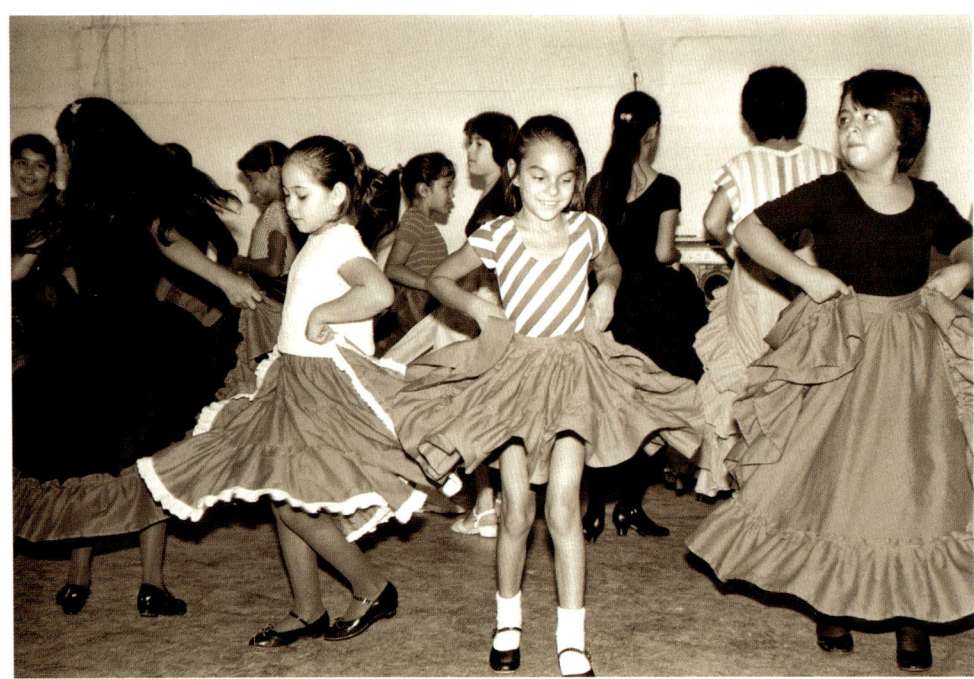

Top: *Zapatero* (1986)
San Antonio, Texas

Bottom: *Young Dancers* (1987)
San Antonio, Texas

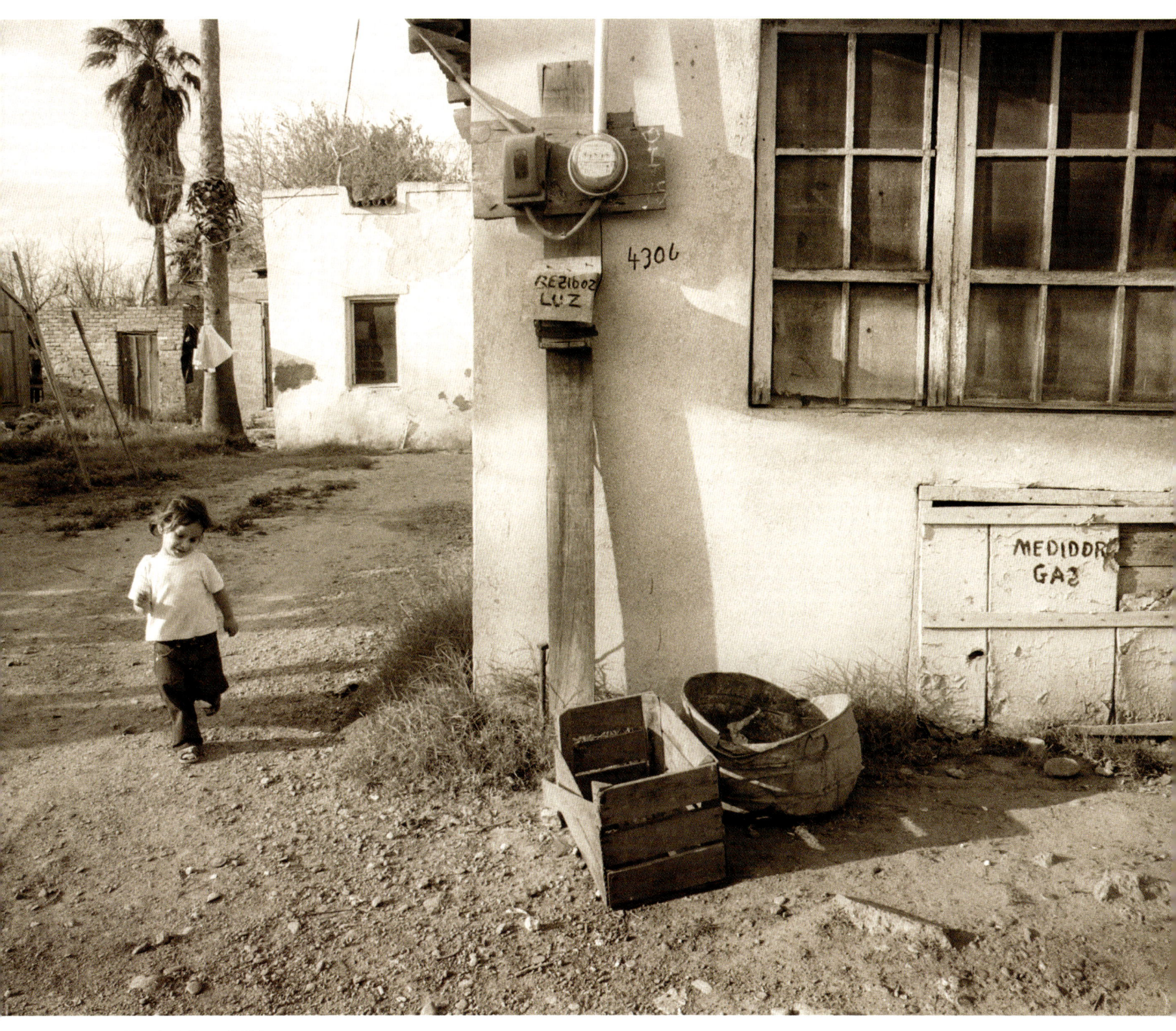

Grandma's House (1985)
Nuevo Laredo, Texas

Artist insight on page 117

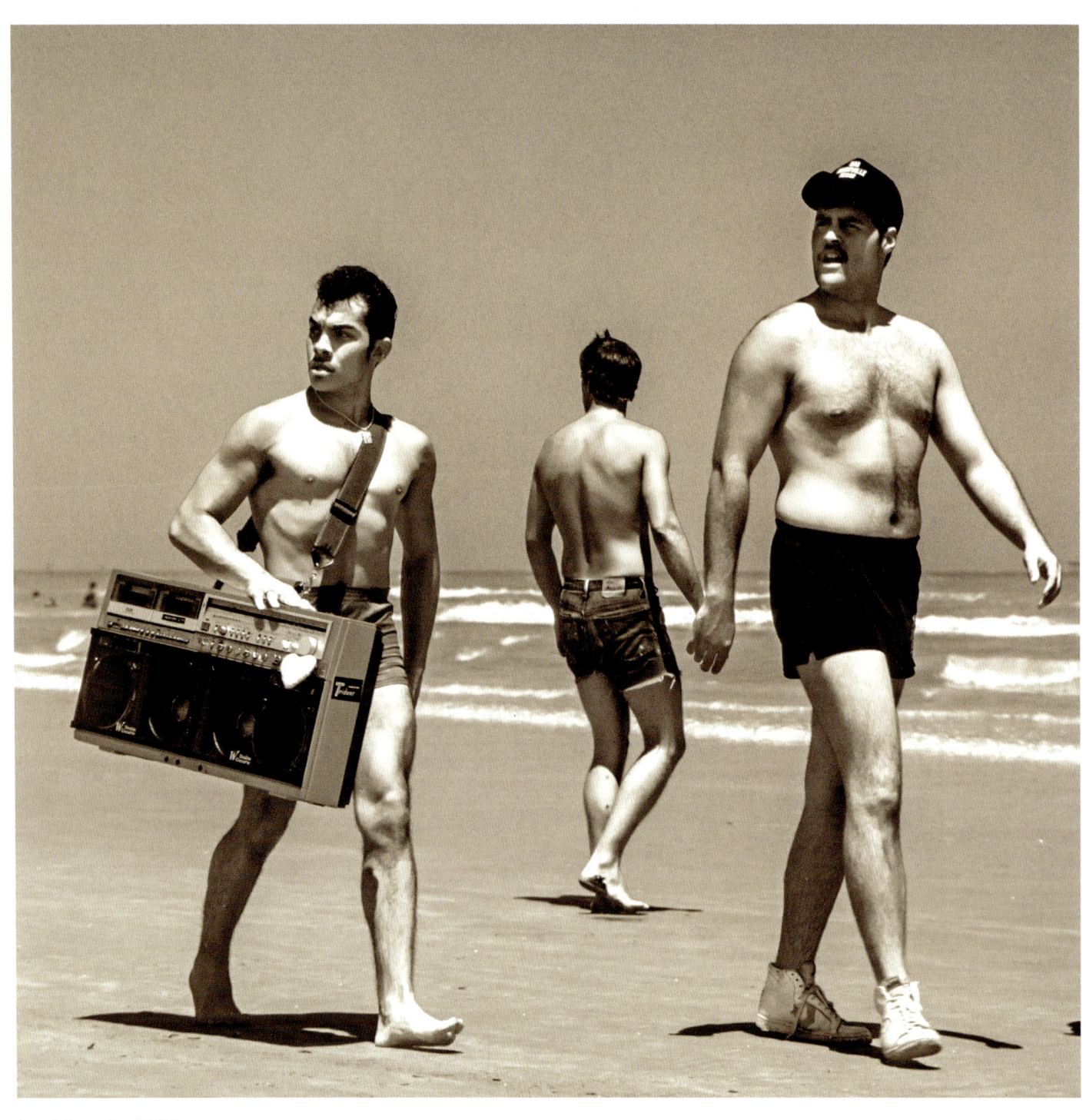

Beach Boom Box (1985)
Port Aransas, Texas

Artist insight on page 118

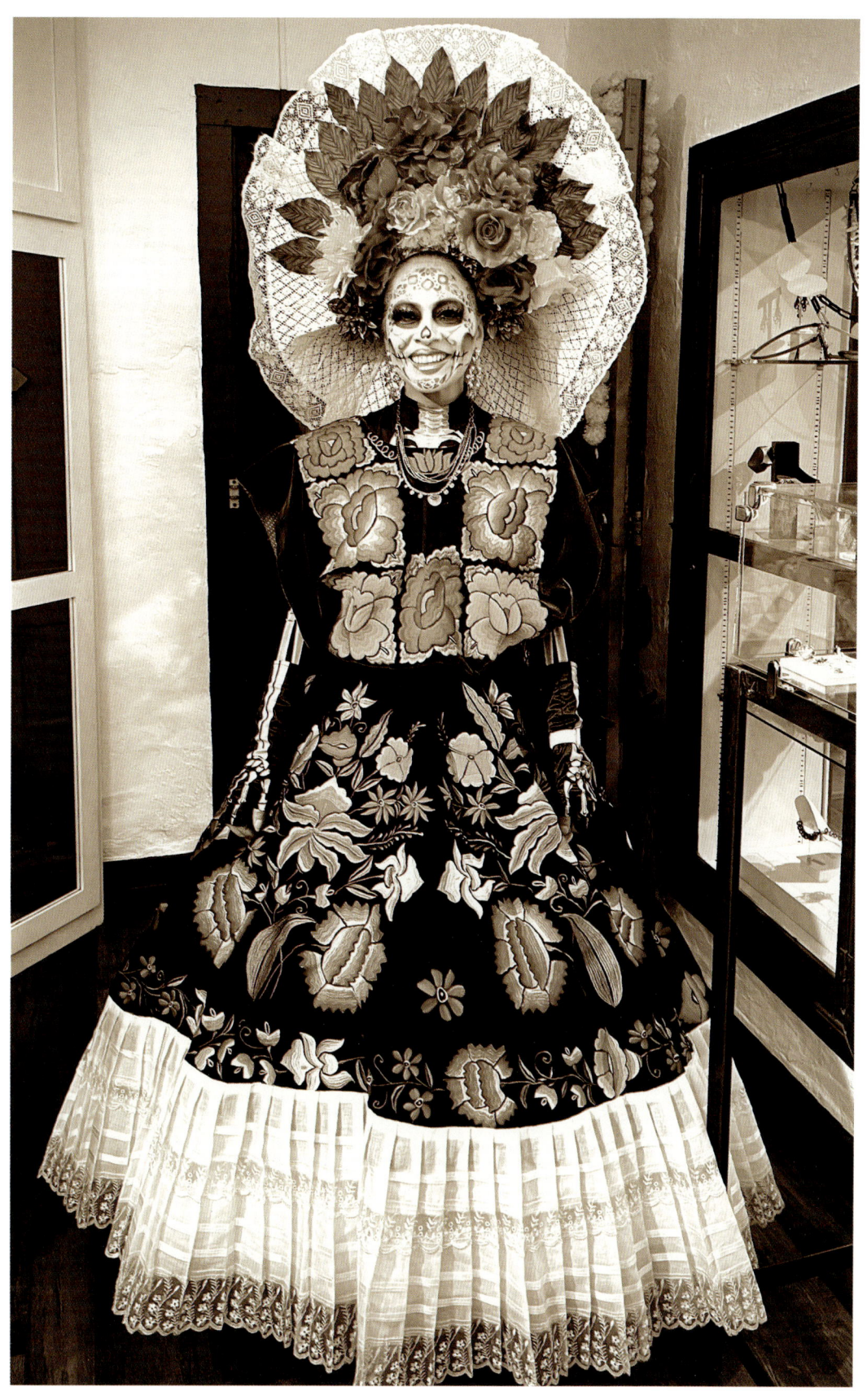

Azul Barrientes (2021)
San Antonio, Texas

Artist insight on page 118

LA VIRGEN

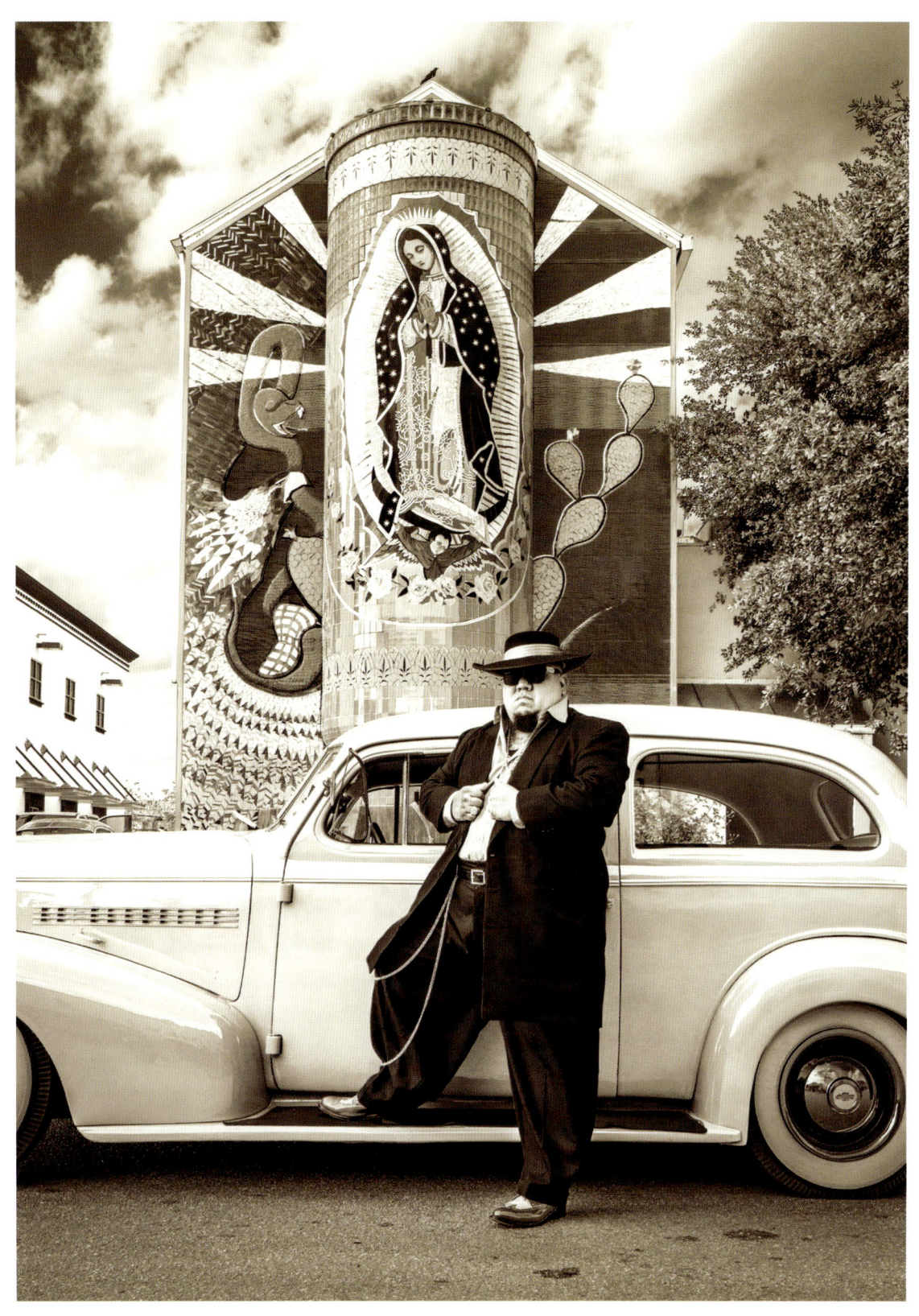

Jose Mosqueda III, Zoot Suiter (2023)
San Antonio, Texas

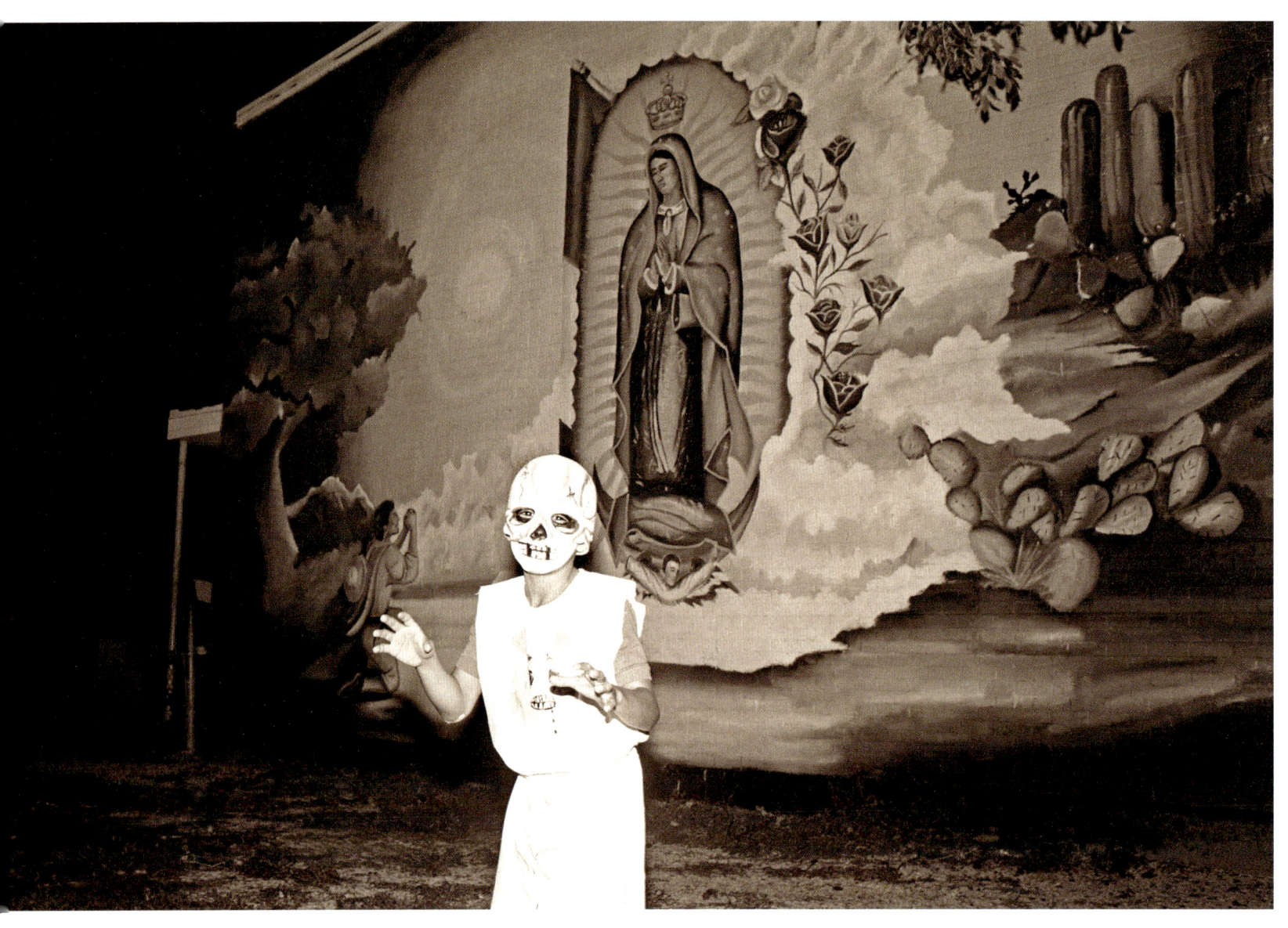

Halloween (1986)
San Antonio, Texas

Artist insight on page 120

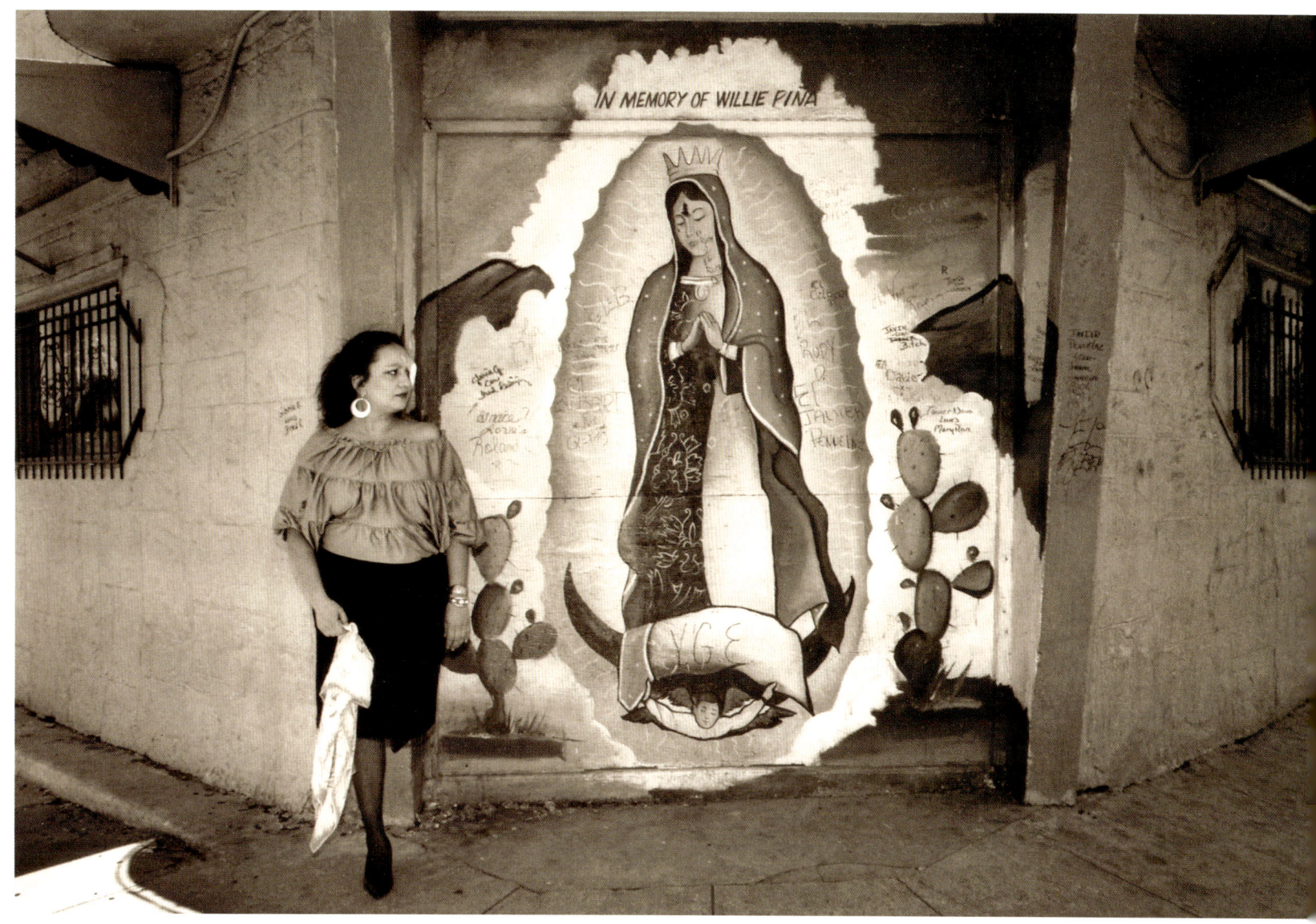

Ruby (1988)
San Antonio, Texas

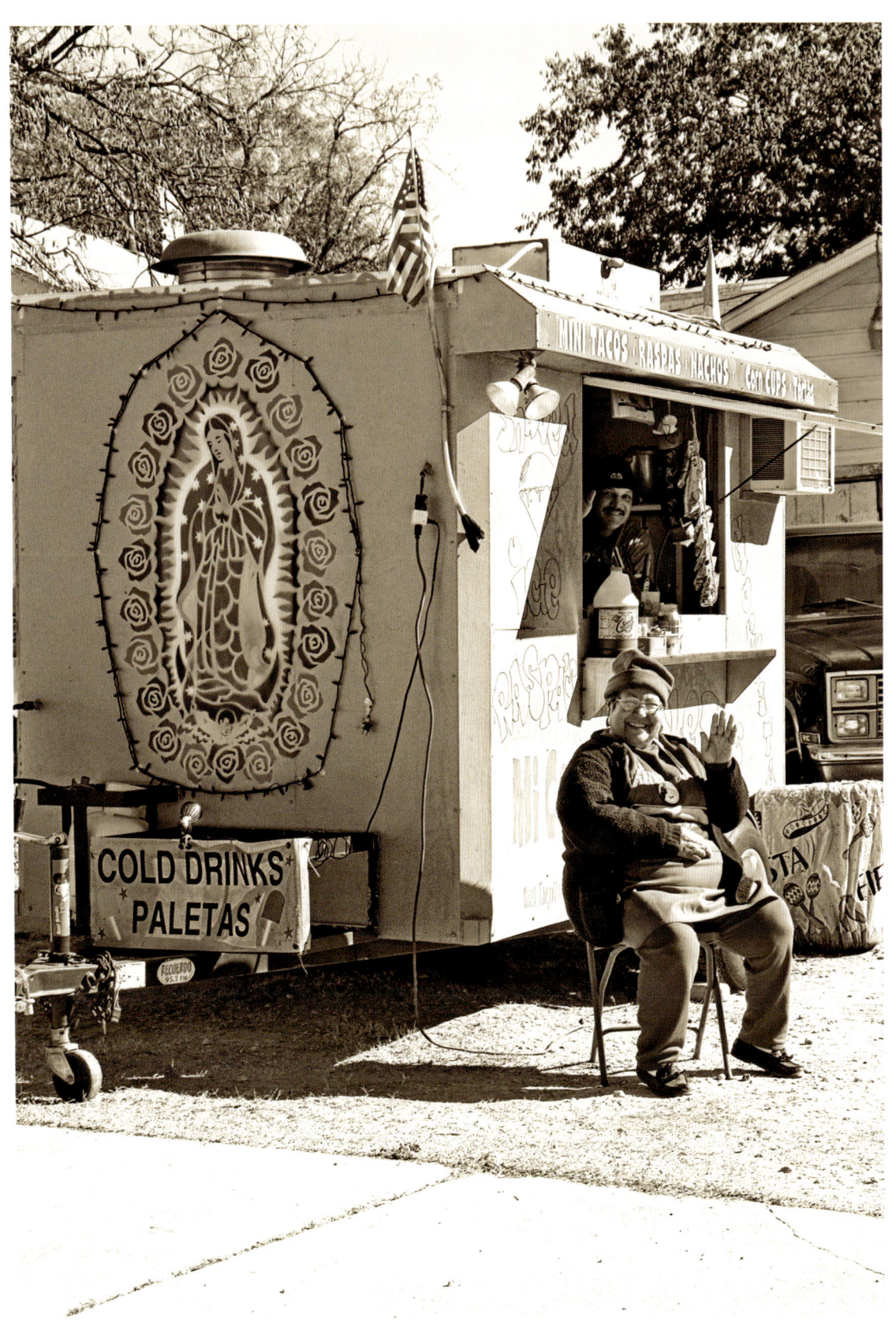

Taco Truck (2008)
San Antonio, Texas

Artist insight on page 121

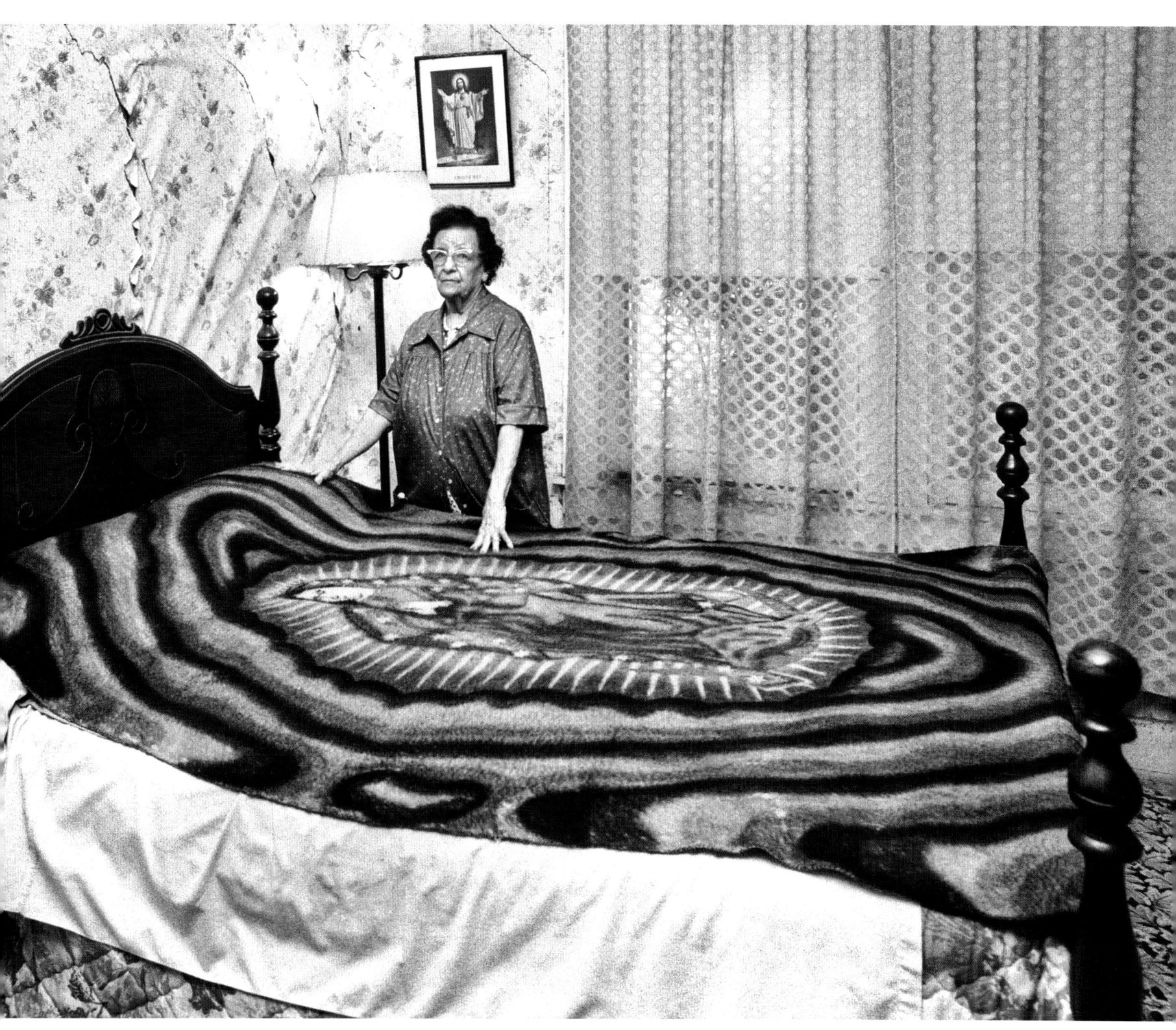

Tia Lupe (1986)
San Antonio, Texas

Artist insight on page 121

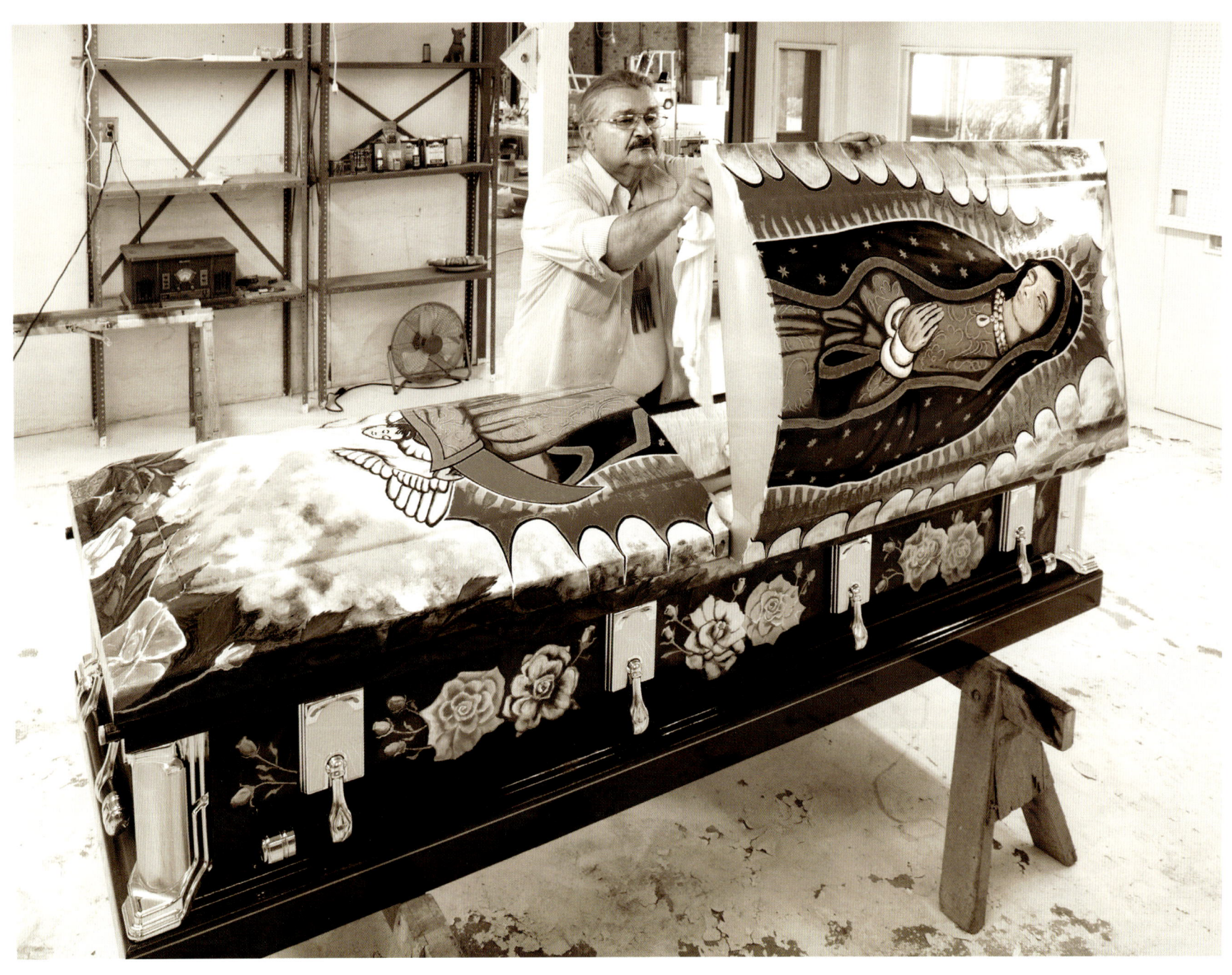

Ronald Rocha (2010)
San Antonio, Texas
Artist insight on page 122

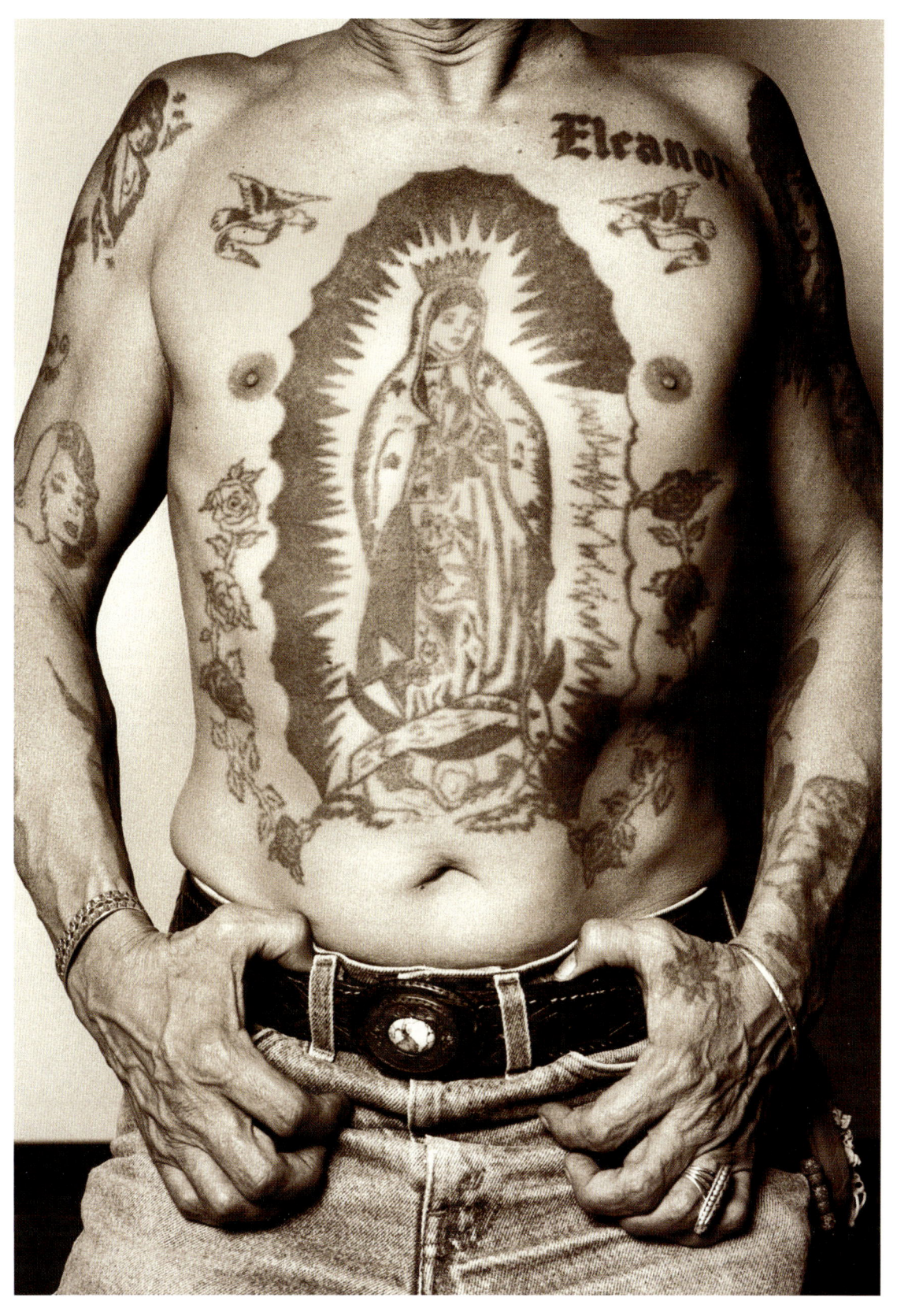

Raul Salinas (1986)
San Antonio, Texas

Artist insight on page 119

CHARREADA

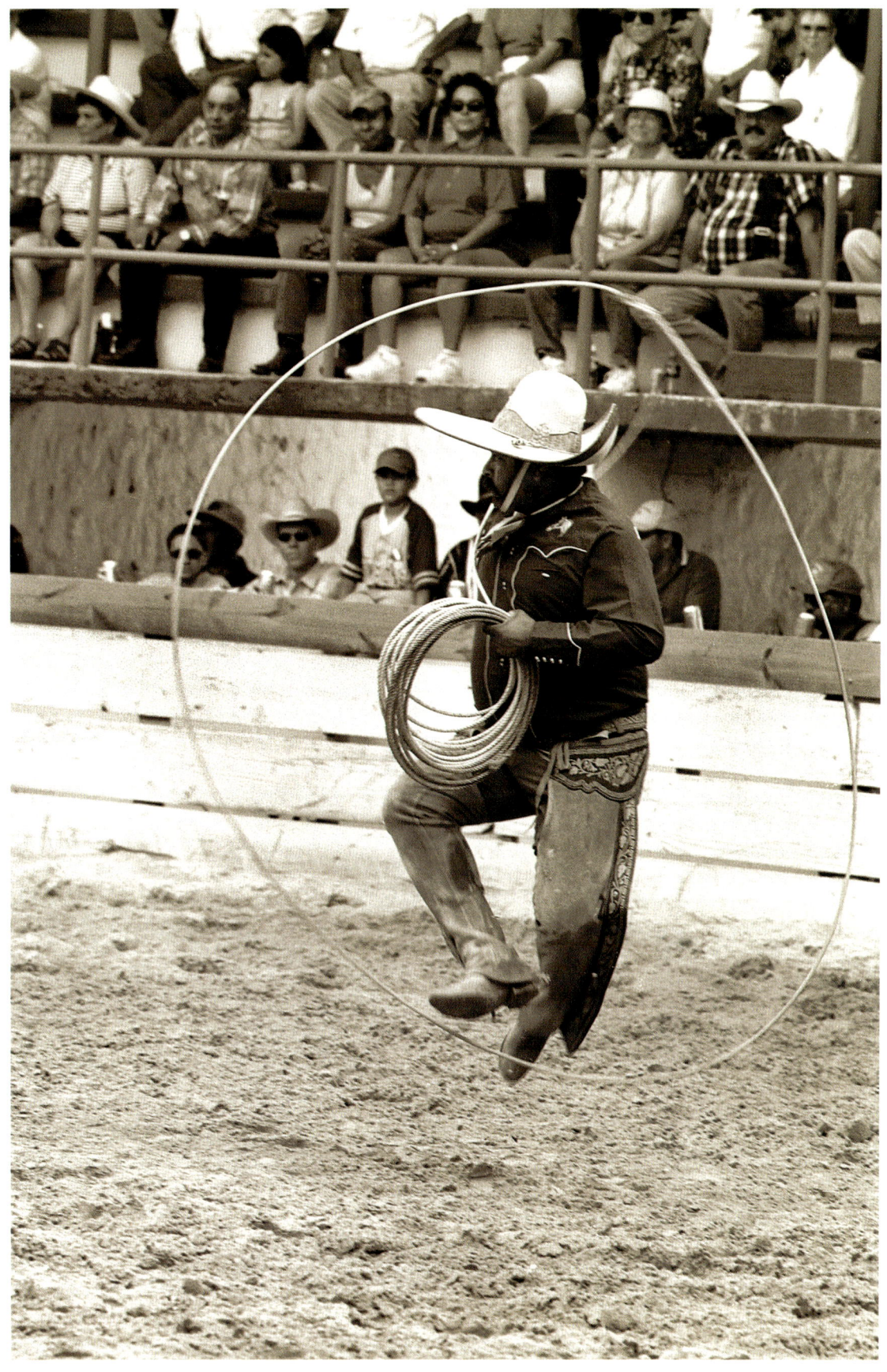

Charro Showing Roping Skill (1998)
San Antonio, Texas
In the collection of the Smithsonian American Art Museum

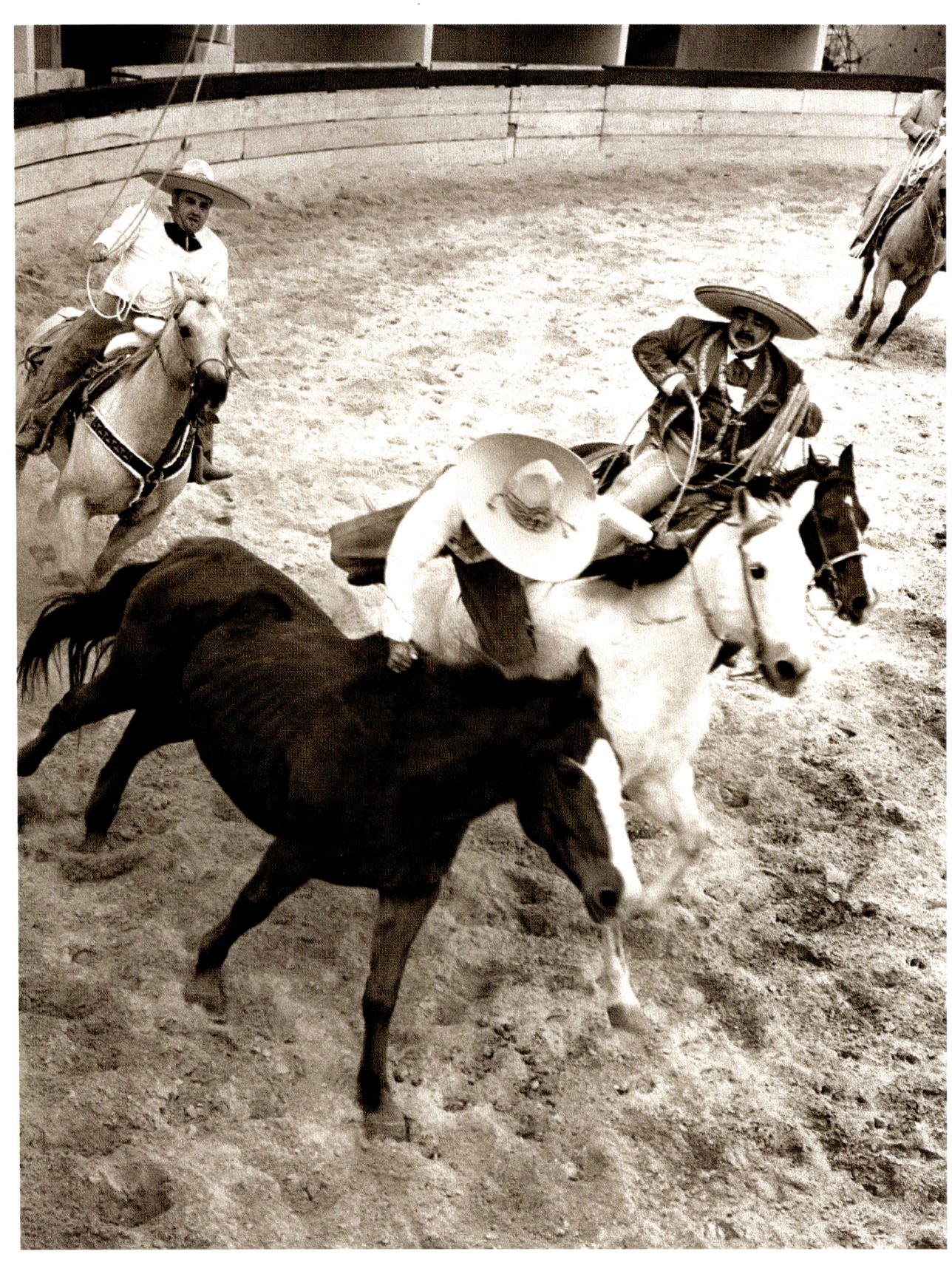

Paso de la muerte (2002)
San Antonio, Texas
In the collection of the Smithsonian American Art Museum

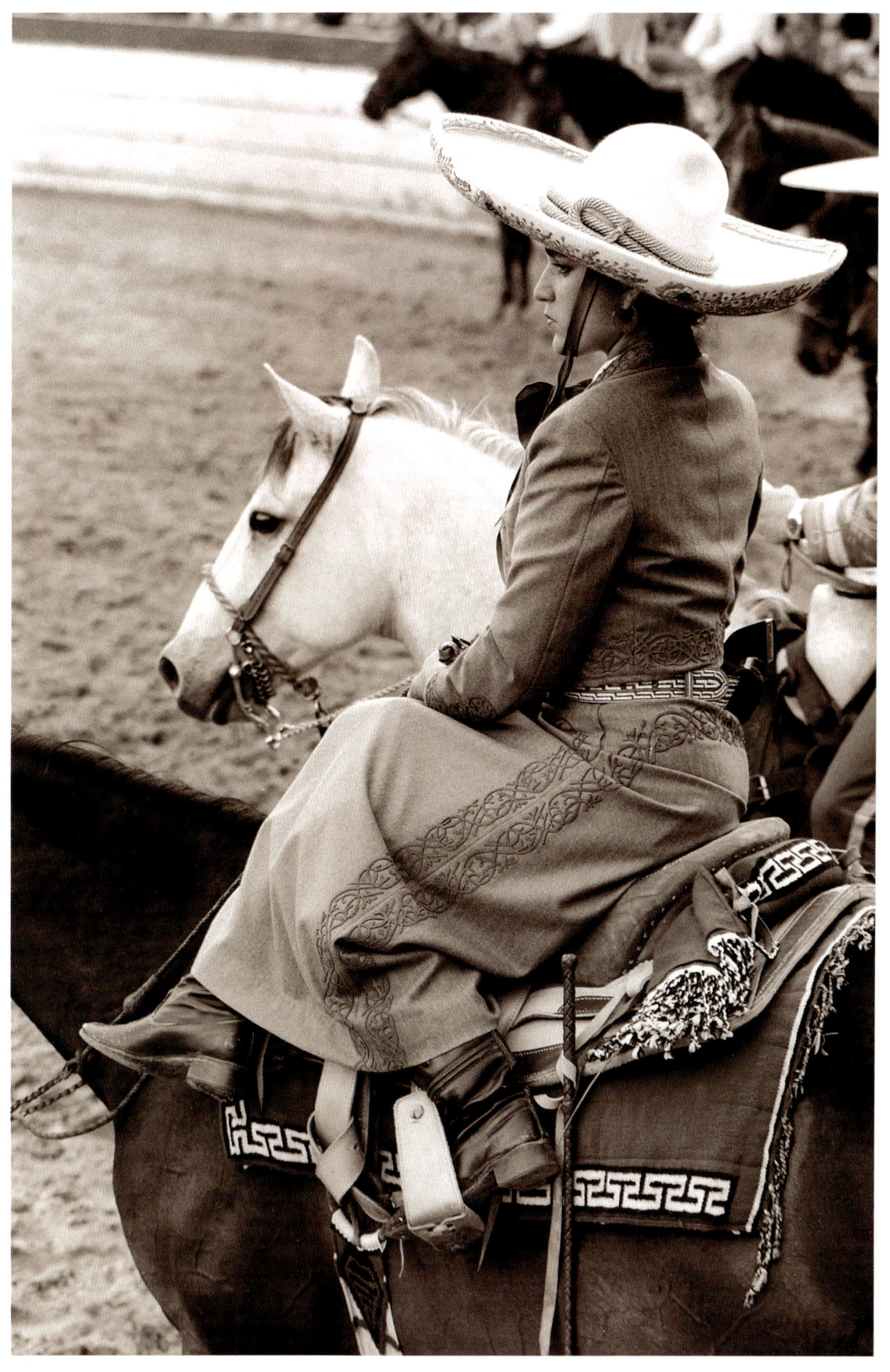

Sylvia Lopez Gaona (1985)
San Antonio, Texas

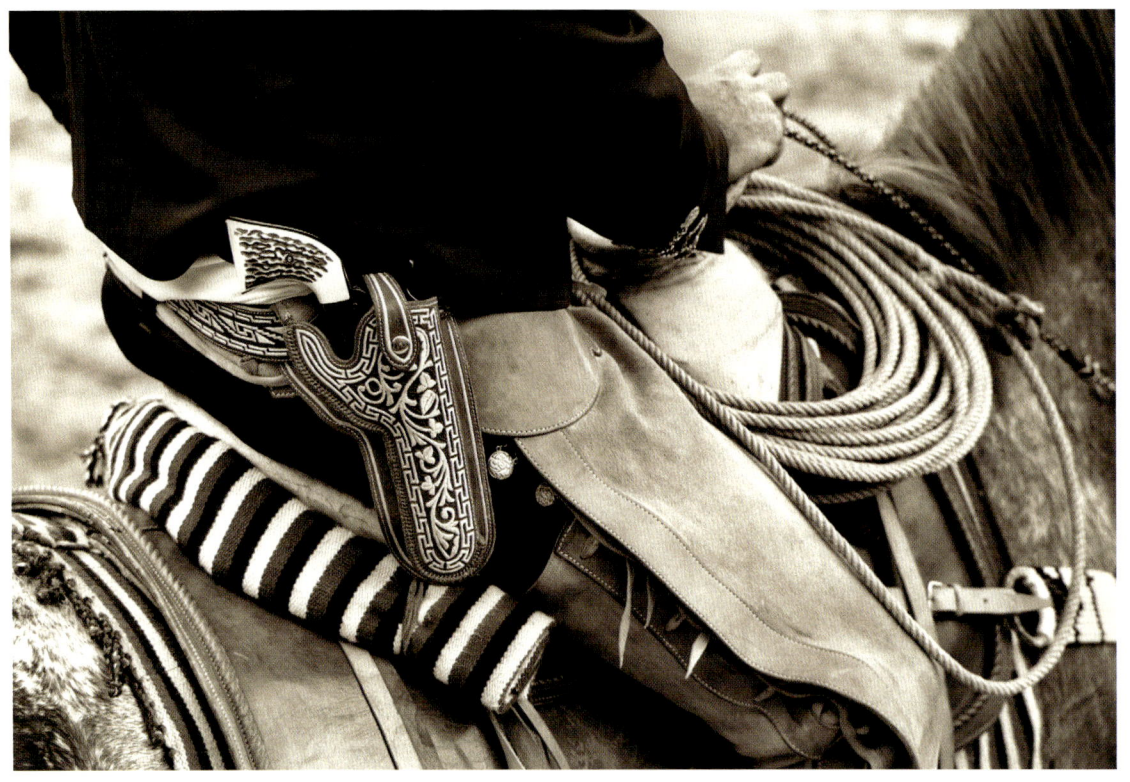

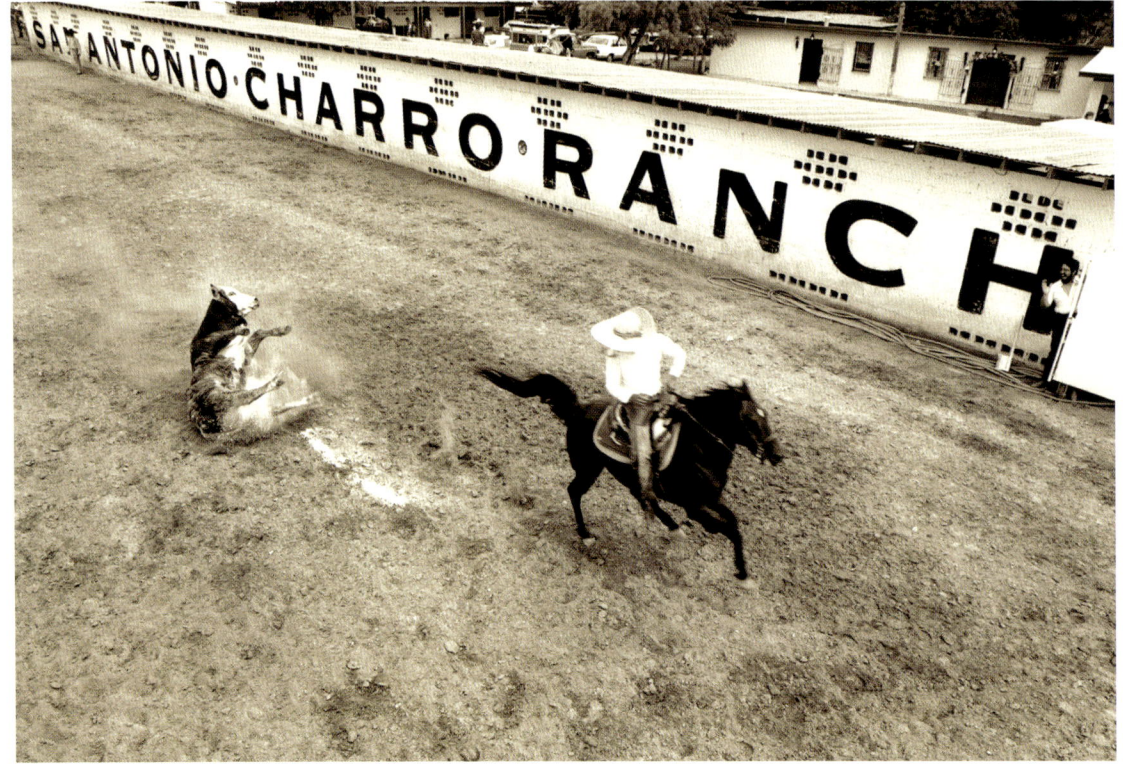

Top: El Charro (1985)
San Antonio, Texas
In the collection of the
Smithsonian American Art Museum

Bottom: Colas (1986)
San Antonio, Texas

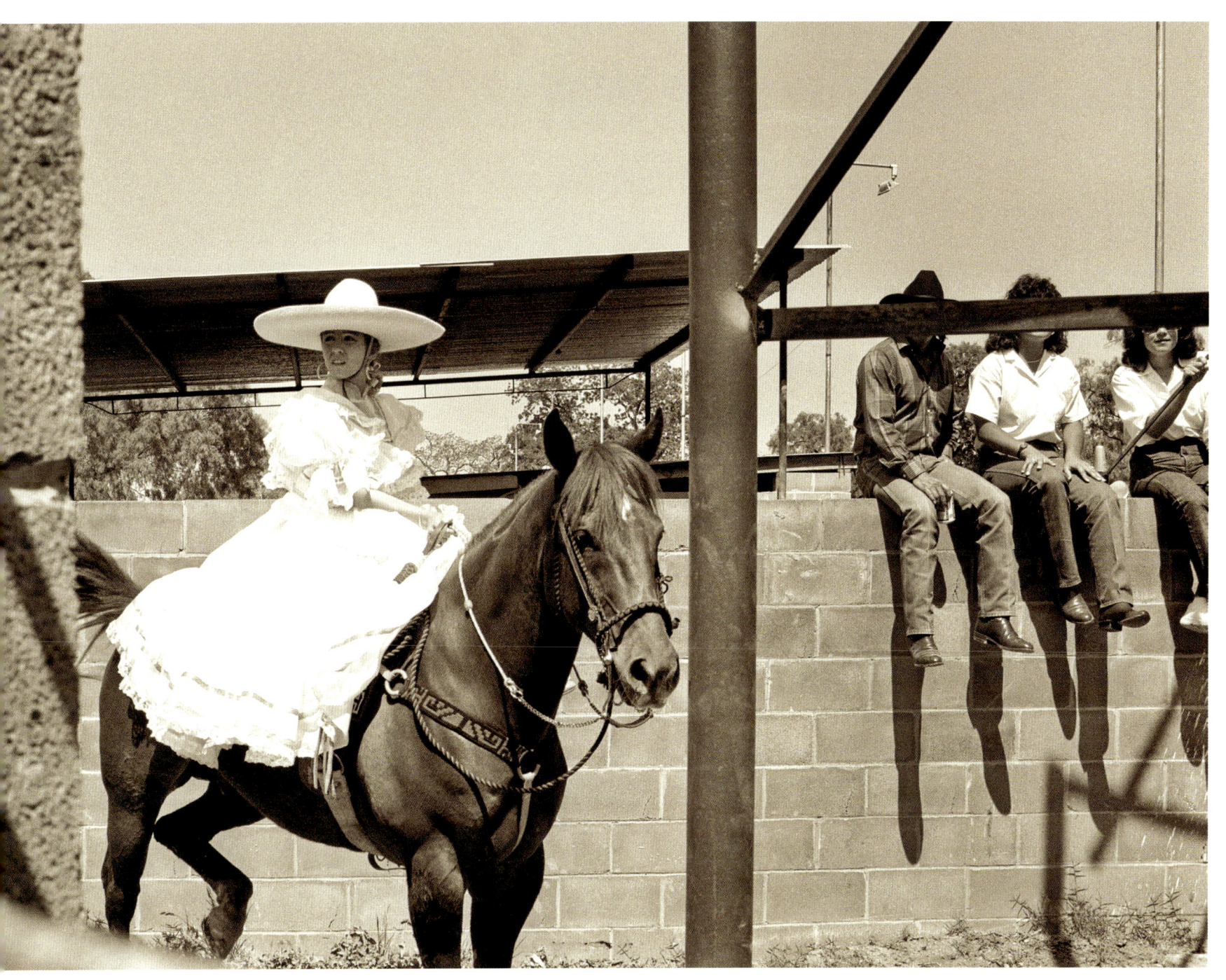

Adelita (1984)
San Antonio, Texas
In the collection of the Smithsonian American Art Museum

CONJUNTO

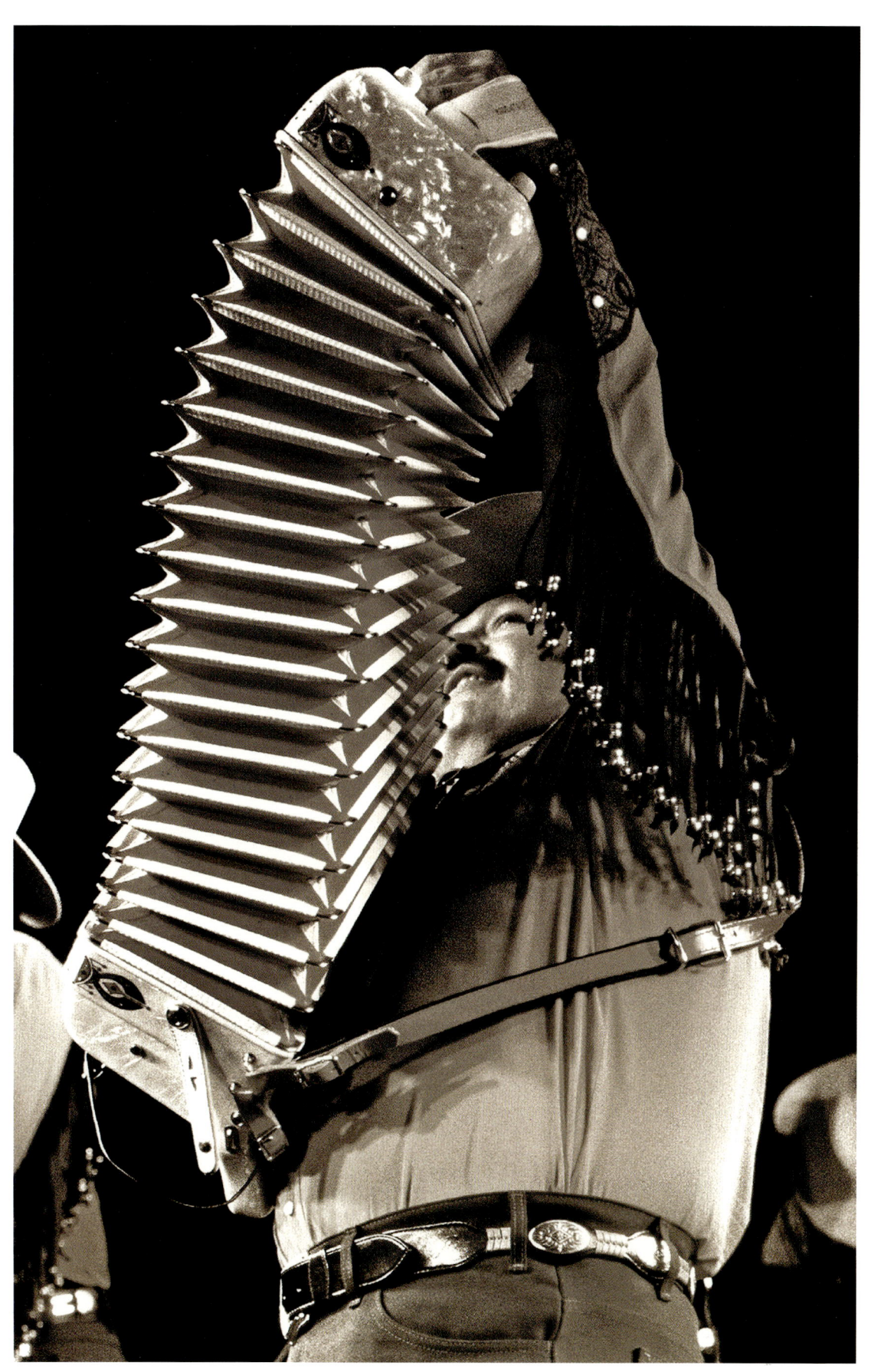

Ramón Ayala (1999)
San Antonio, Texas

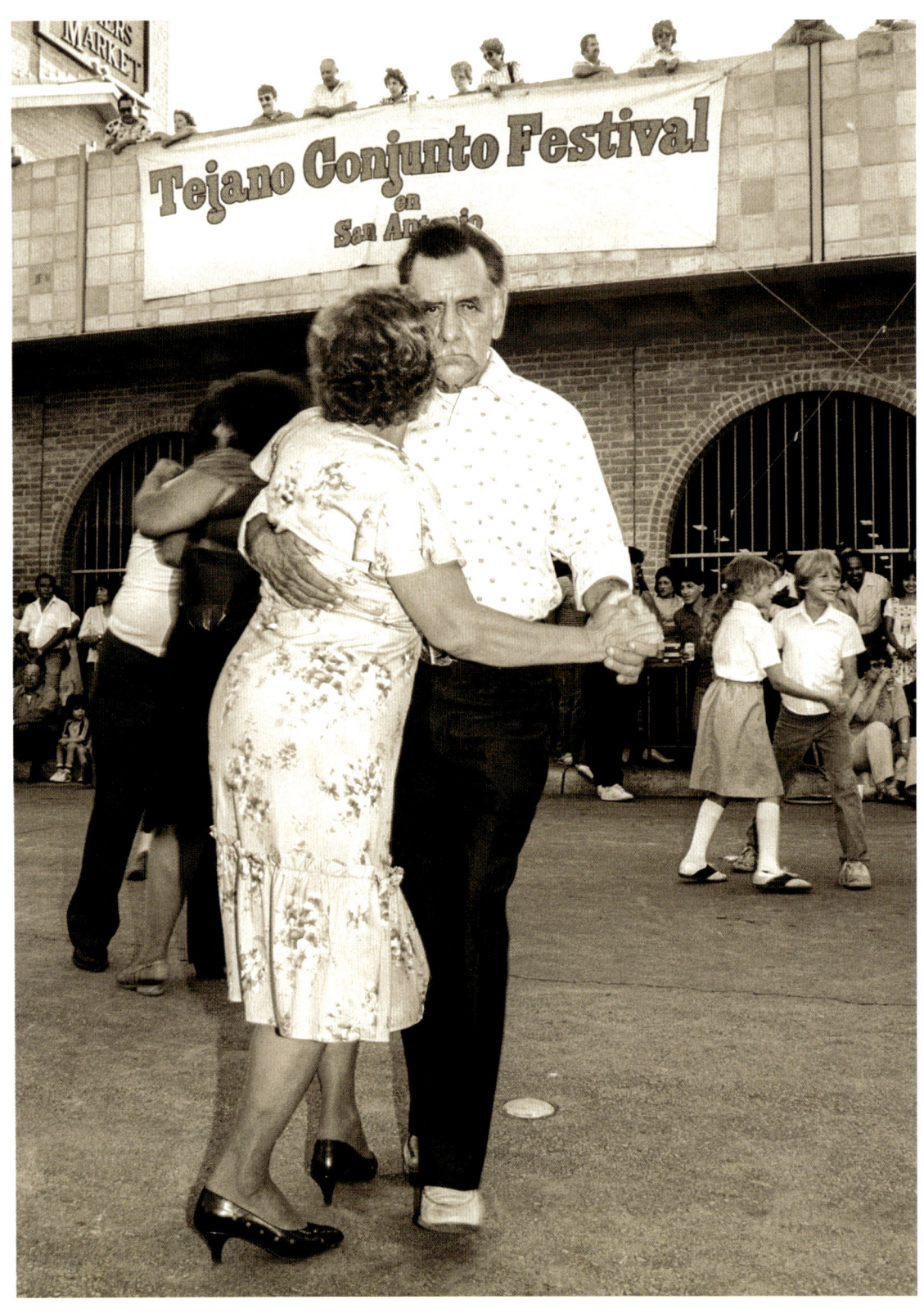

La Movida (1985)
San Antonio, Texas

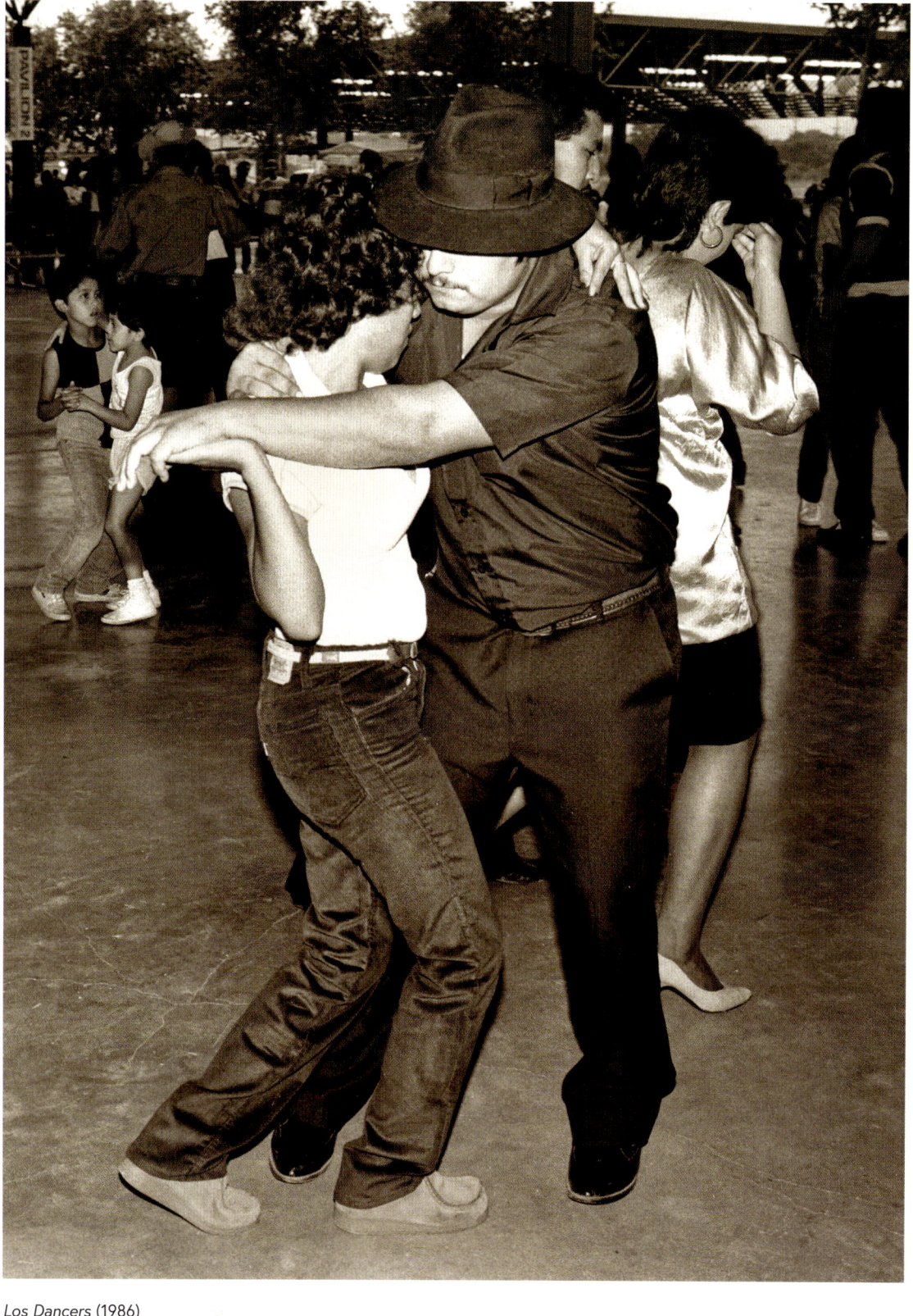

Los Dancers (1986)
San Antonio, Texas

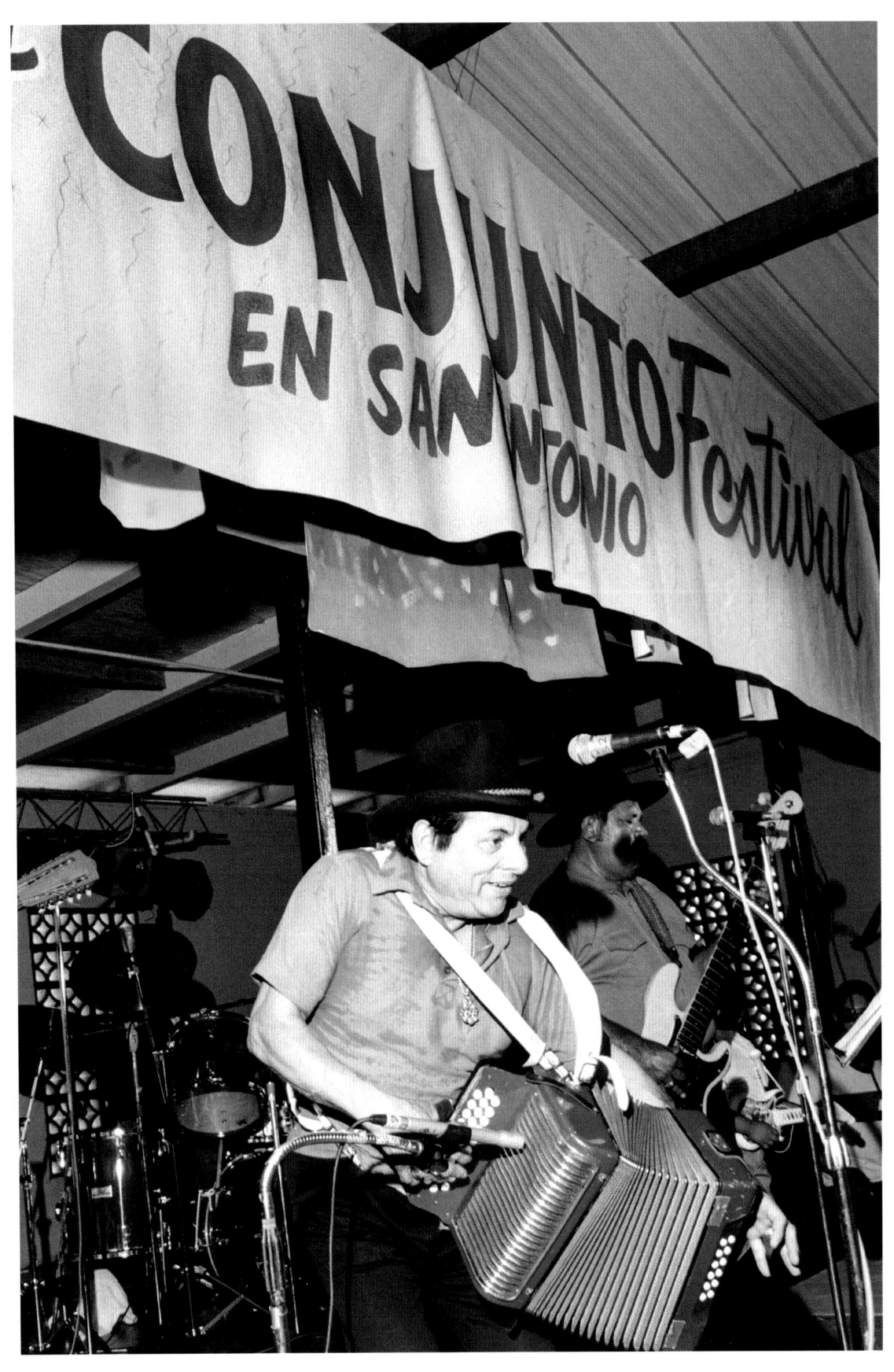

Mingo Saldivar (1988)
San Antonio, Texas

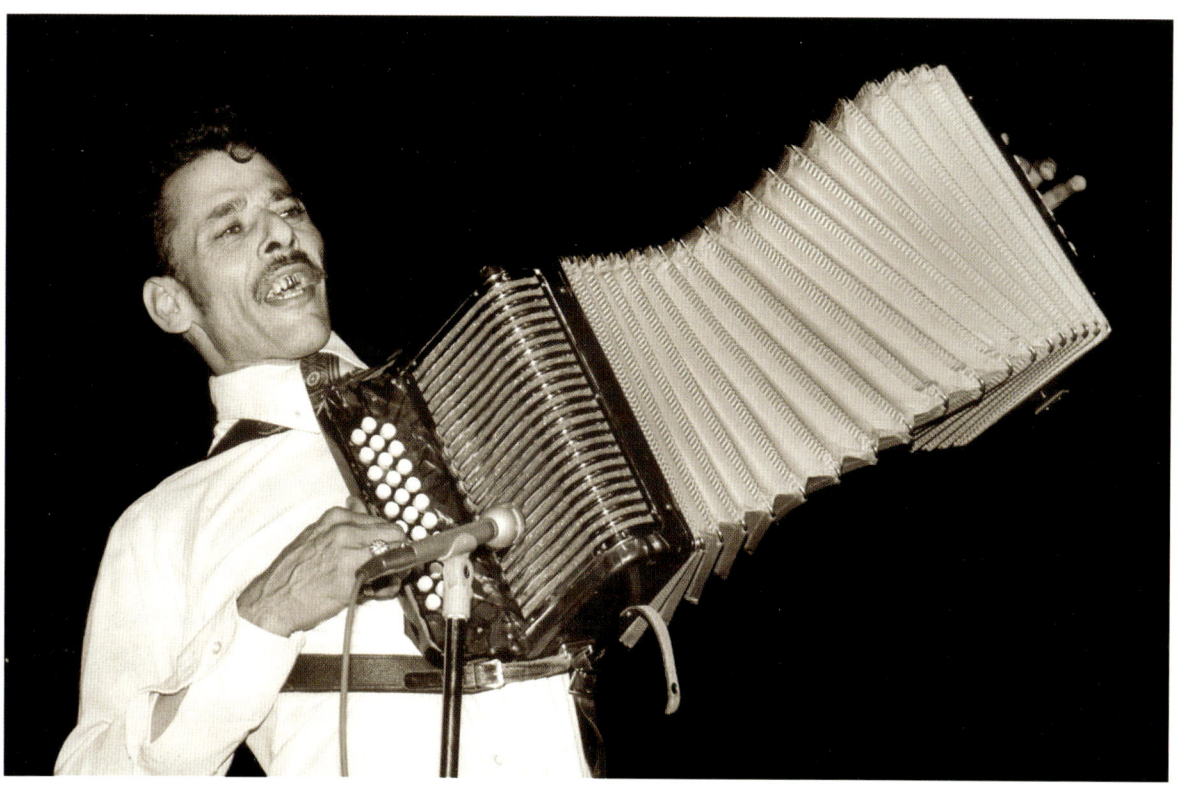

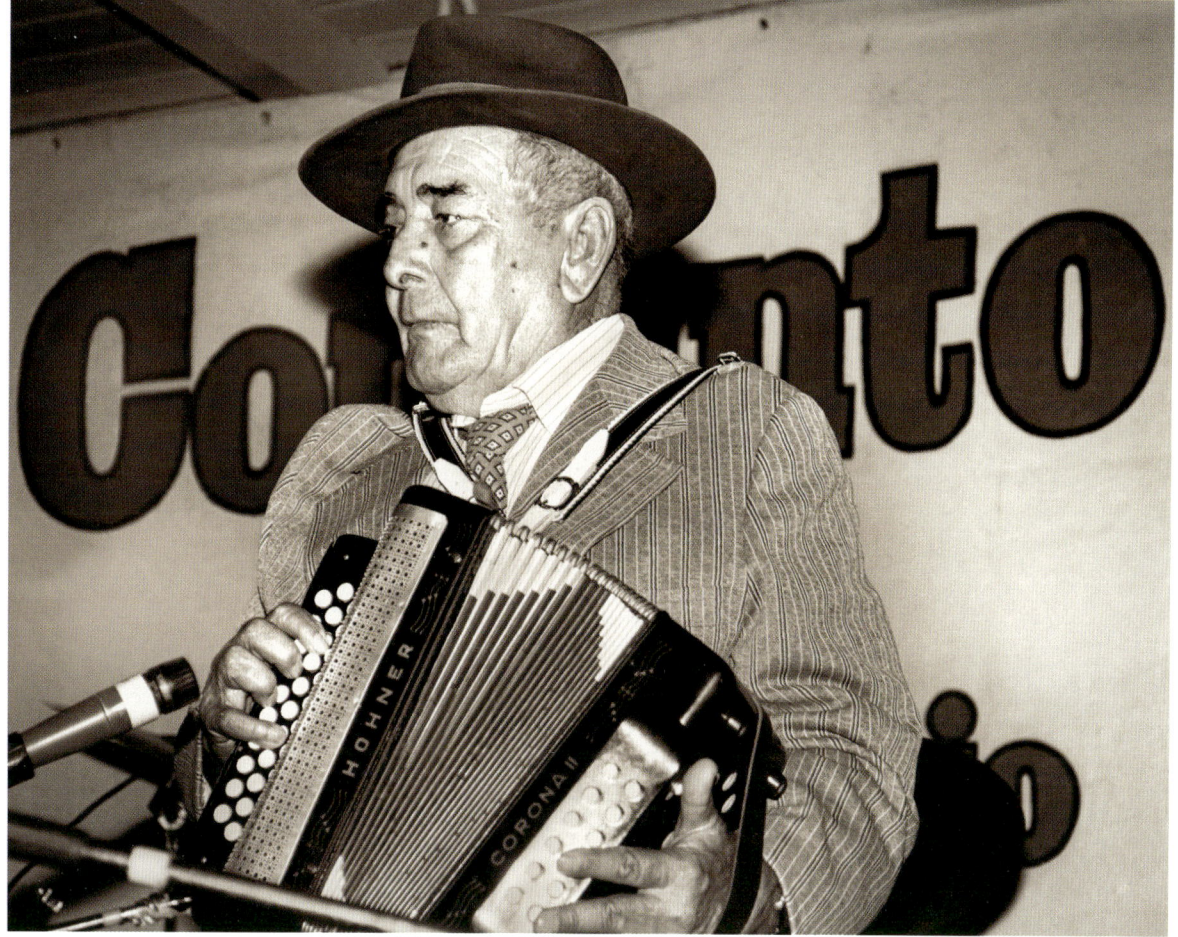

Top: Santiago Jiménez (1987)
San Antonio, Texas

Bottom: Narciso Martínez (1987)
San Antonio, Texas

RETRATOS

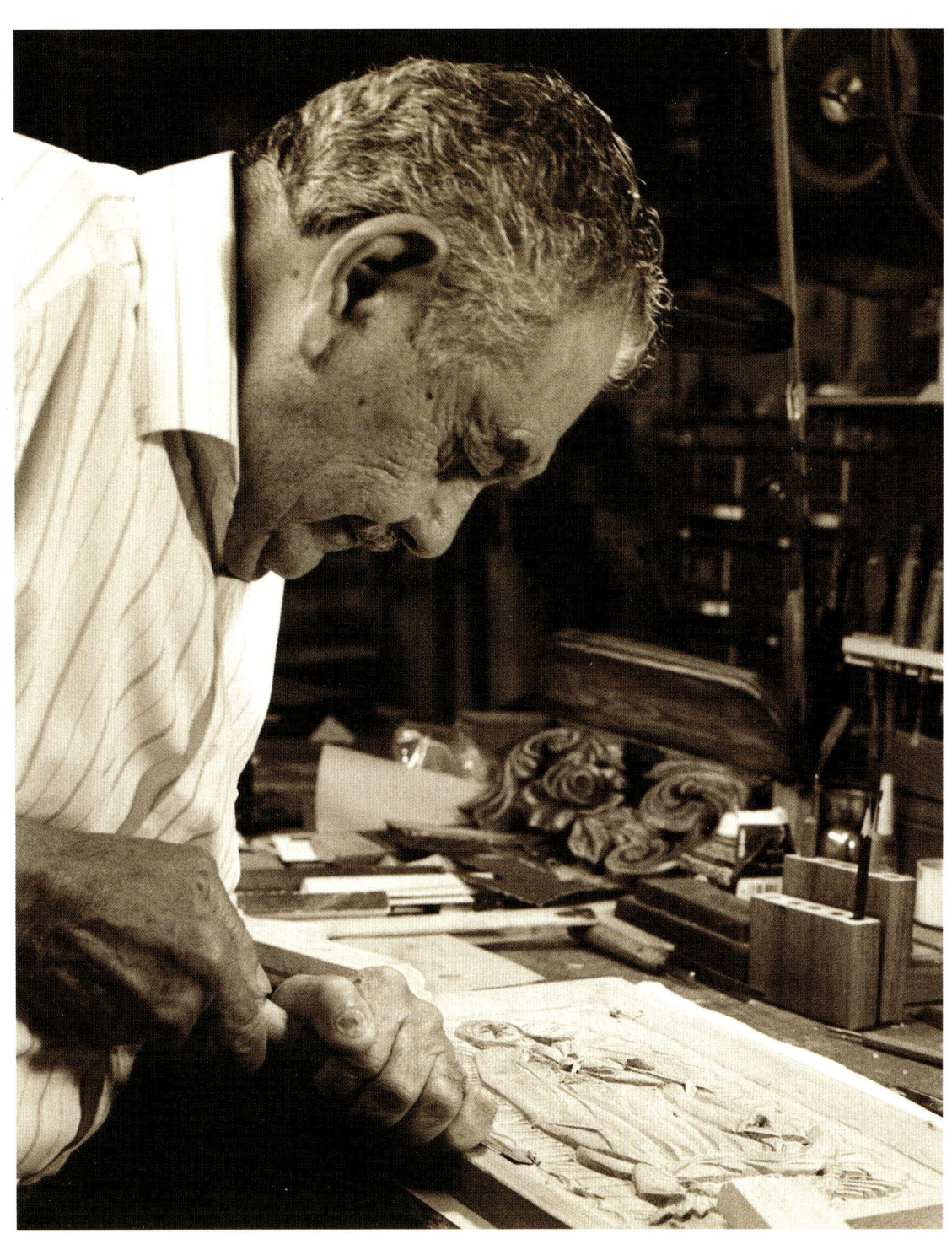

Papá (1998)
San Antonio, Texas

Artist insight on page 124

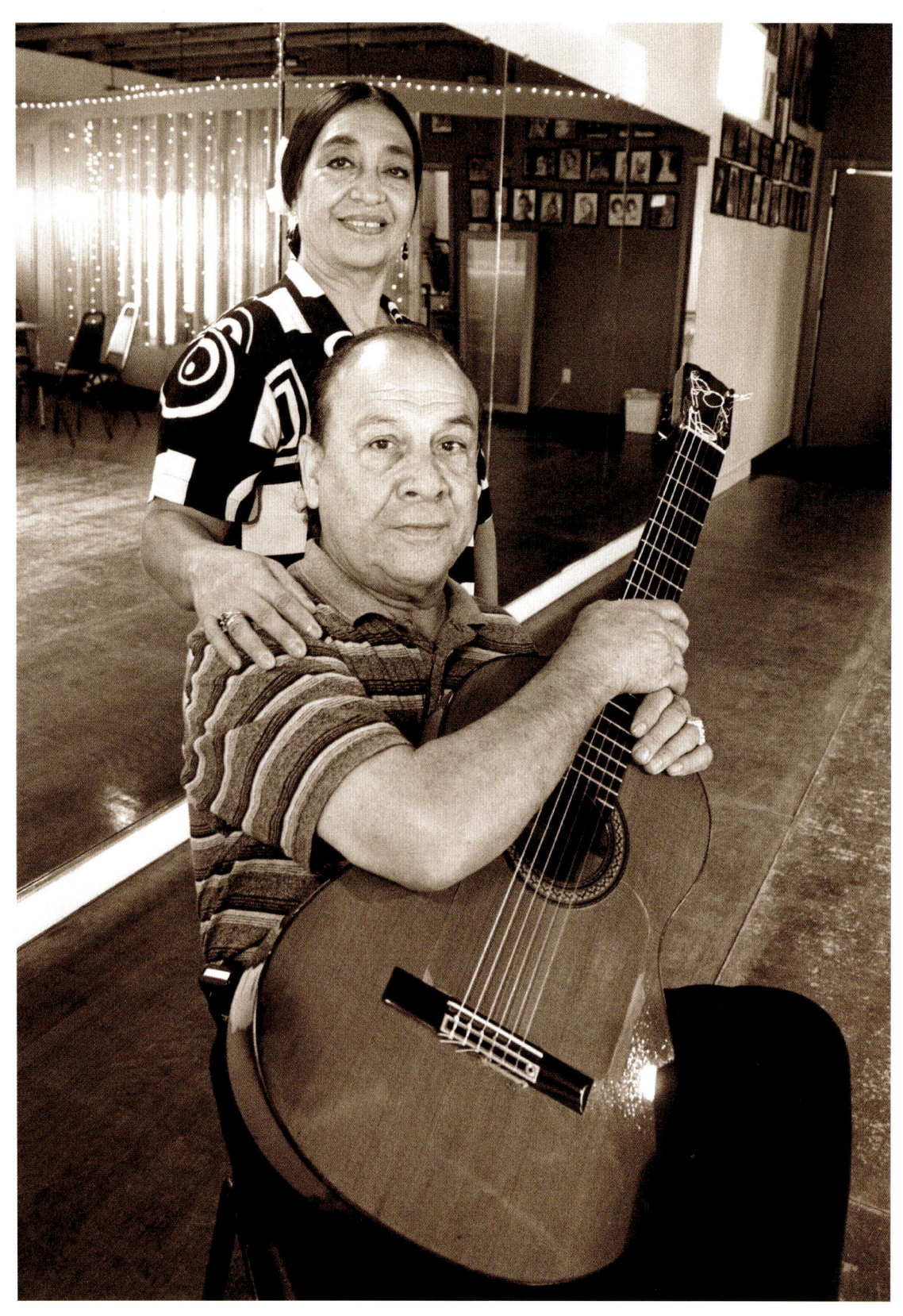

El Curro and Teresa Champion (2000)
San Antonio, Texas

Artist insight on page 124

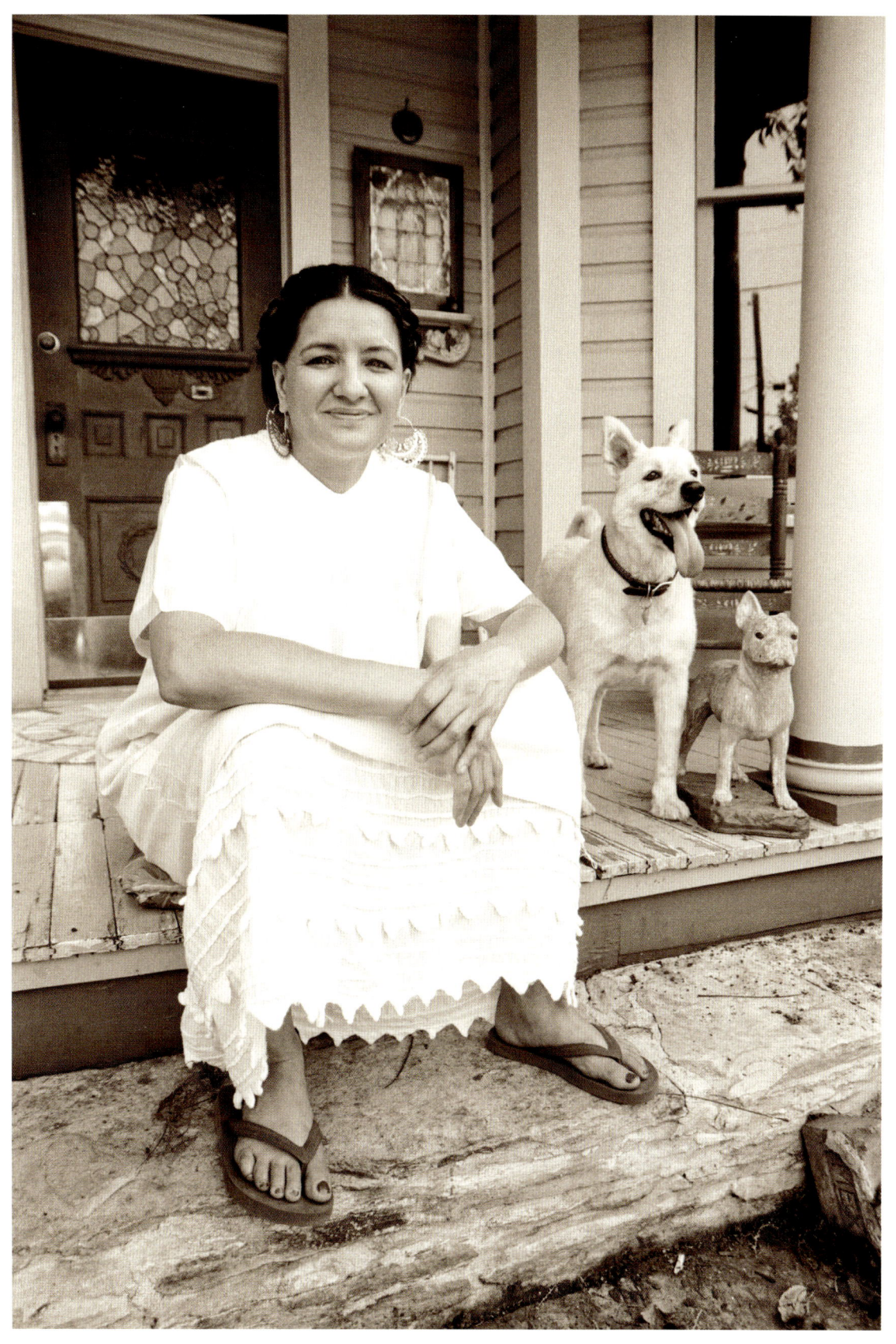

Sandra Cisneros (1998)
San Antonio, Texas
In the collection of the National Portrait Gallery

Artist insight on page 125

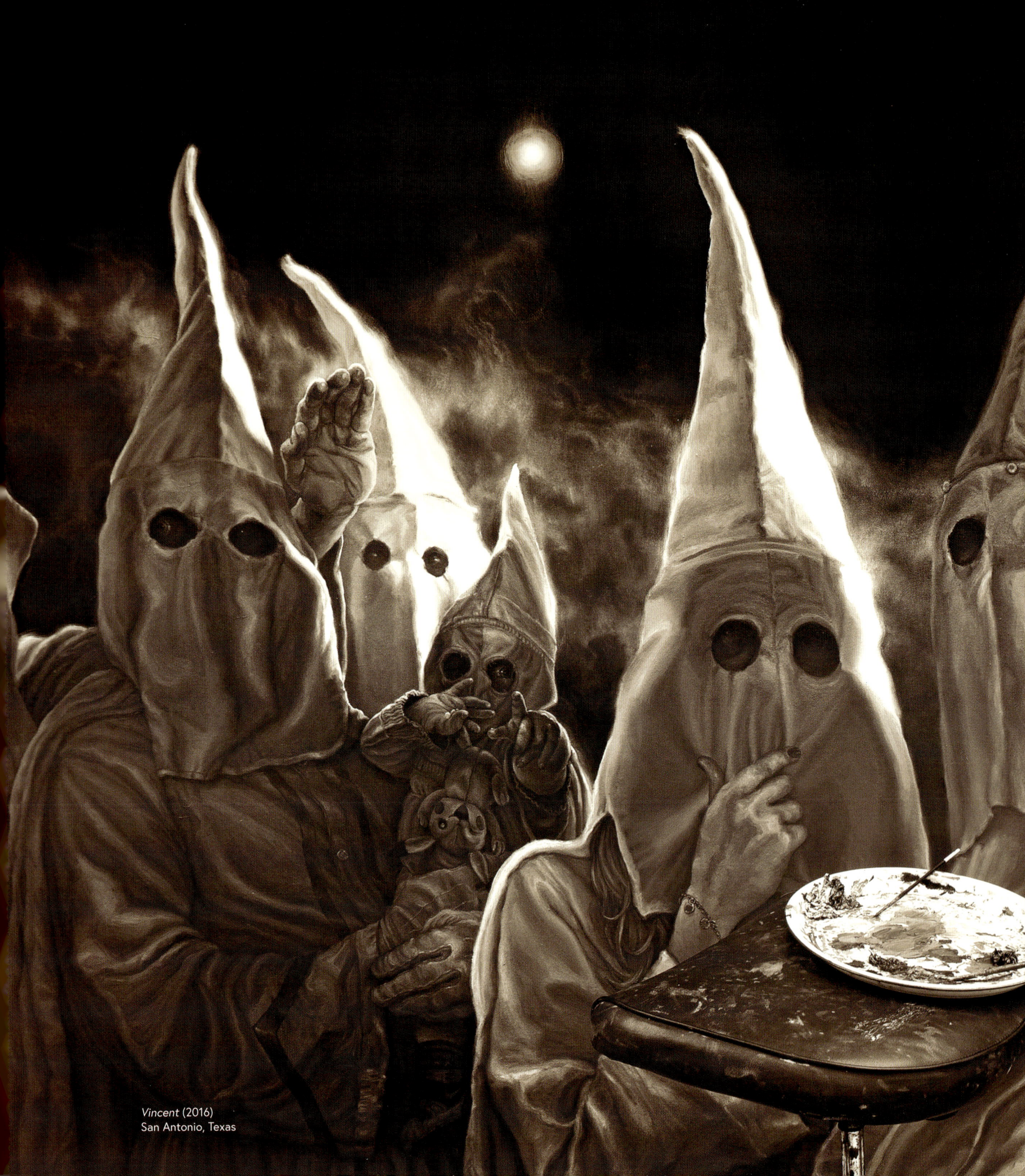

Vincent (2016)
San Antonio, Texas

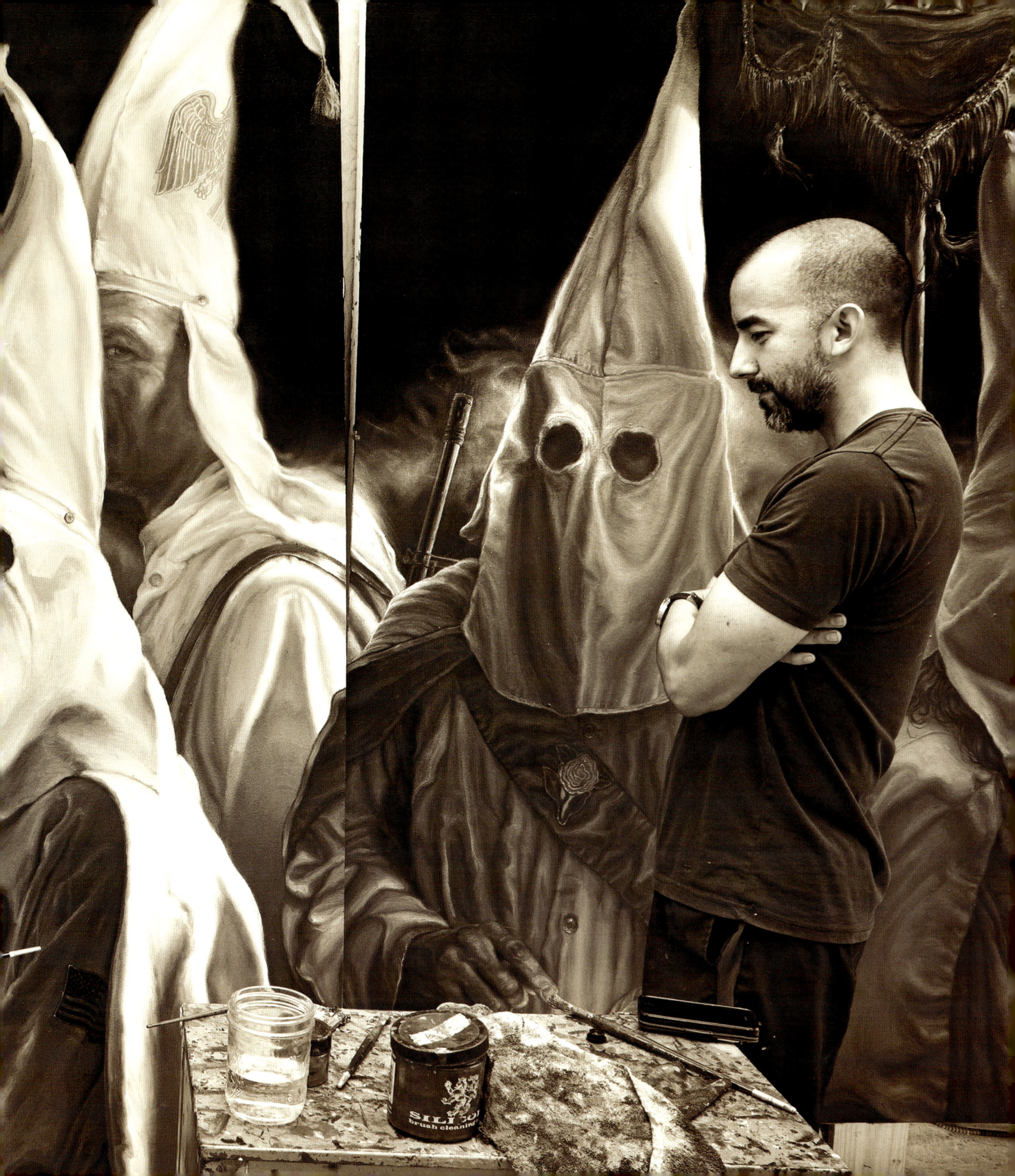

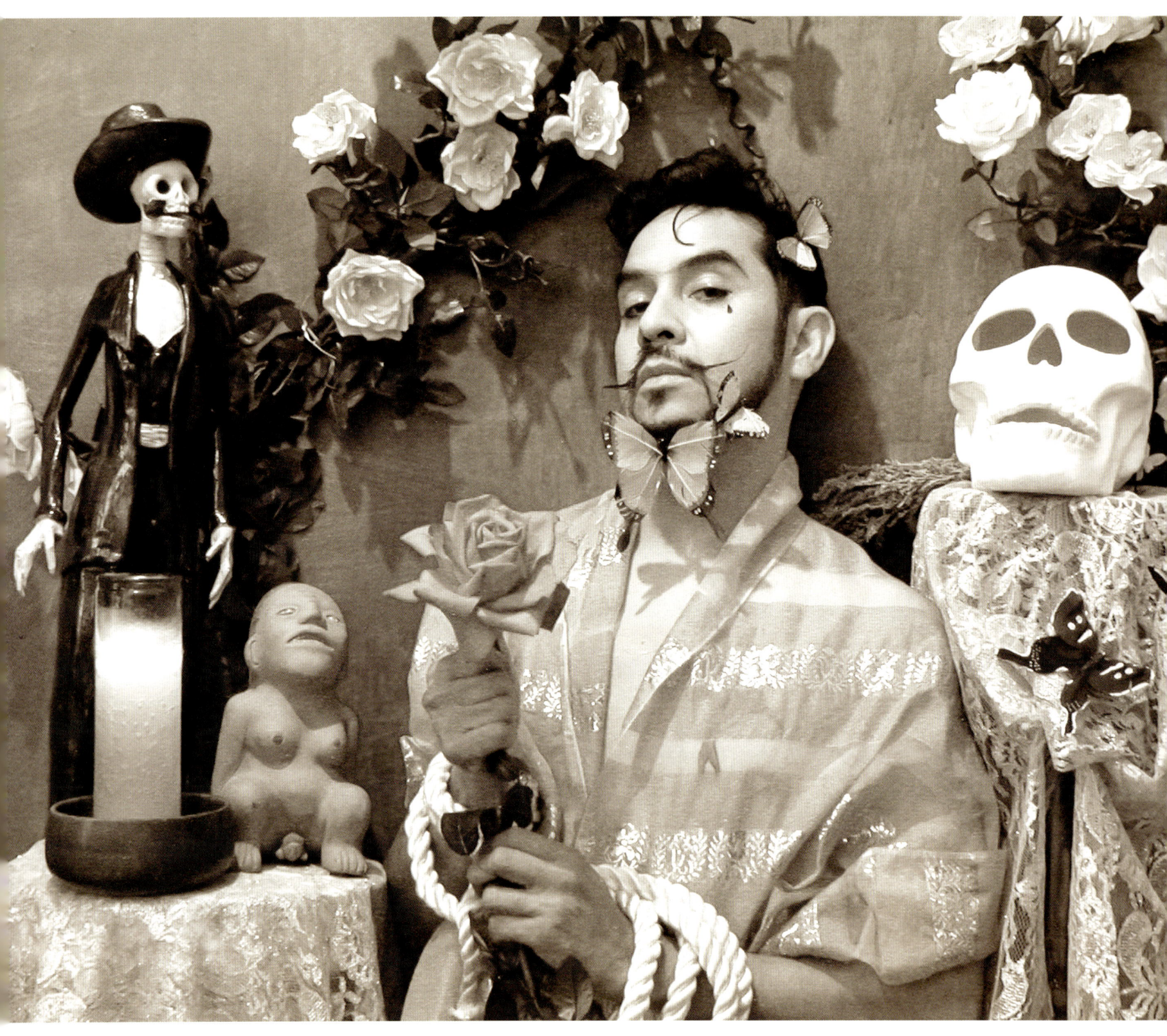

David Zamora Casas (1999)
San Antonio, Texas

Artist insight on page 126

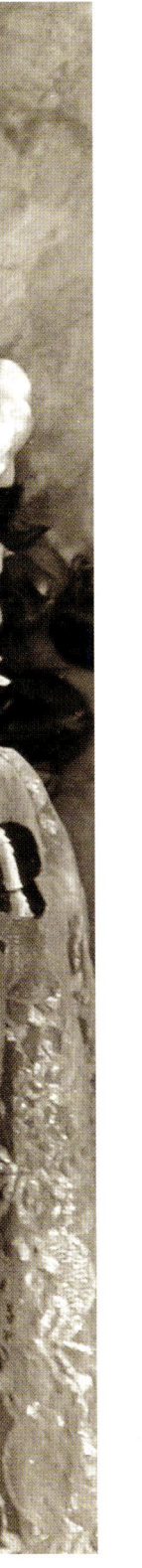

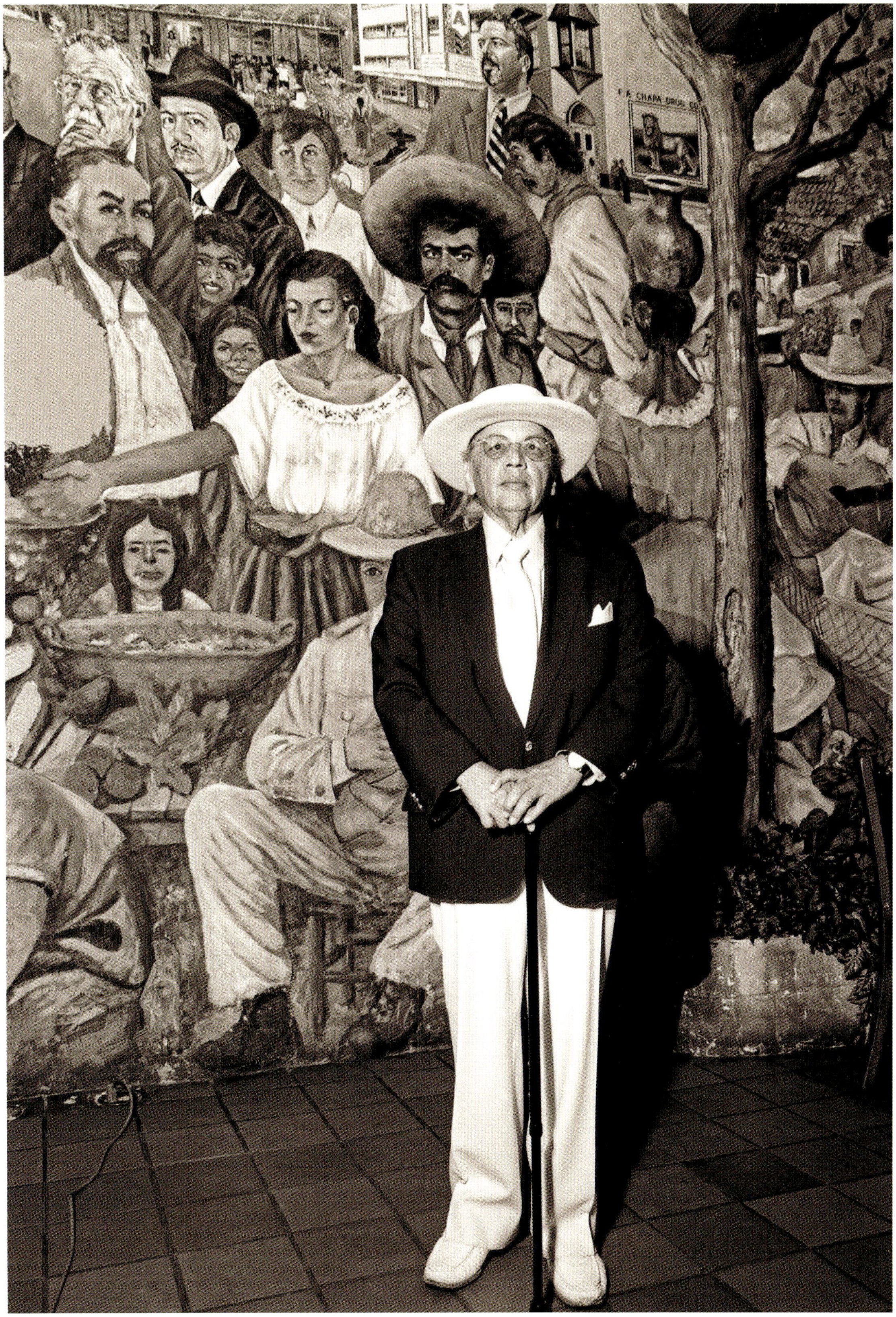

Jorge (2000)
San Antonio, Texas

Artist insight on page 126

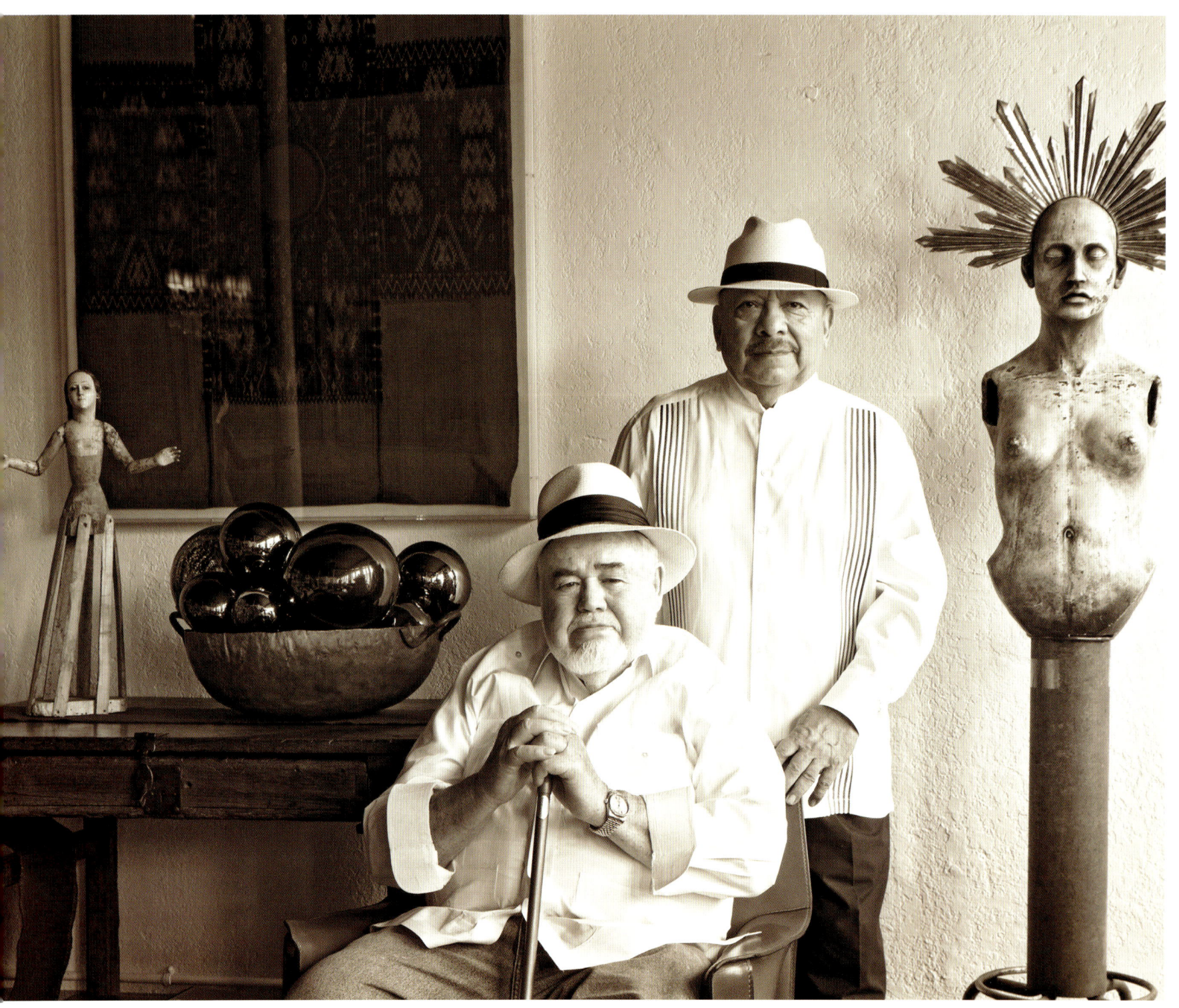

Tomás Y Dudley (2010)
San Antonio, Texas

Artist insight on page 127

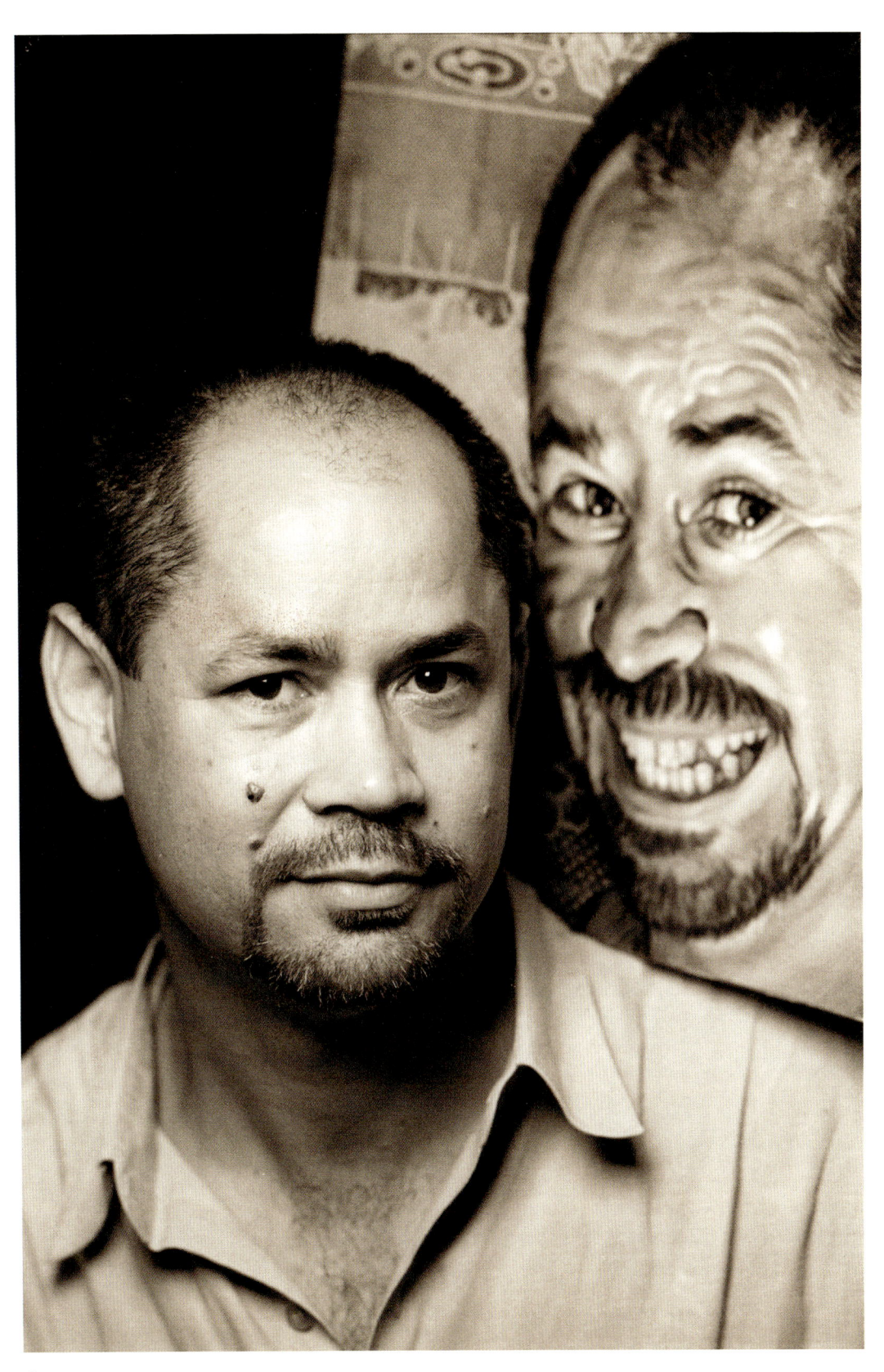

Ángel Rodriguez-Diaz (1995)
San Antonio, Texas

Artist insight on page 128

FRAGILE ROMANCE

WORDS BY GARY WHITFORD

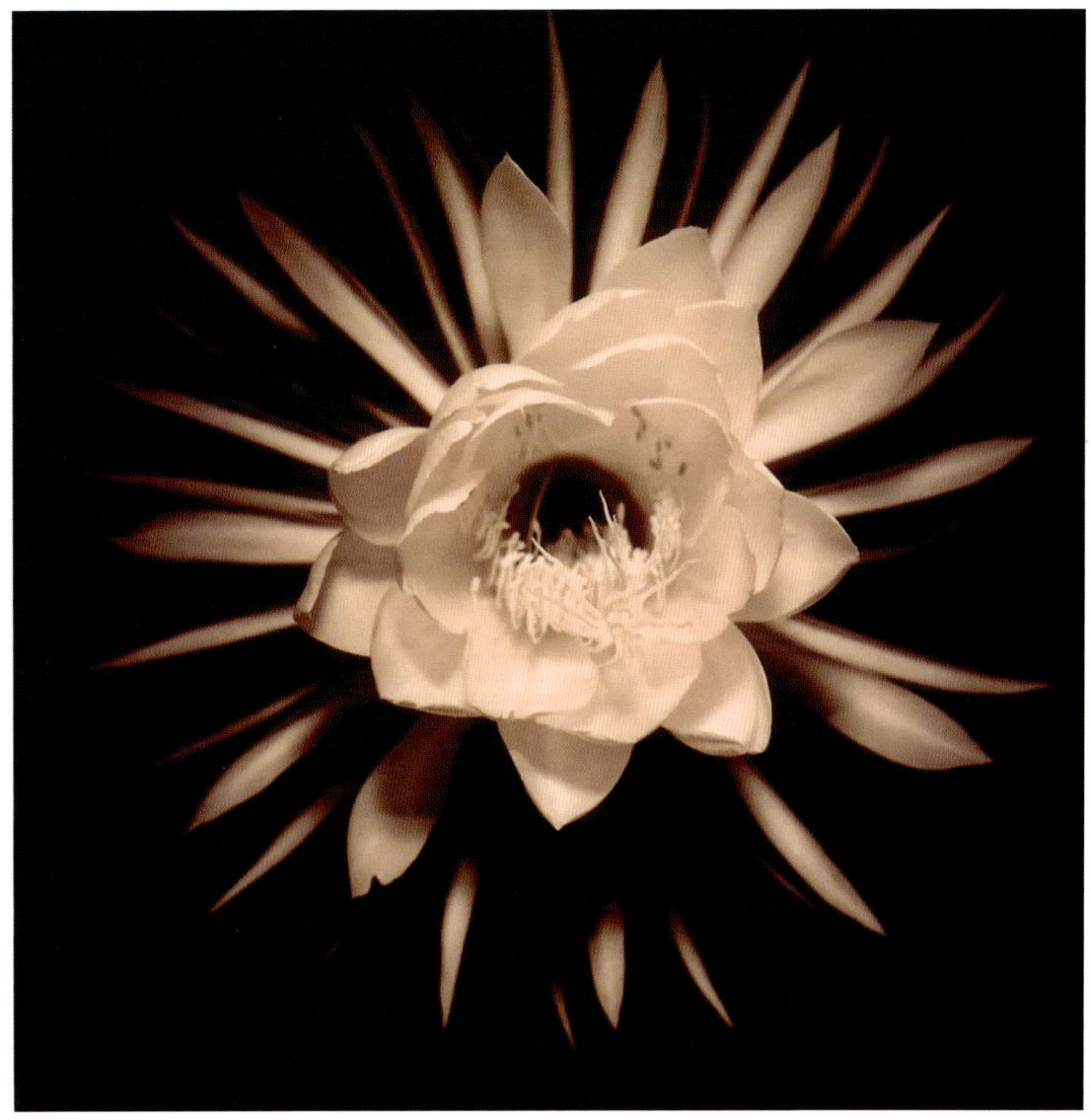

In Midnight Privacy (1996)
San Antonio, Texas

In midnight privacy, love opens wide.
Beyond tongue and tonsil,
Tonight's conversation digests.
Assessment feeds her bloodstream
To open her inviting glow.

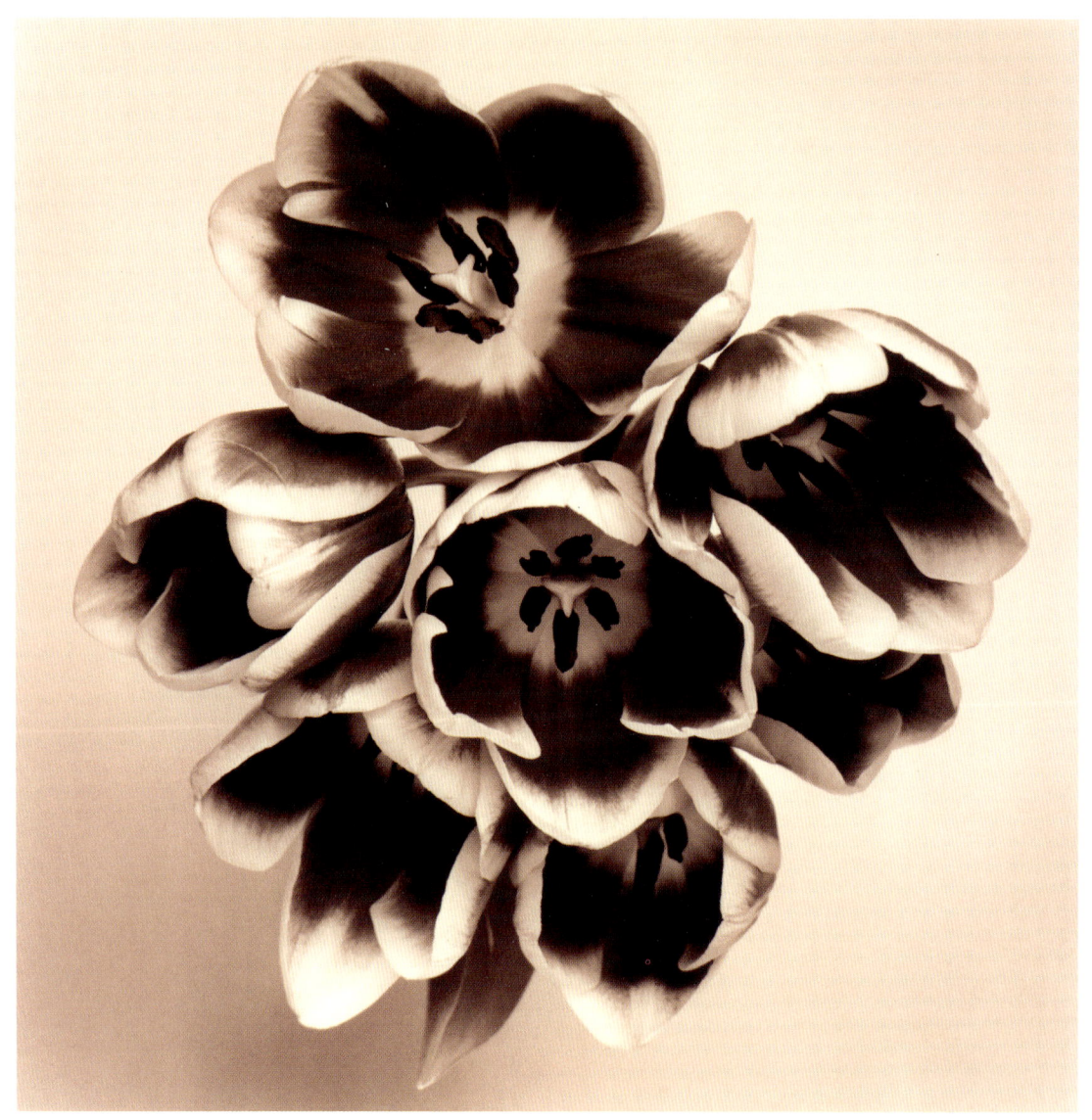

Sacred Vanity (1996)
San Antonio, Texas

Gazing without seeming to notice,
She reviews the suitor band:
Which honors sacred vanity
Enough to repeat his name?

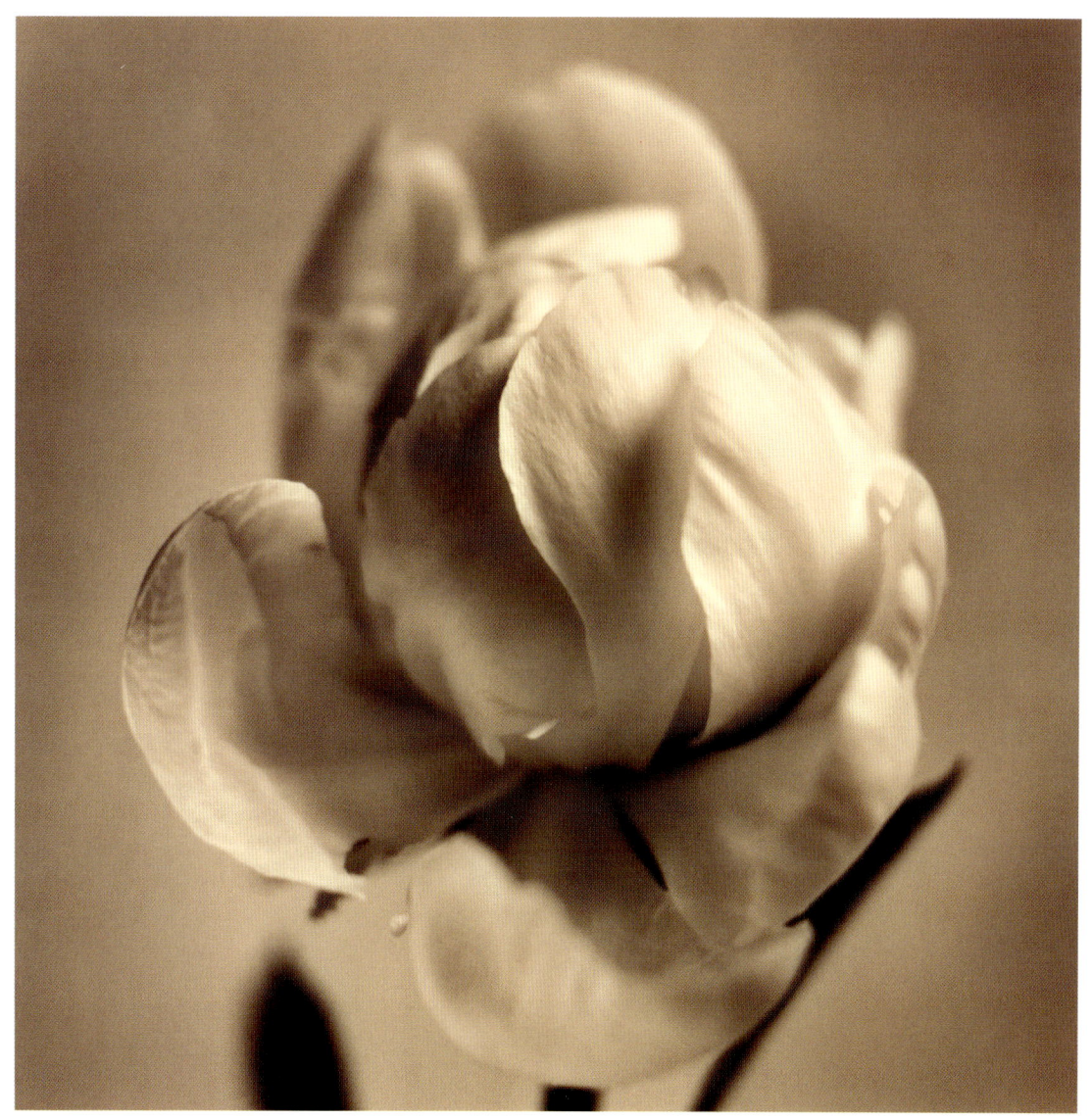

Nude Glowing (1996)
San Antonio, Texas

She crosses from bathroom to bed
Nude, glowing in the afternoon light.
The roundness of her,
The colors of her,
Memory burns indelible
Walking to me alive and easy.

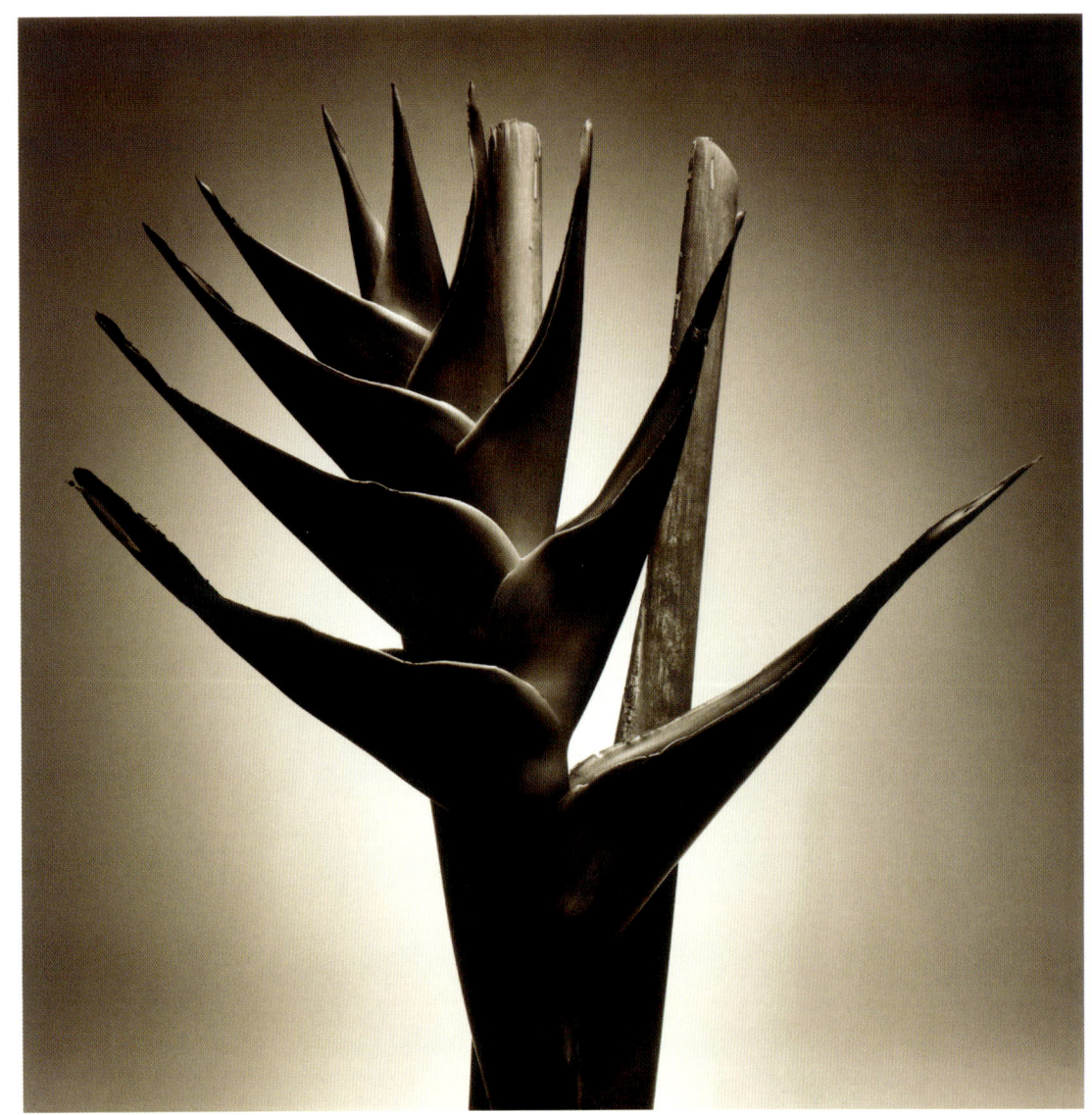

Exotica (1996)
San Antonio, Texas

This morning, we awake
Alive as we will ever,
As close as we get.
Light crowns your exotica,
Your face relishes my adoration.

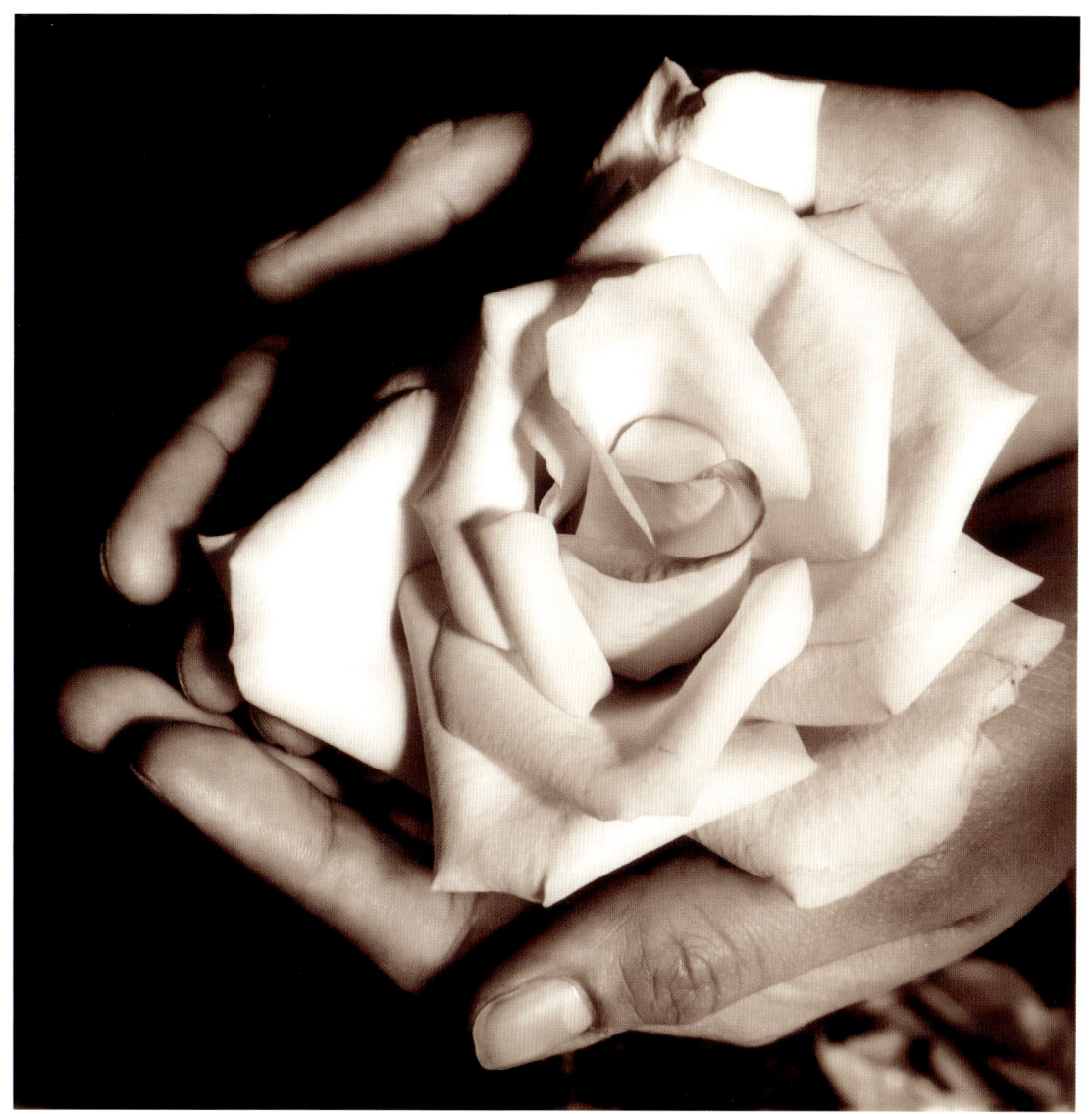

Ardent Feeeling (1996)
San Antonio, Texas

Not the whole world in her hands,
Merely the part that determines
The validity of my most ardent
Feelings, dreams, intention, sex.

ANGELS

WORDS BY GARY WHITFORD

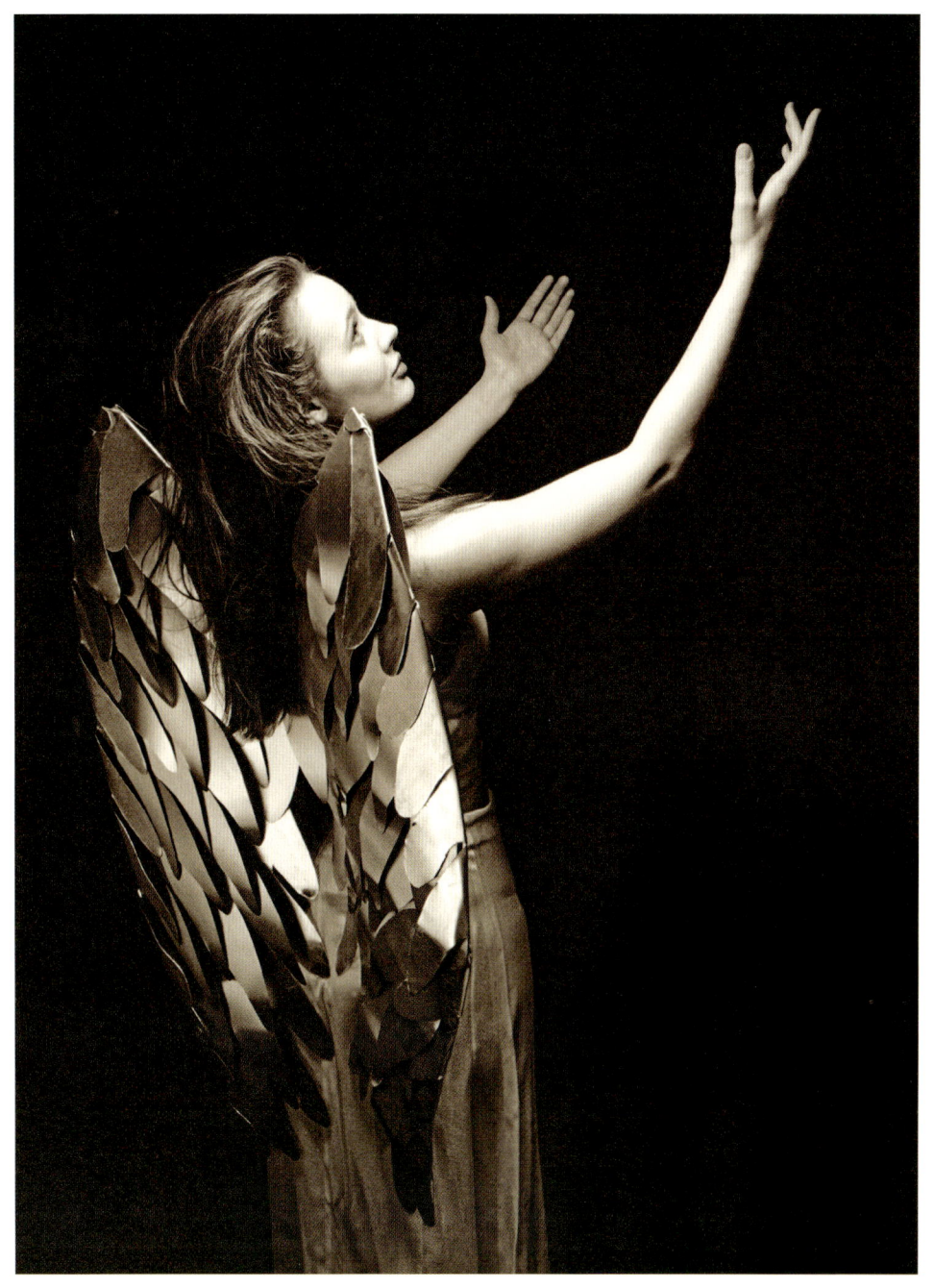

Guardian Angel (2002)
San Antonio, Texas

Angel, guard my heart against love unmet;
Angel, reveal True Self that I may meet
True Love with able spirit and enduring faith.

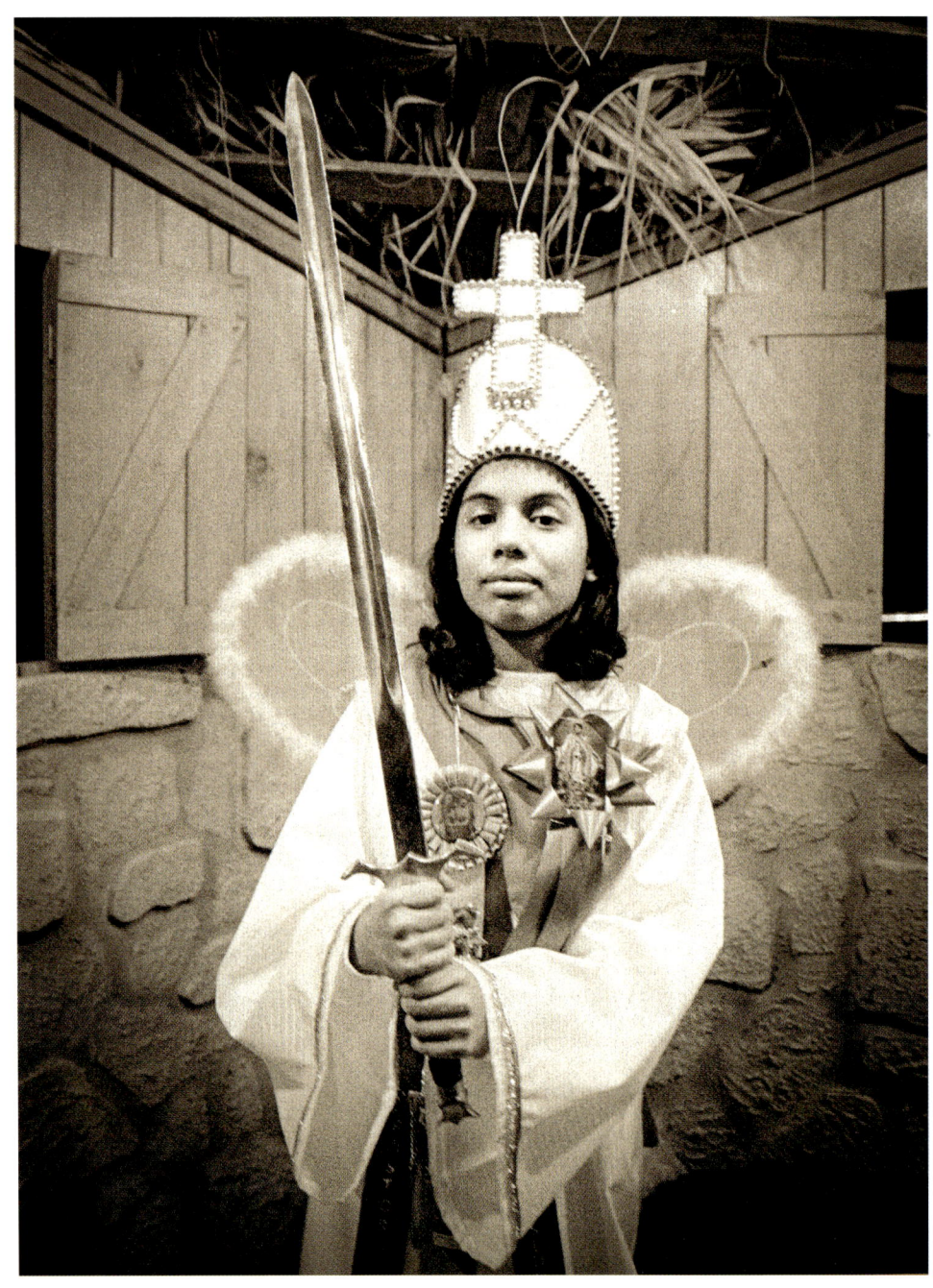

Angel of Faith (2003)
San Antonio, Texas

When no peace can be negotiated,
When trouble impends,
Angel of Faith bear your Light,
Lead me to strength and honor.

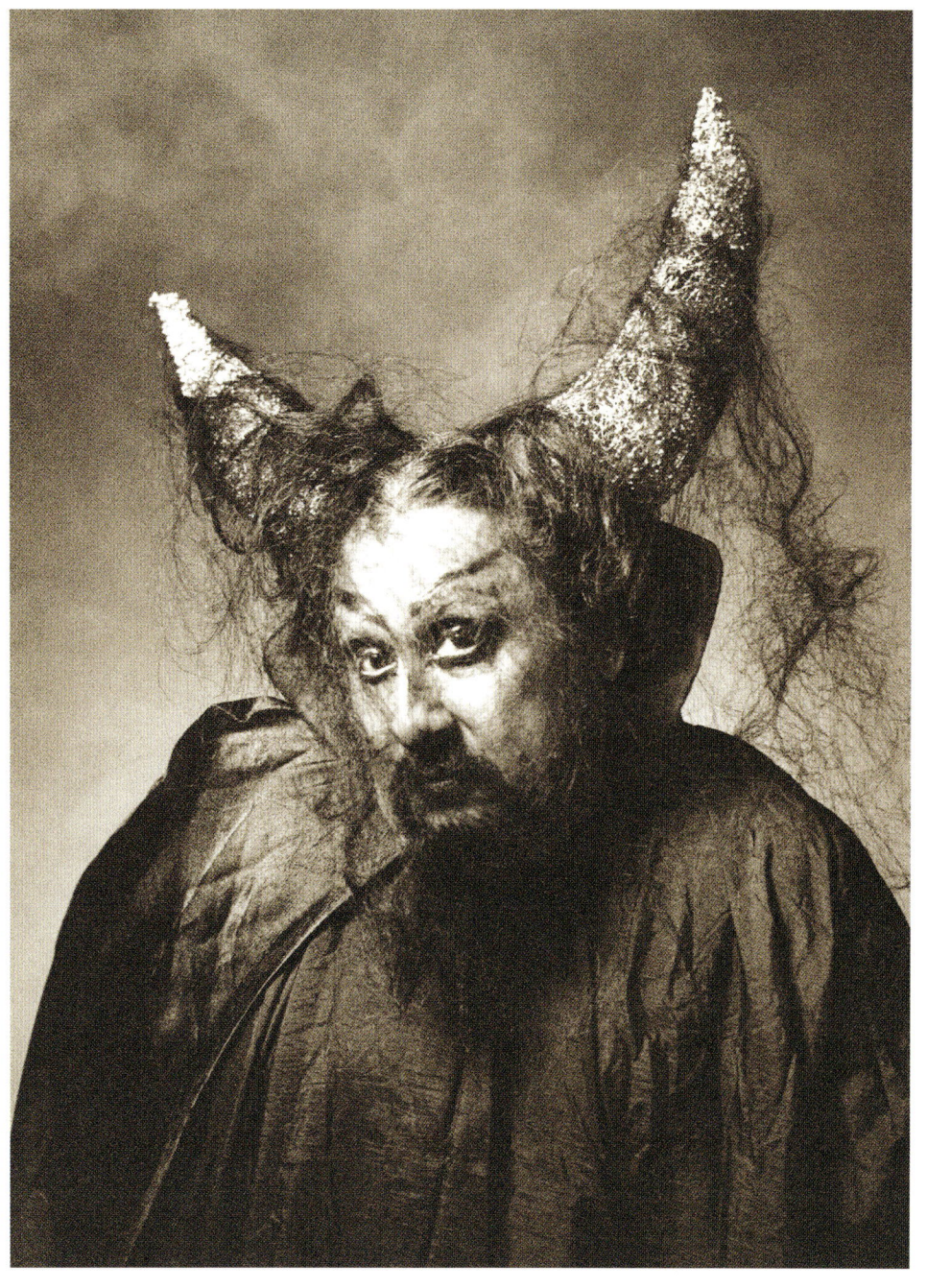

El Satanico (2002)
San Antonio, Texas

Fame, glamor, wealth
Deceit, greed, corruption
War, famine, drought:
Devil in the details.

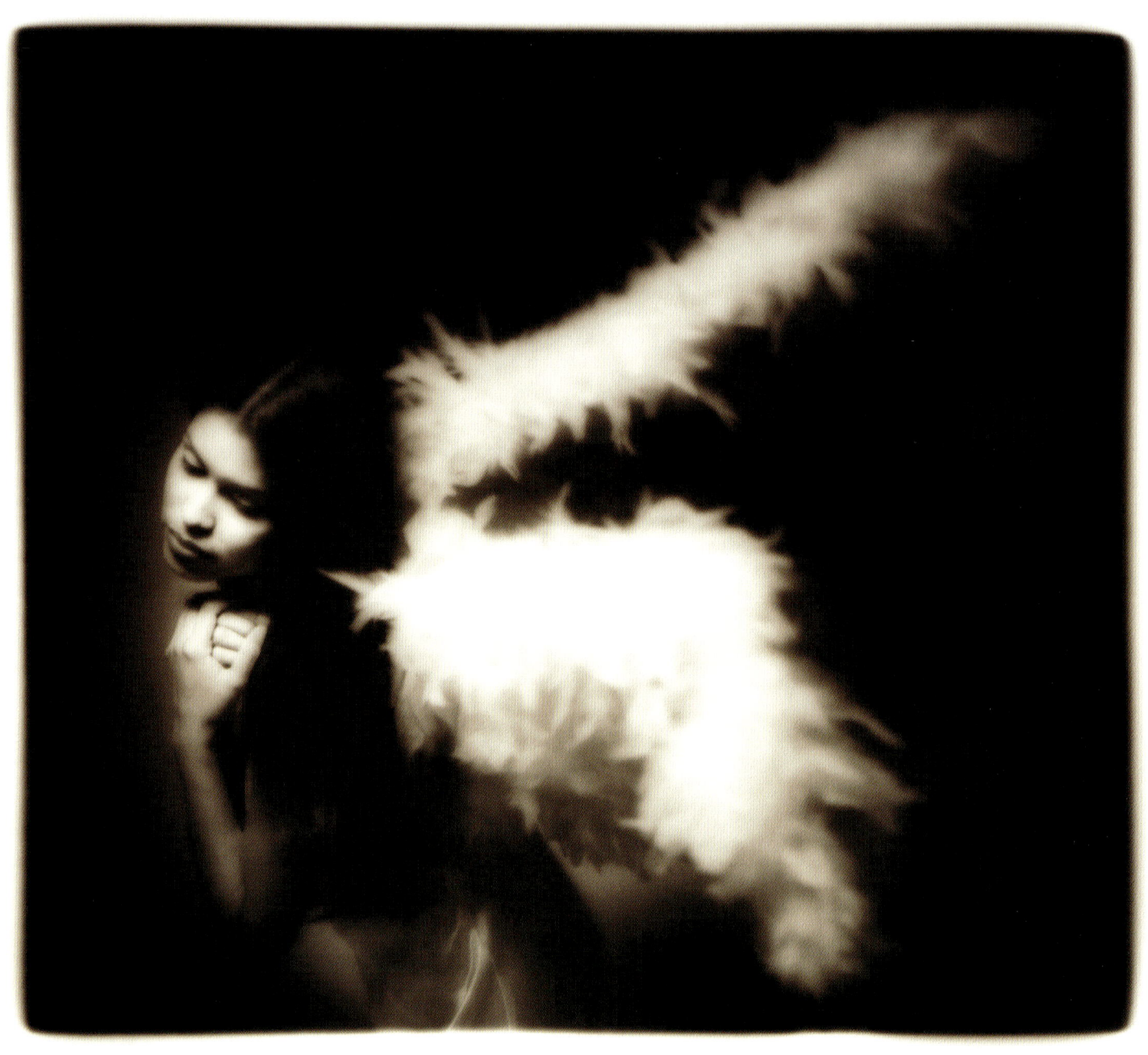

Angel of Love (1998)
San Antonio, Texas

Seraphim's Epiphany
You look at me,
Eyes need no words,
"Love unlimited by reason endures."

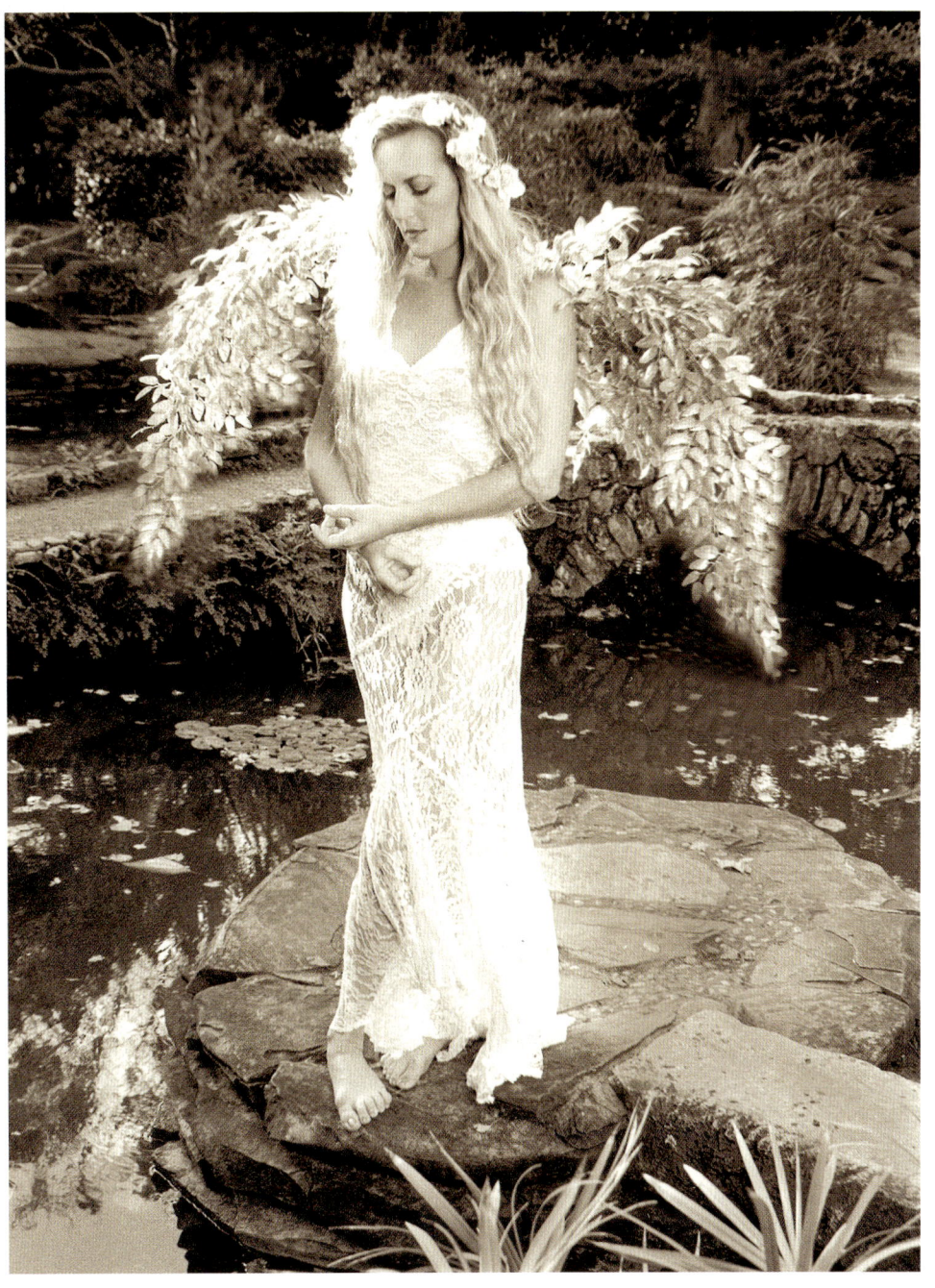

Angel of Serenity (2004)
San Antonio, Texas

Serenity, constant Angel of Still Voice
beneath busy-ness of days and dreams
your Blessings and Bliss
are but a deep breath away

SELENA

INSIGHT BY SUZETTE ARRIAGA

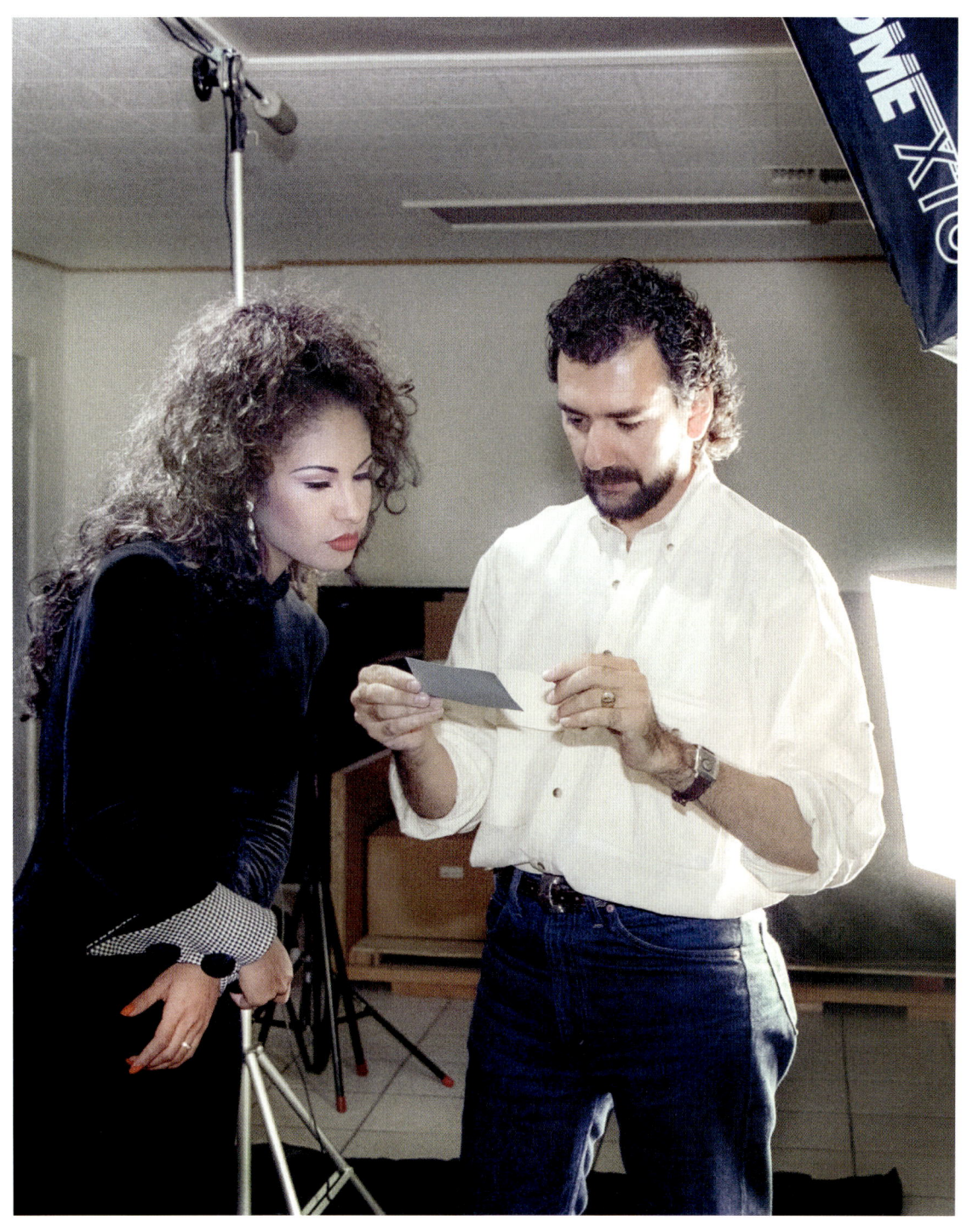

Selena and Al (1994)
San Antonio, Texas

We asked Al to come and take new promotional photos of Selena y Los Dinos. The background concept was inspired by a photo of the grupo Extreme. They happened to have one of Selena's favorite songs entitled, "More Than Words."

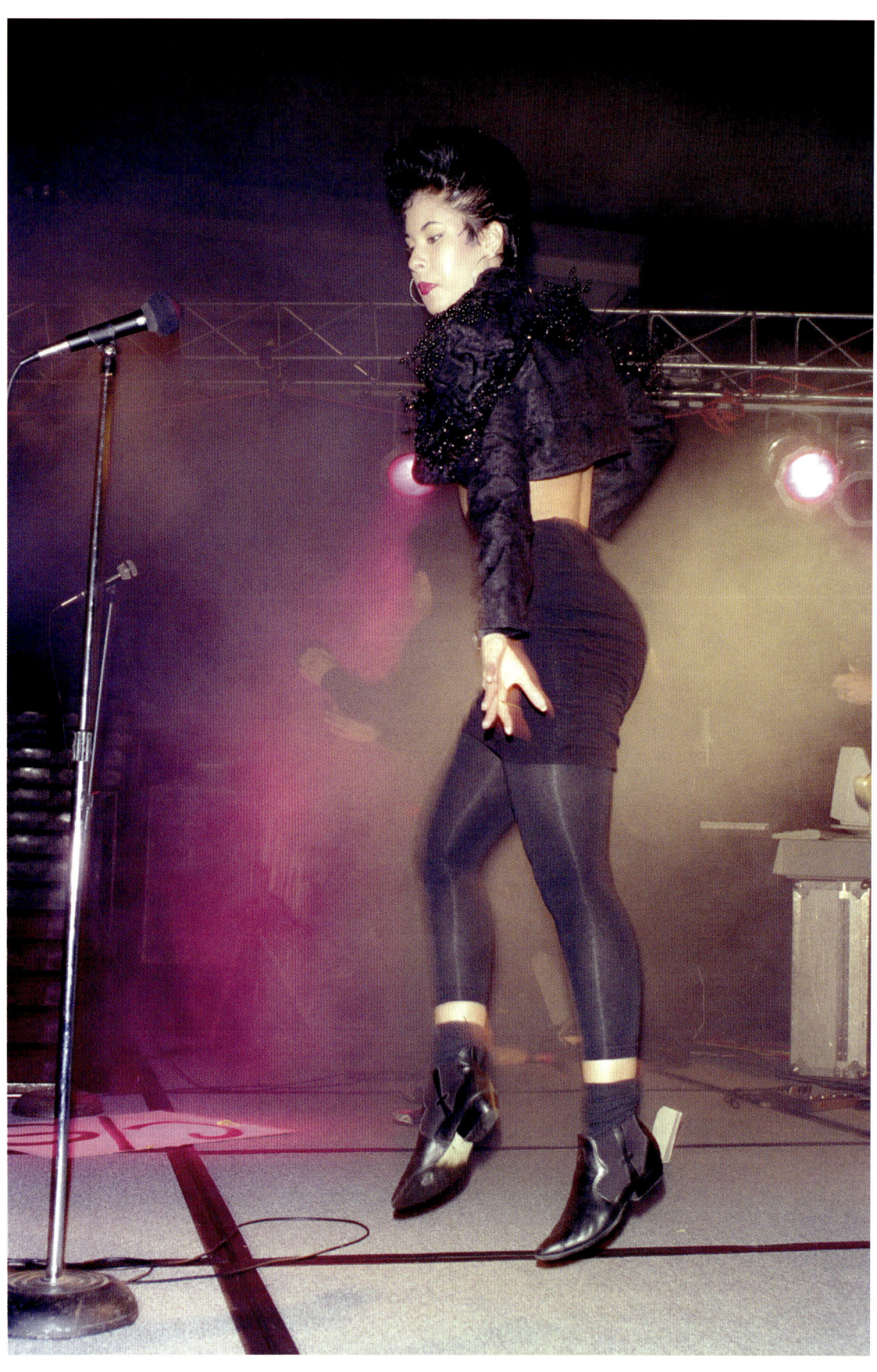

Selena Bailando (1990)
San Antonio, Texas

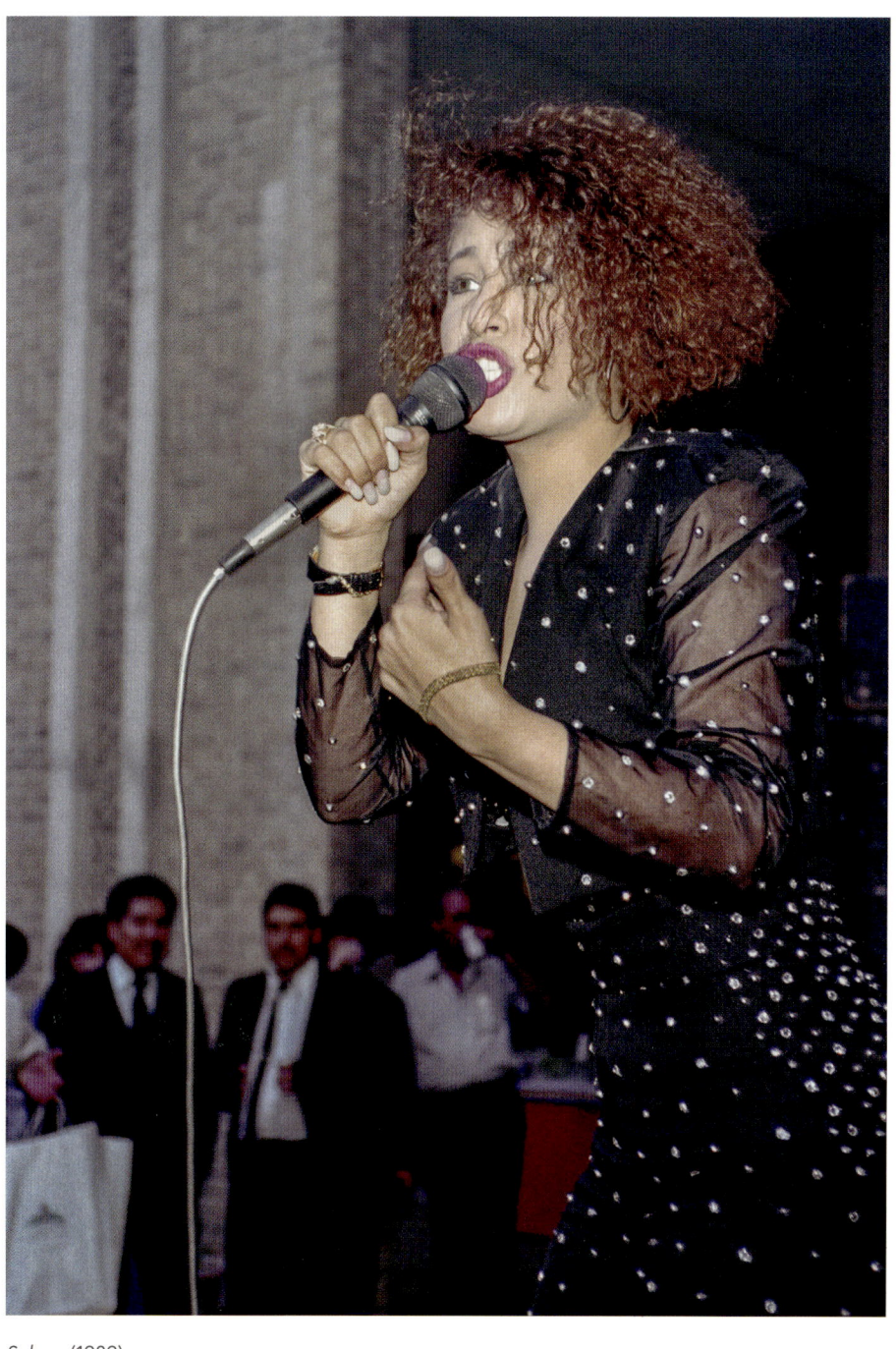

Selena (1989)
San Antonio, Texas

Selena performing at a kick off party event for the Tejano Music Awards in San Antonio, Texas. Always a bit intimidating performing during the day.

In 1994, Selena celebrating a huge win over the KXTN radio station DJs. As you can tell, Selena enjoyed giving DJ Marco a pie to the face for talking so much smack on air. San Antonio always has felt like our second home filled with so many wonderful people.

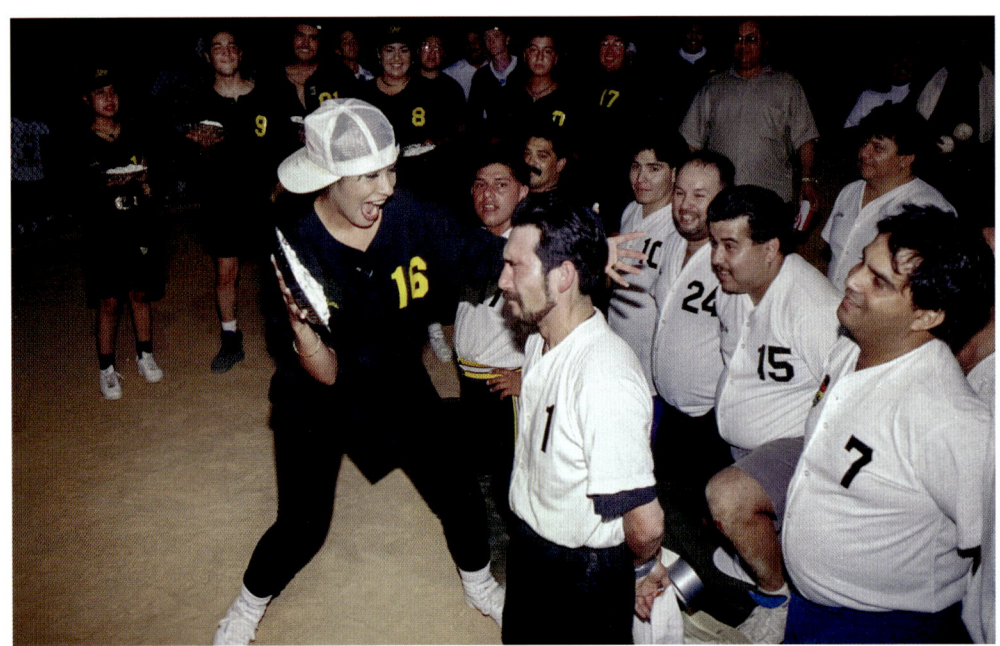

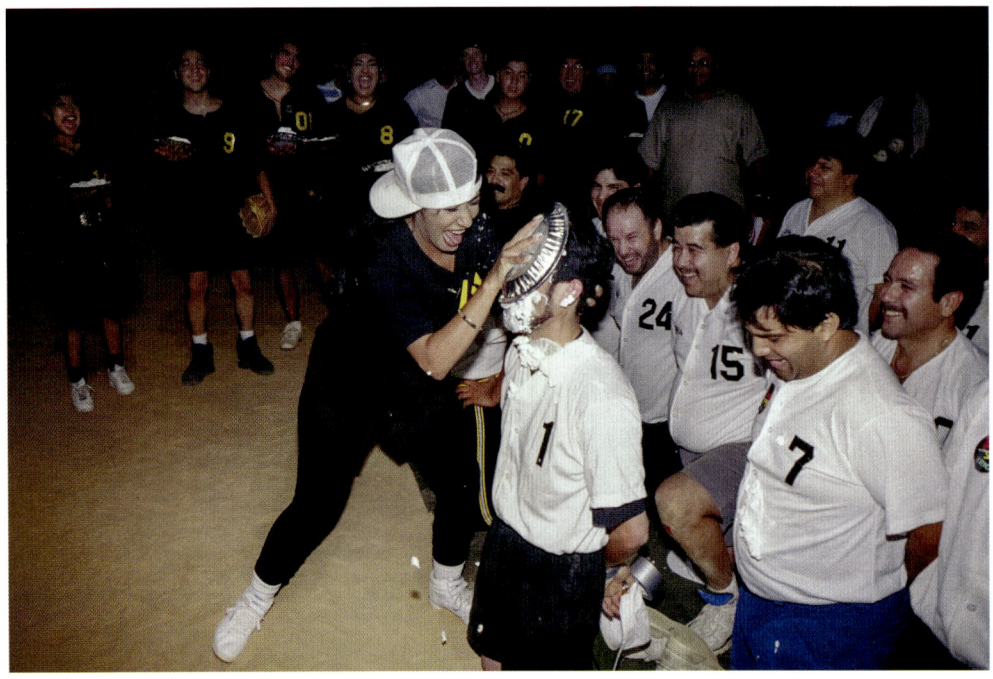

Selena (1994)
San Antonio, Texas

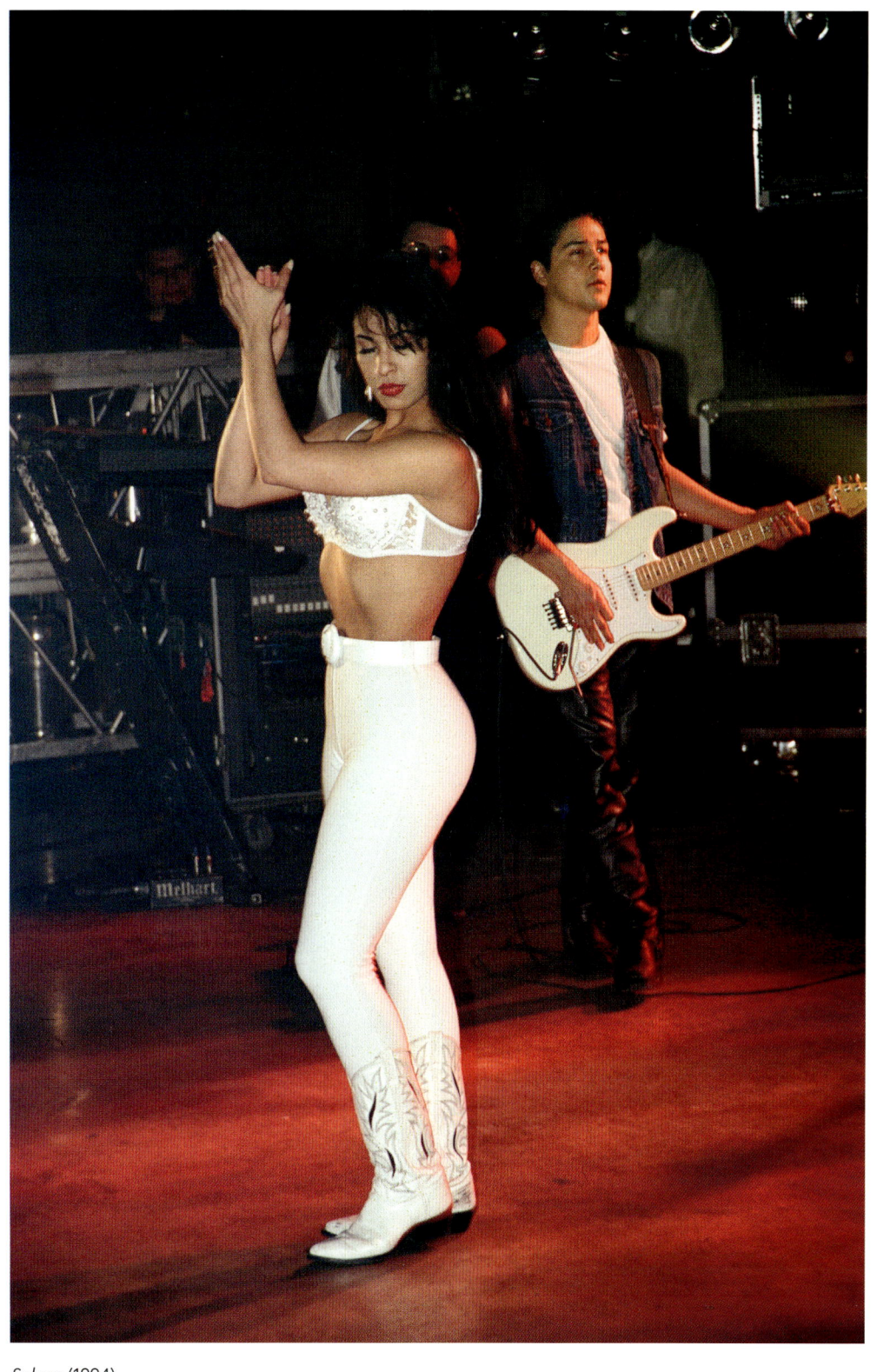

Selena (1994)
San Antonio, Texas

Selena captured in a signature pose in 1994 while performing with her band, Los Dinos.

This photo of *Selena y Los Dinos* was photographed at the Memorial Coliseum in Corpus Christi in 1993. This photo showcases the confidence of each band member individually and as a group.

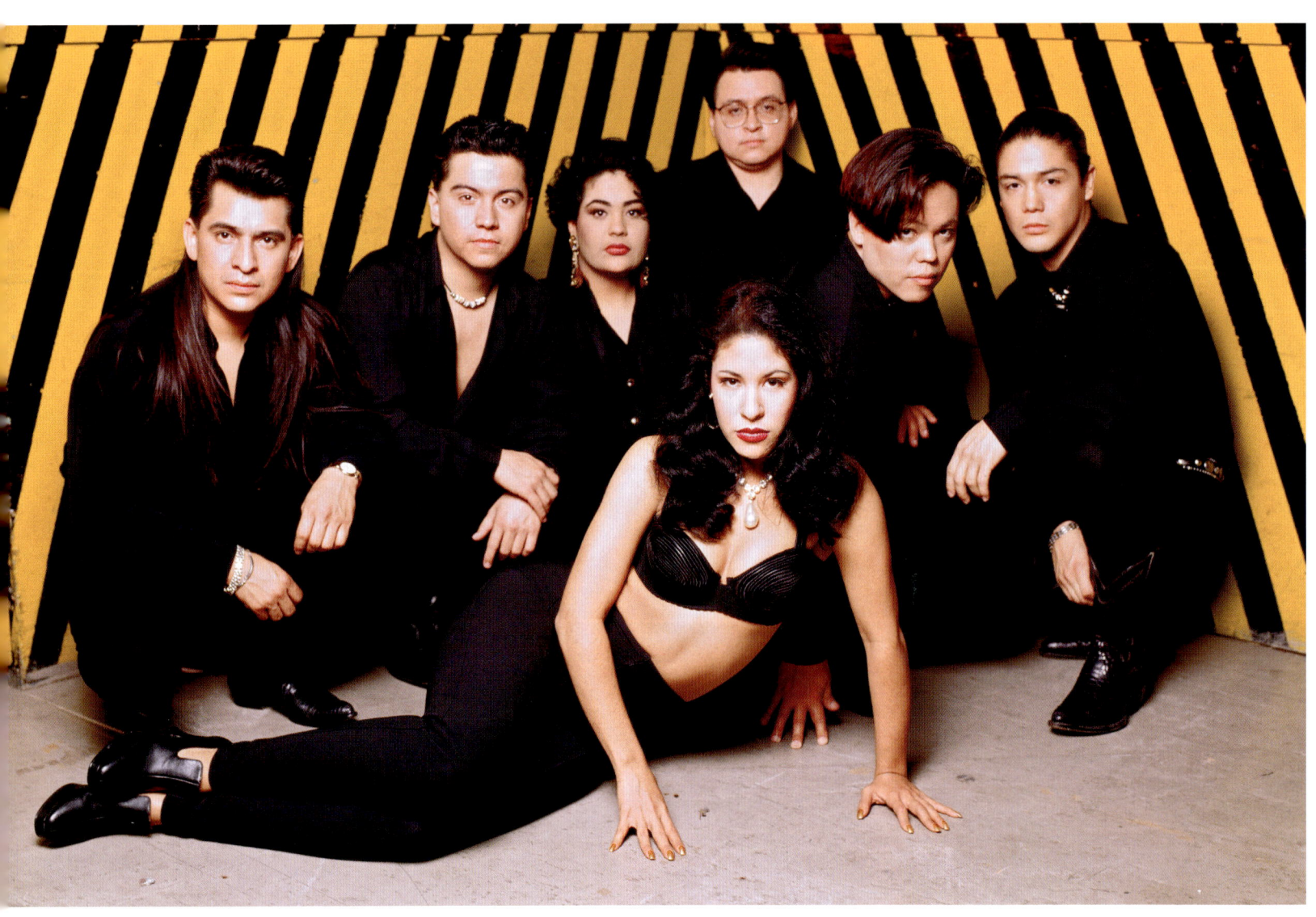

Selena y Los Dinos (1993)
San Antonio, Texas

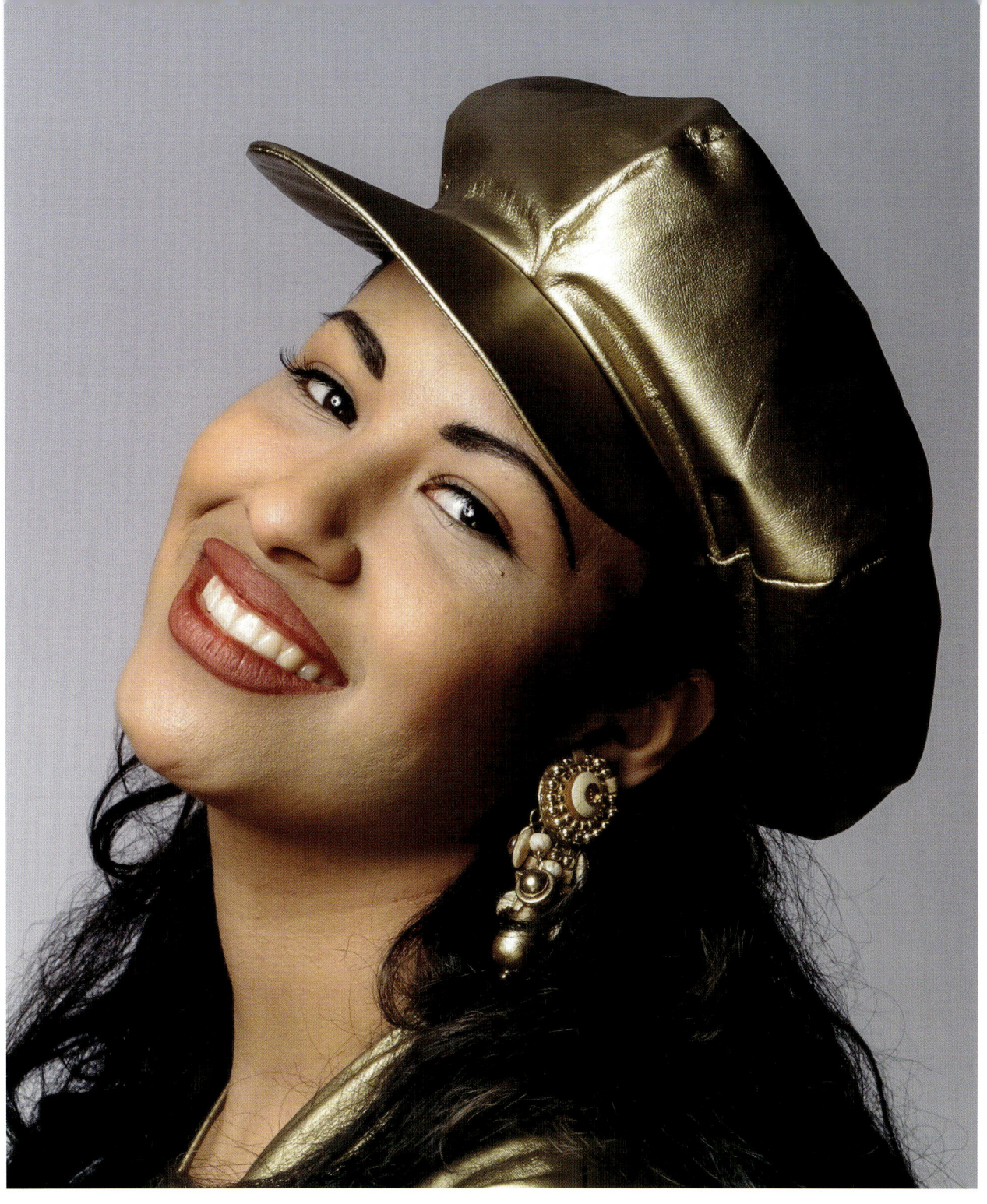

Selena for Coca Cola (1994)
San Antonio, Texas

Selena wearing her own line of clothing from her Moonchild design house in 1994 for the new Coca-Cola campaign. She was extremely excited and proud to showcase some of her new line of clothing.

One of the most iconic pictures taken of Selena performing with her band, Los Dinos, at the 1994 Tejano Music Awards. This performance was mesmerizing.

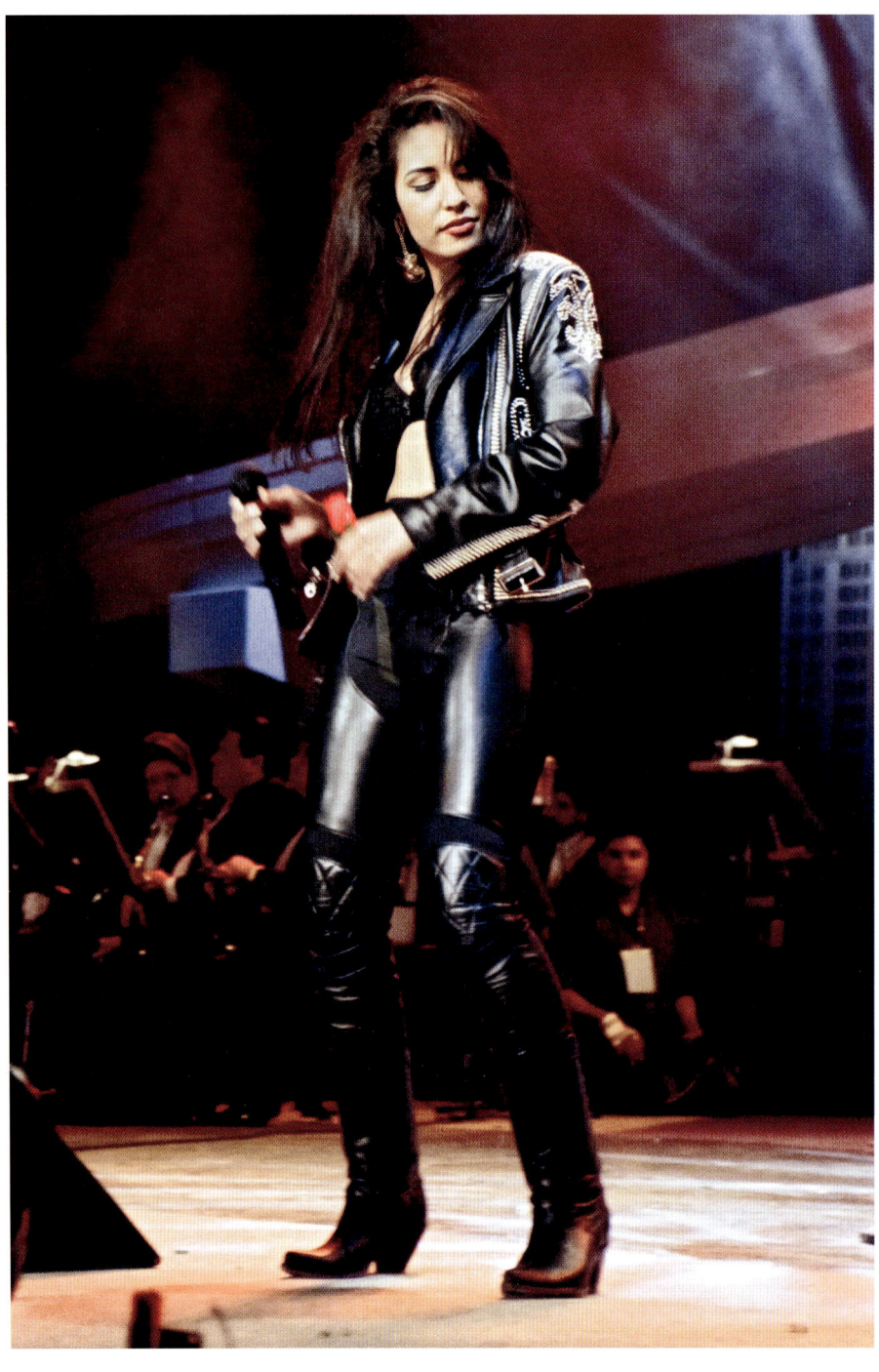

Selena Live (1994)
San Antonio, Texas

Having a good time during our photoshoot in our cheetah era.

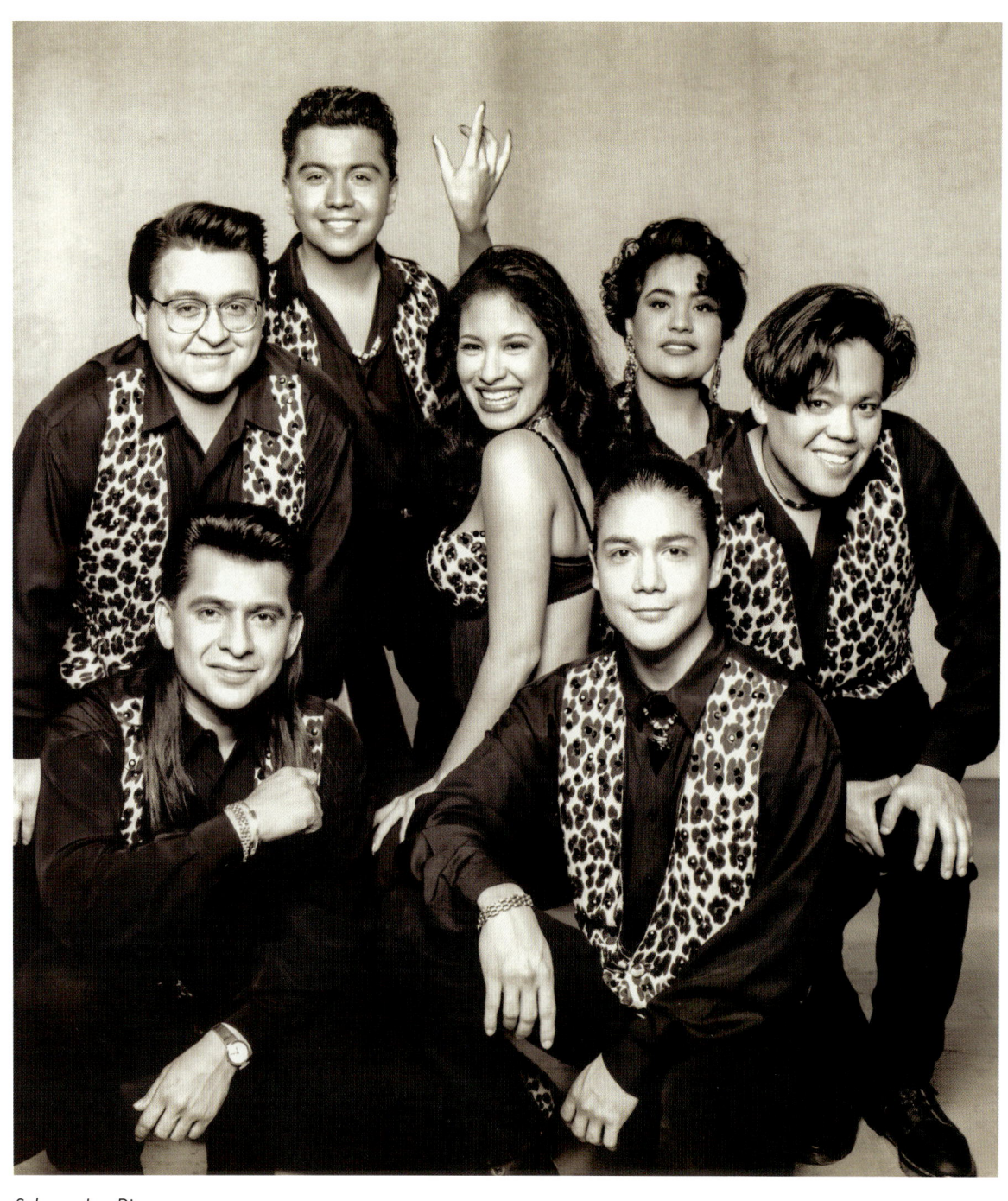

Selena y Los Dinos
San Antonio, Texas, 1994

CATCHING LIGHTNING IN A BOTTLE: THE OPPORTUNITY OF A LIFETIME

by Al Rendón

By 1987 I had shifted my photographic interests from Rock & Roll to the Conjunto and Tejano bands of my own culture, and was working on photo assignments for several of the regional Tejano record labels.

Selena Quintanilla grew up in Corpus Christi. Her father, Abraham Quintanilla, managed Los Dinos, which included Selena's brother A.B. Quintanilla and sister Suzette Quintanilla. The band had been performing since she was nine years old. Abraham's life was all about music, and his children were learning the business as well as becoming accomplished performers. Selena recorded with the Freddie, Cara and GP record labels before signing with Capitol EMI—they had signed her thinking she would be the next Gloria Estefan. She would prove to be so much more.

In 1989, as I was covering the Tejano Music Awards, I happened to catch Selena and Los Dinos band as they did an early performance on a stage set up outside the awards hall. I had photographed some of the most dynamic acts in the world, but I had never seen anything like this band with a young seventeen-year-old girl. She was an amazing performer and had a special bond with her audience.

I had already been working for Capitol EMI Latin and was pushing to photograph Selena's next album cover. In 1992, the industry was excited about *Entre A Mi Mundo*, Selena's third album, written and engineered to be her commercial breakthrough. The album was due to come out soon when I got a call from EMI. The album photography they had from another photographer wasn't acceptable to the record company, and they needed a quick reshoot. Accustomed to working with shoe-string budgets, I was really pleased that the label's generous budget would cover studio rental, a professional makeup artist, and all the film I could shoot. With direction from the record company requesting I use a white background and better lighting, I rented a friend's studio, borrowed a white parachute backdrop, set up my lights, and awaited Selena's arrival.

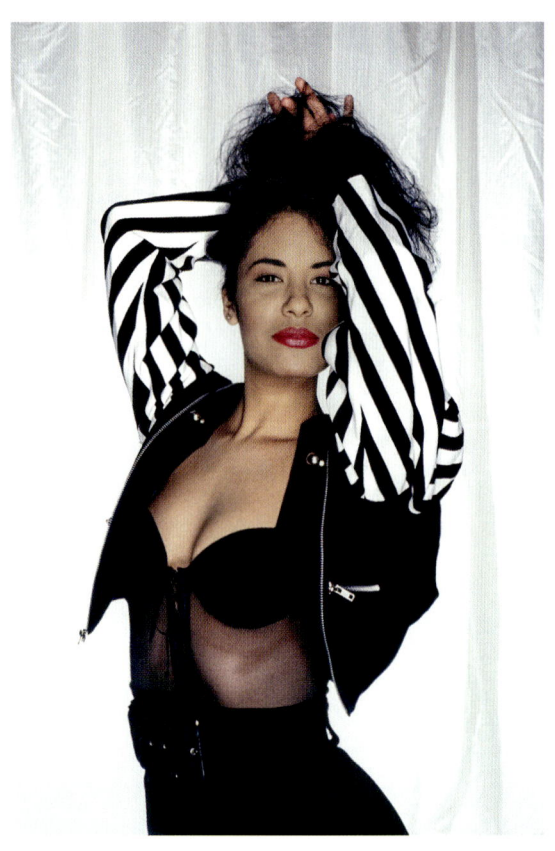

Selena Entre a Mi Mundo (1992)
San Antonio, Texas

Album cover photo of Selena in 1992 for Entre a Mi Mundo. *This album opened so many doors with hits that include* Como La Flor, La Carcancha *and* Missing My Baby *to name a few.*

The session was scheduled for early evening. The band was traveling from Corpus Christi, heading out on tour. When they arrived, Abraham was first off the bus. We made our introductions and I showed Mr. Quintanilla the studio. He was professional and collaborated with me on the photography concept. Selena and Suzette came off the bus, carrying Selena's wardrobe into the dressing room. Working professionally for more than a decade, Selena was quiet, but open and welcoming. Up to that point I had not yet worked with a Tejano band with a female lead singer, so when she came out of the dressing room, I was blown away. This wasn't the teen I first saw outside the Tejano Awards. She had matured beautifully, wearing a bustiere with a see-through midriff, bold striped top, black spandex pants and sizzling heels. She soon would be designing and producing her own unique costumes for herself and the band.

As the photo shoot went on and she changed into several outfits, John McBurney, who is still my go-to makeup artist, hovered in the background. Occasionally, Selena would come out and choose a lipstick, borrow a brush, or ask for John's opinion. I was so impressed that Selena didn't need a lot of direction and was very comfortable, natural, and had fun in front of the camera. Everything she did for the camera was the expression of a star in bloom. This cover shot is known to fans around the world.

EDIBLE
IMMIGRANTS

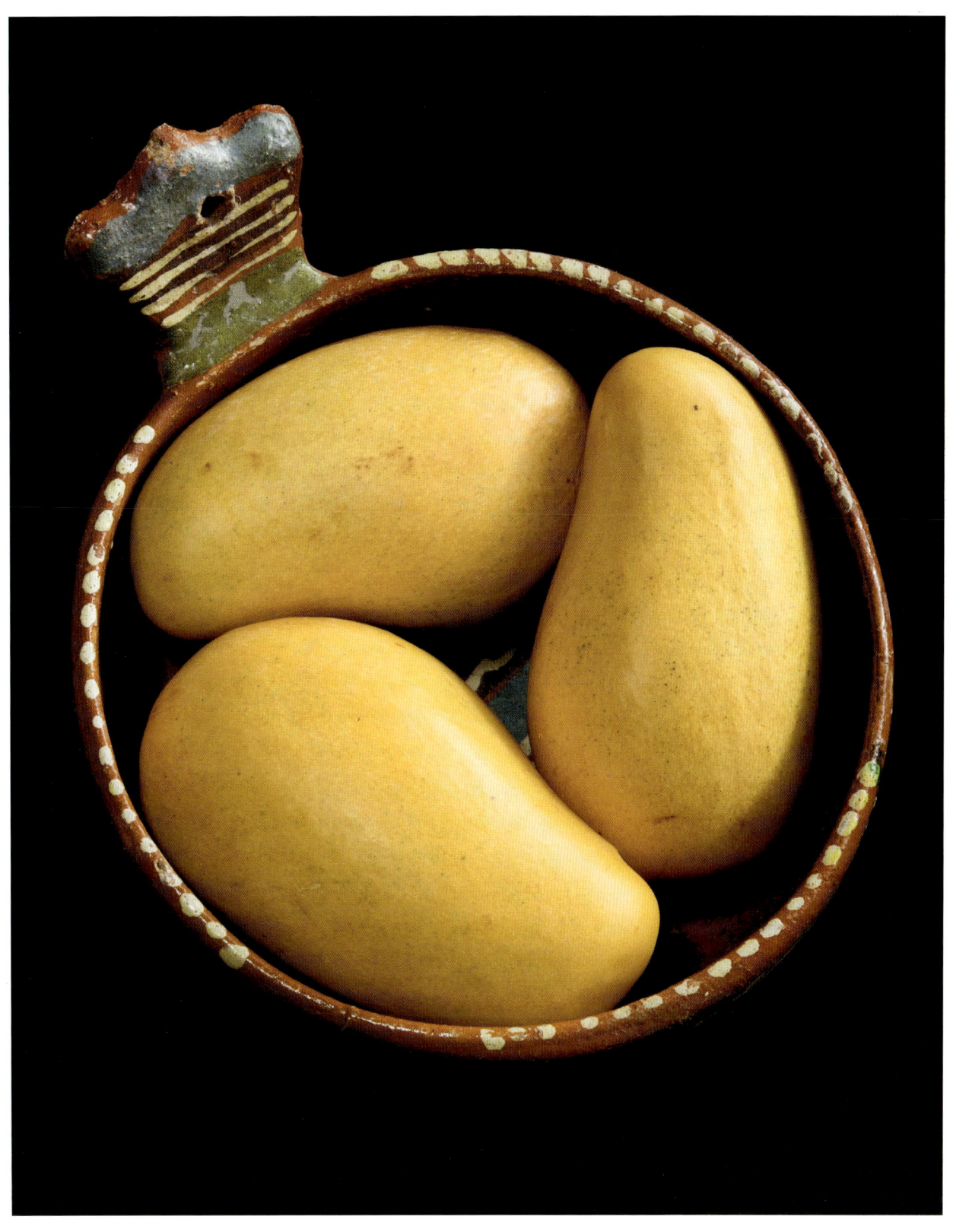

Honey Mango (2018)
San Antonio, Texas

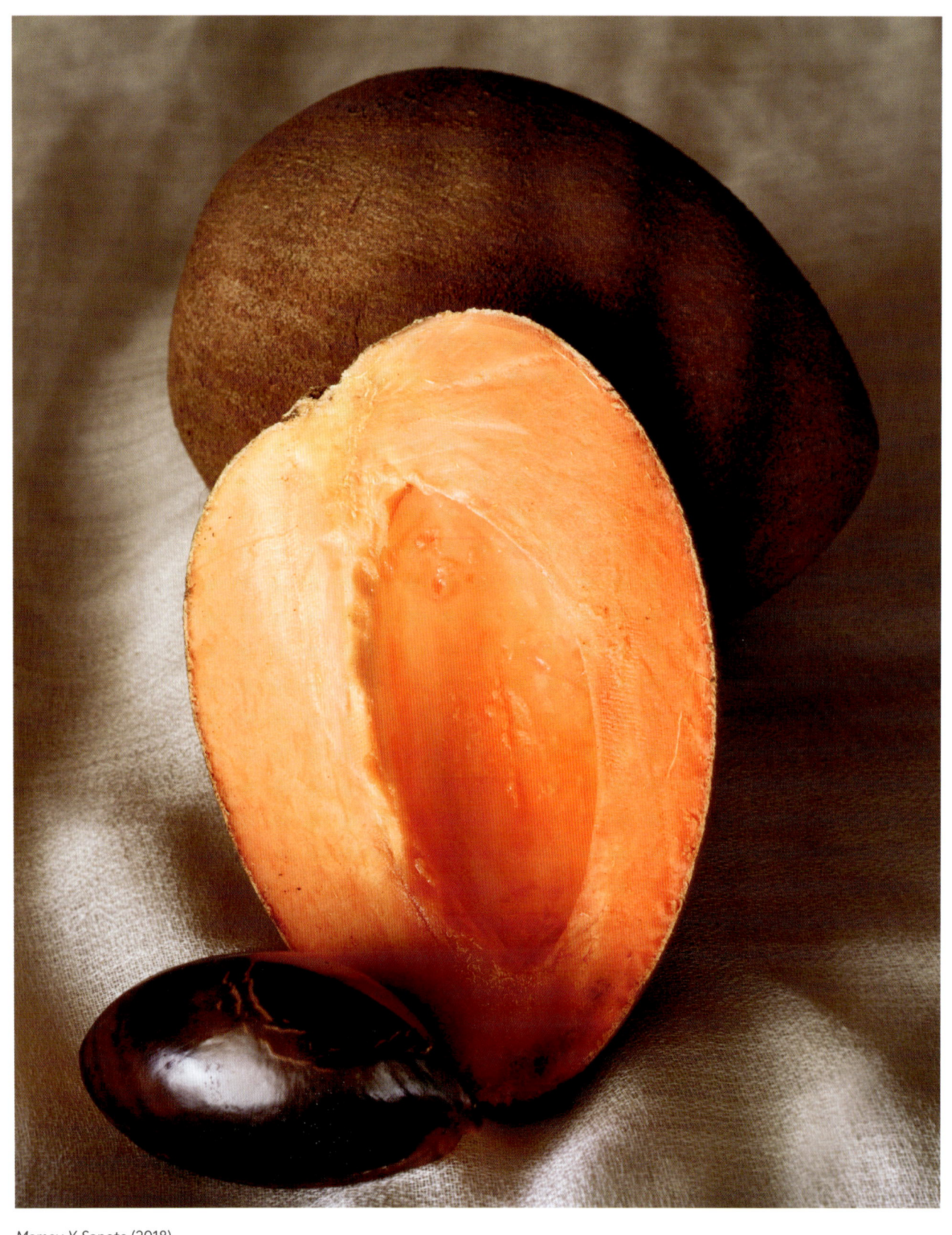

Mamey Y Sapote (2018)
San Antonio, Texas

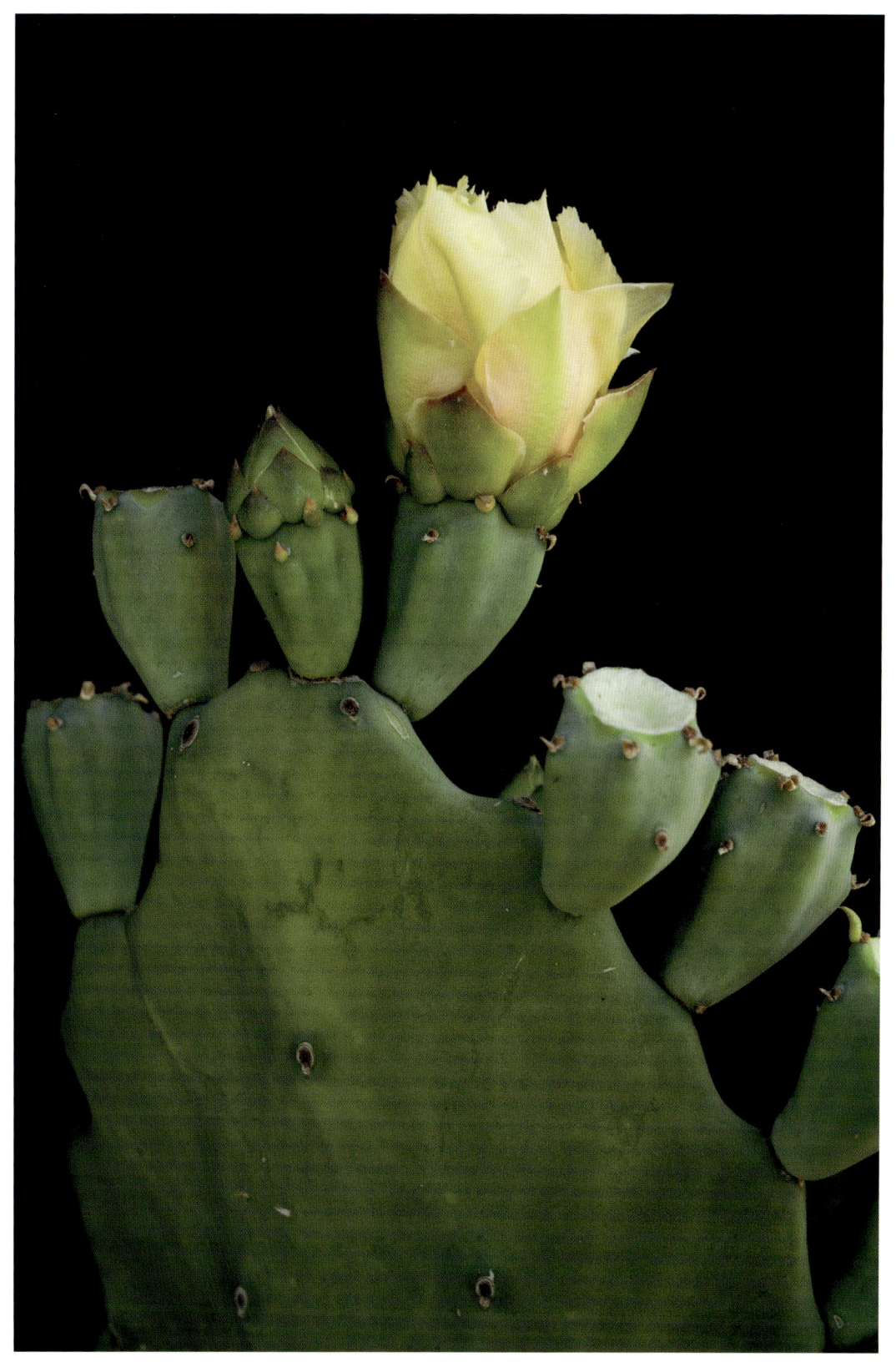

Nopal y Tuna (2018)
San Antonio, Texas

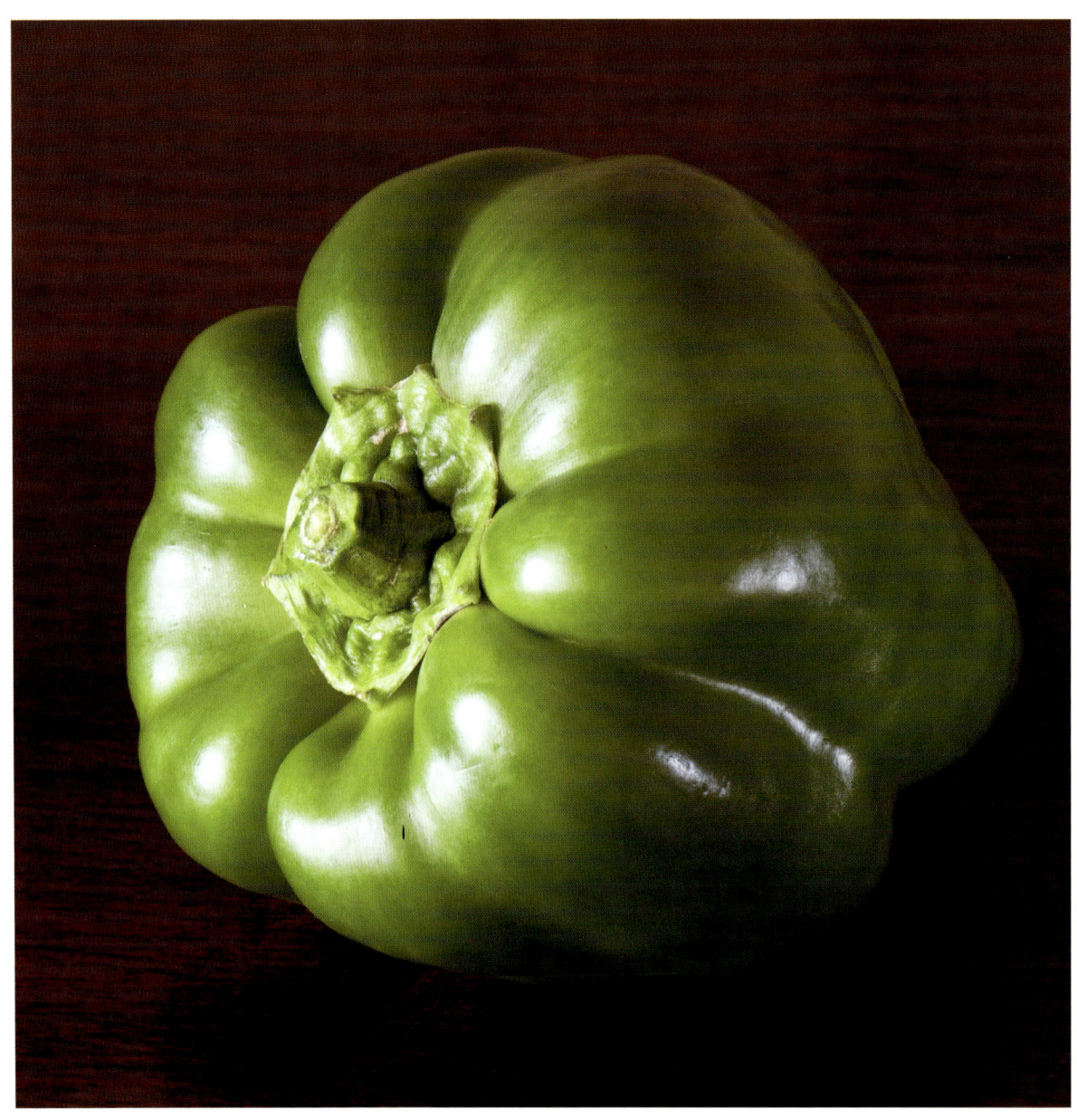

Bell Pepper (2018)
San Antonio, Texas

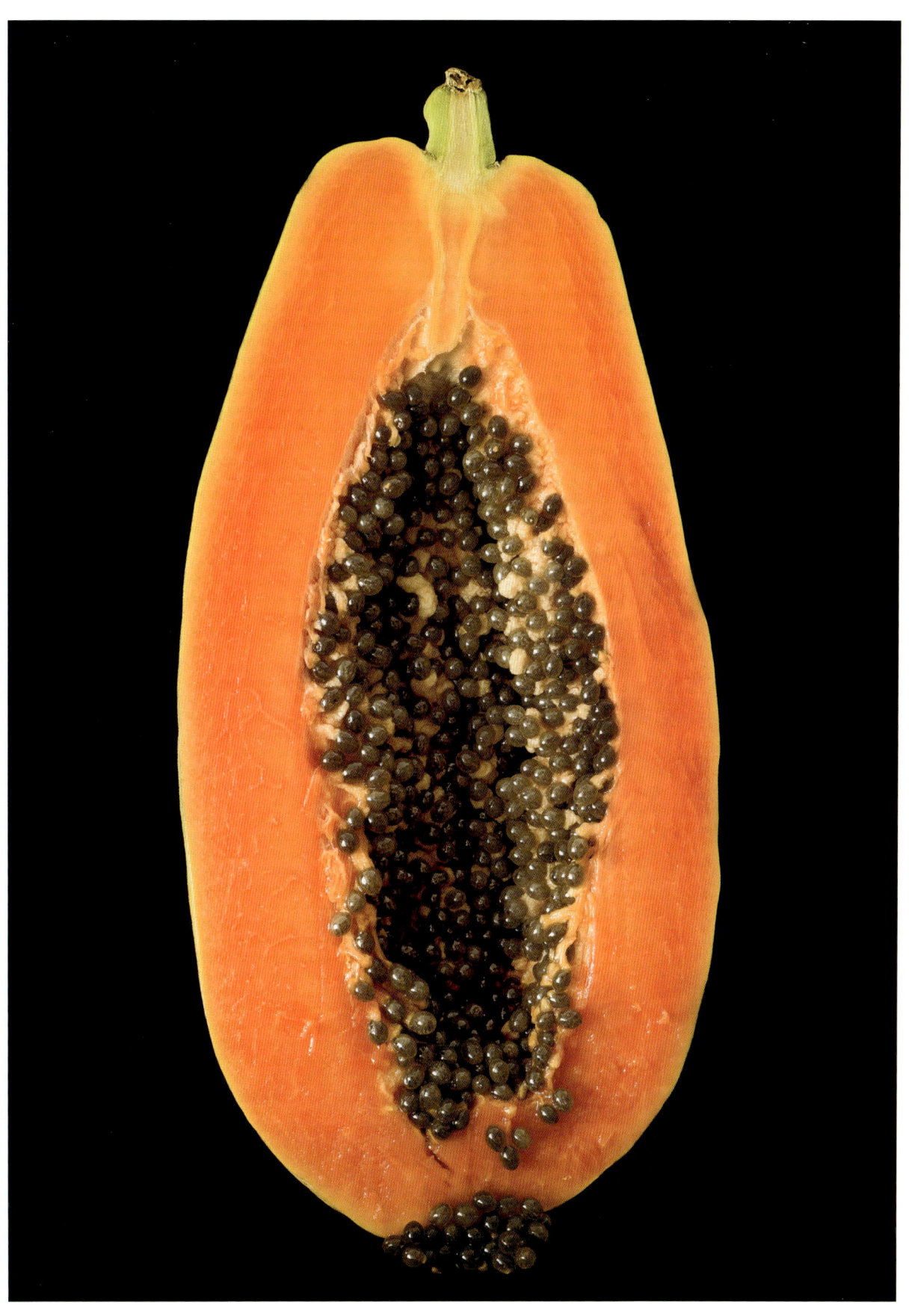

Papaya (2018)
San Antonio, Texas

FACES OF
RESILIENCY

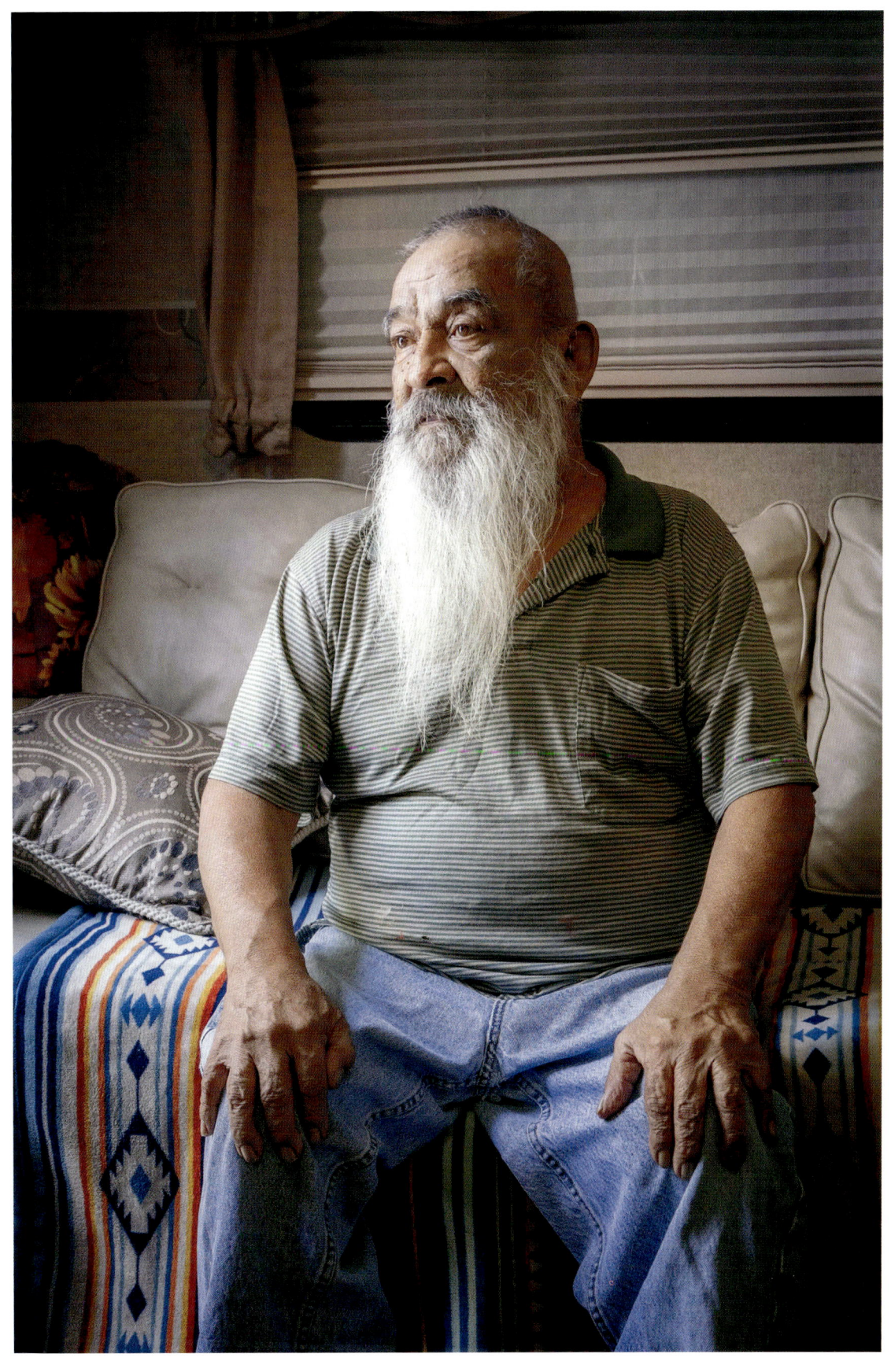

Nicolas Paz (2021)
San Antonio, Texas

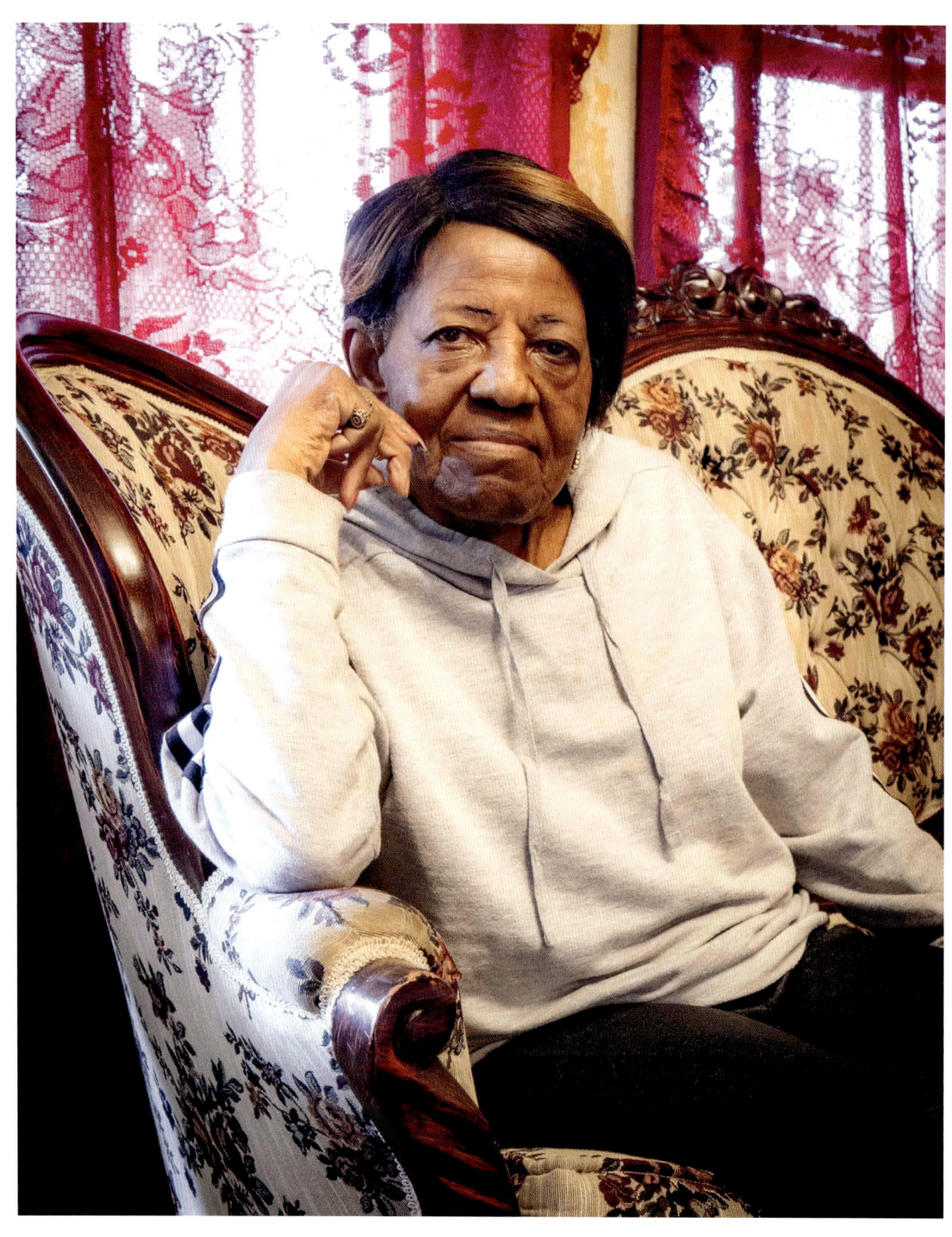

Bobbie Benton (2021)
Fort Worth, Texas

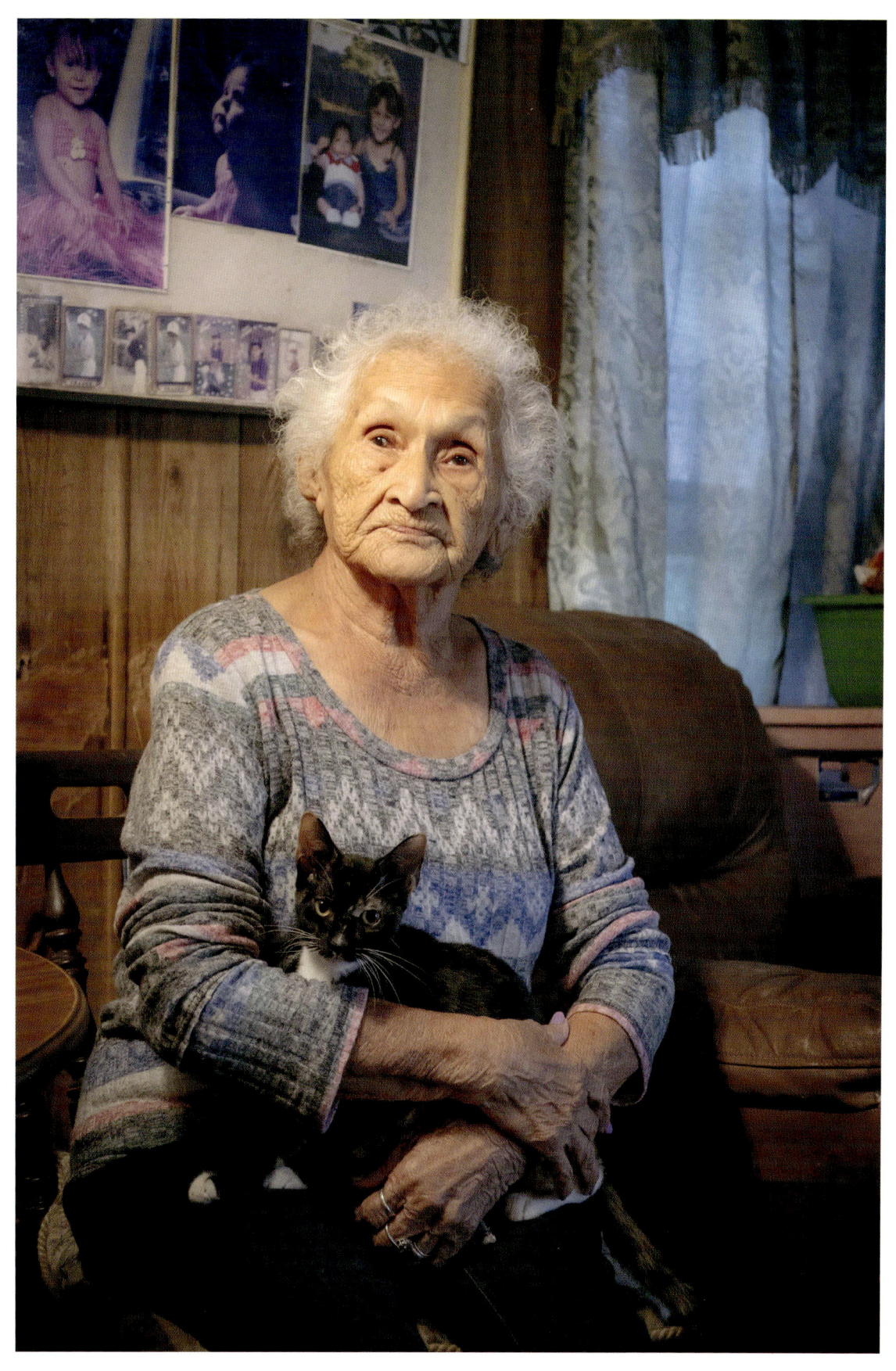

Ofelia Salinas (2021)
Edinburg, Texas

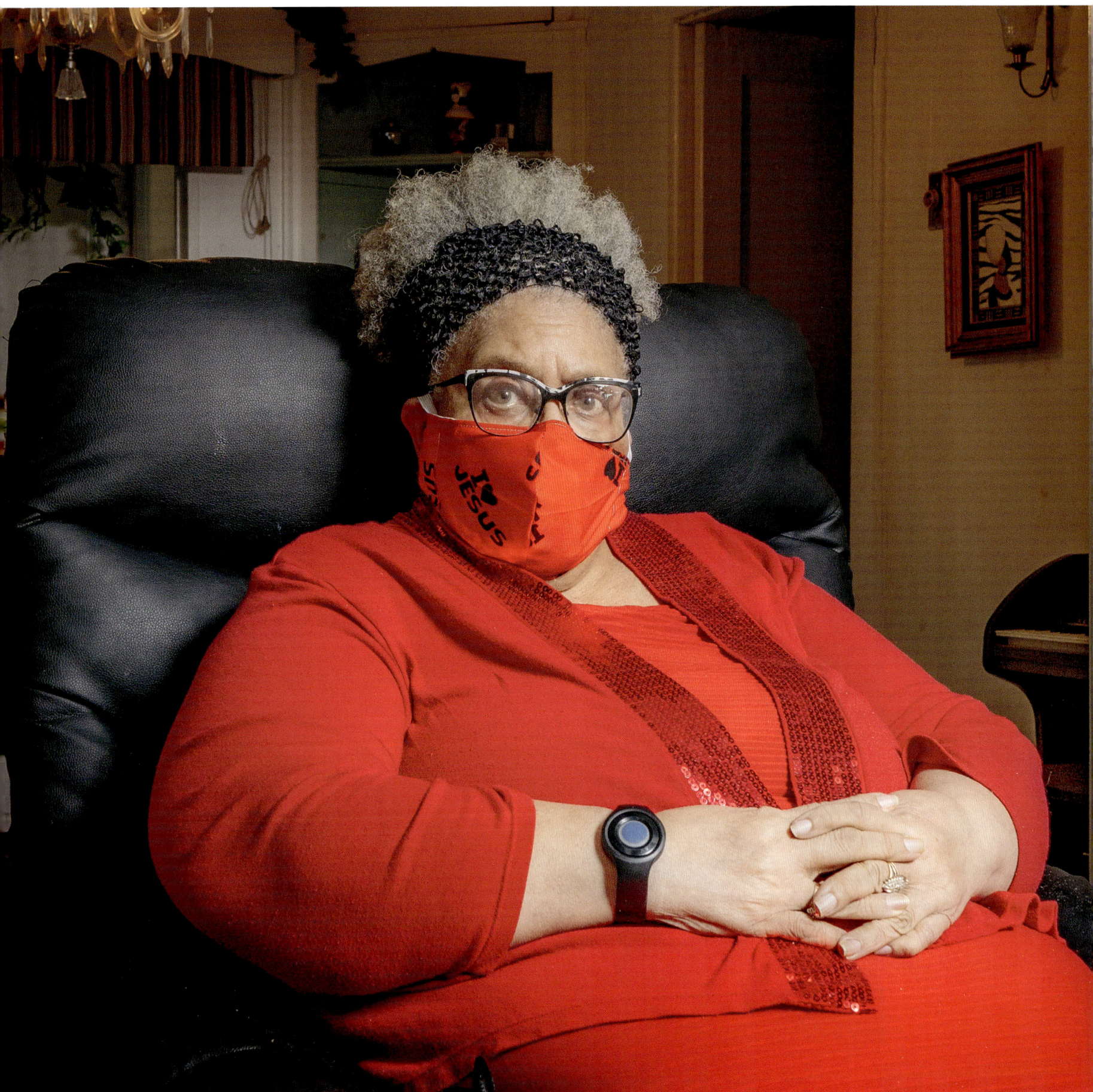

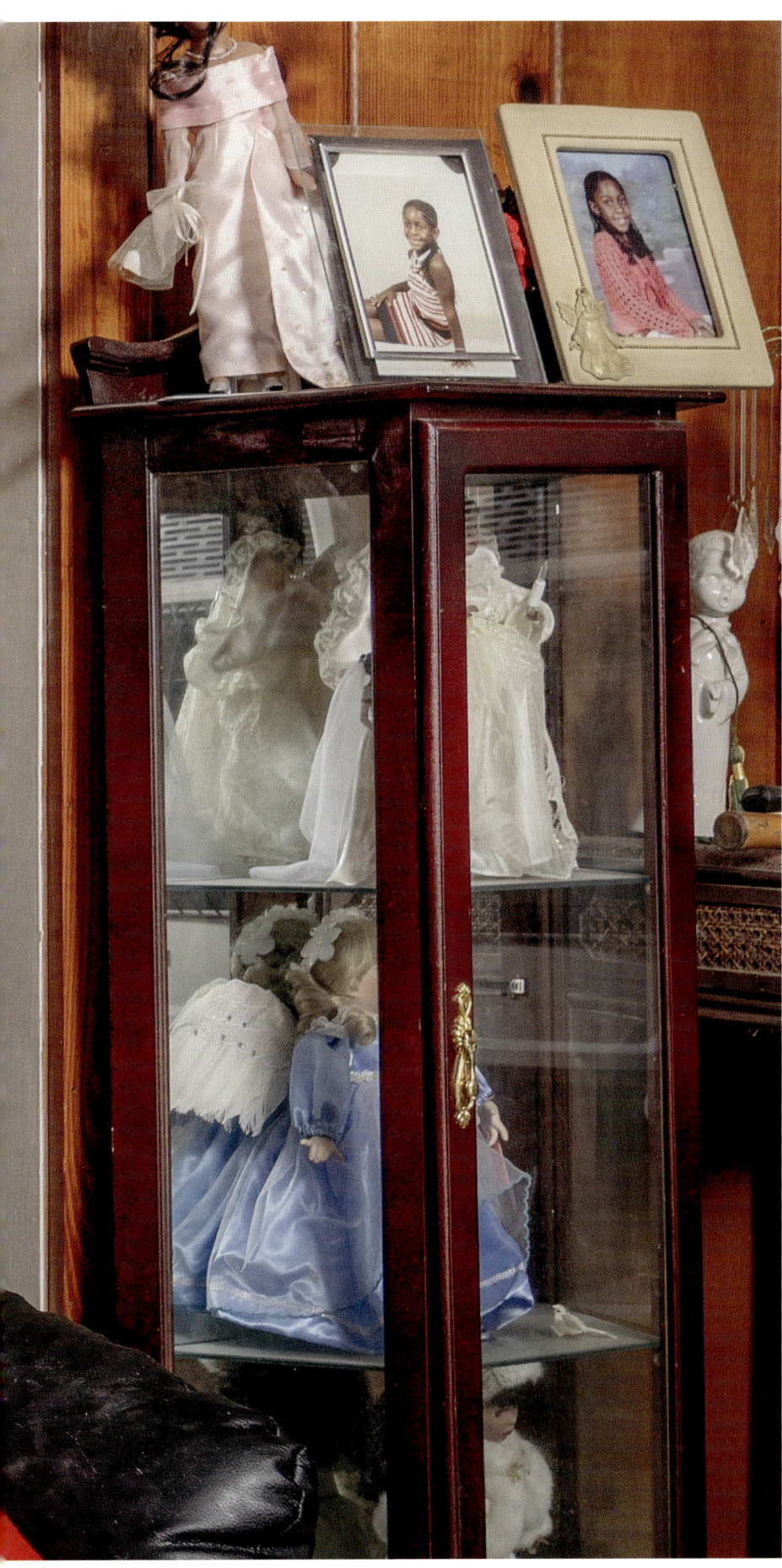

Sophronan Webber (2021)
Dallas, Texas

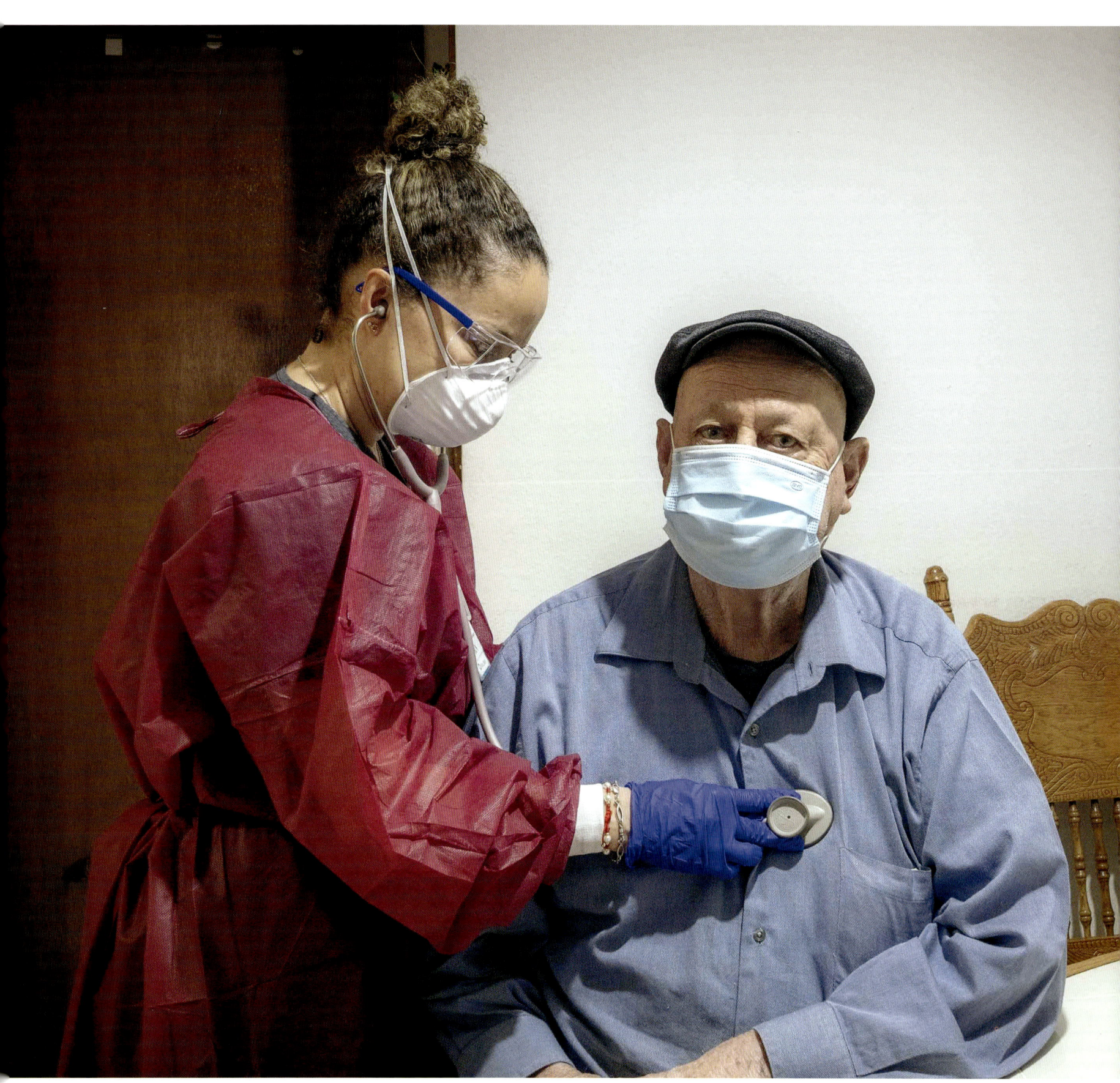

Rene Benavides (2021)
McAllen, Texas

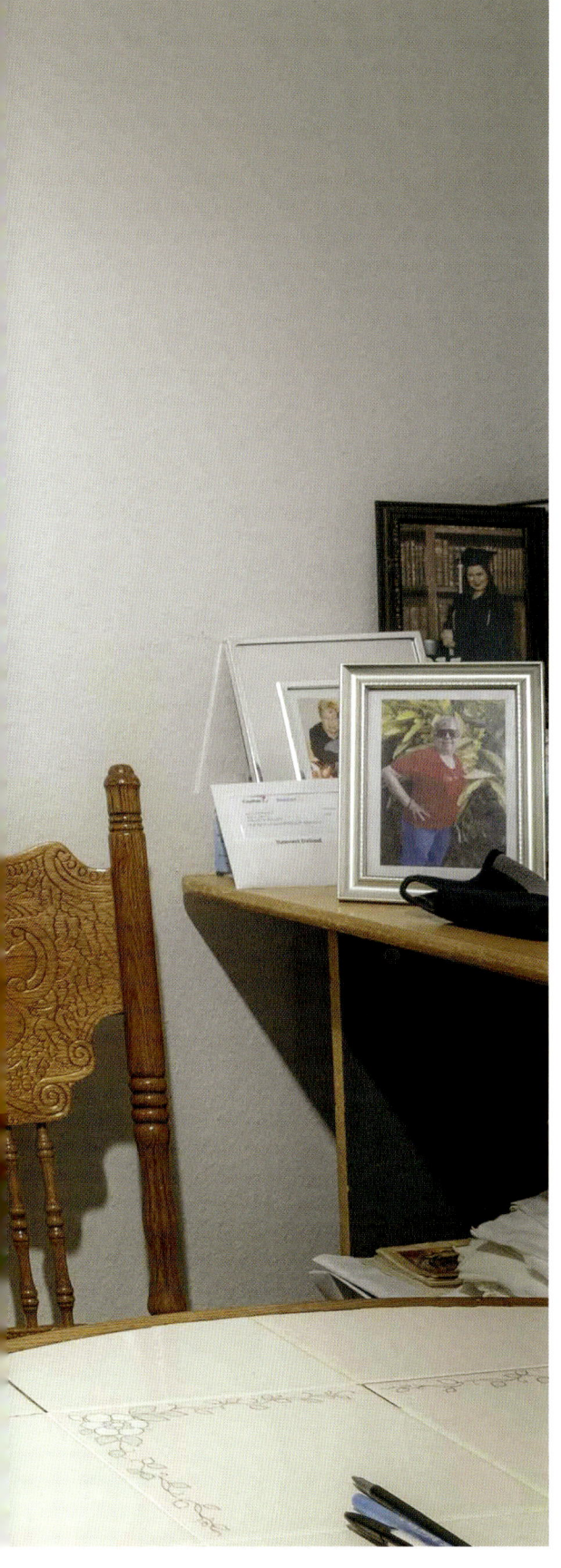

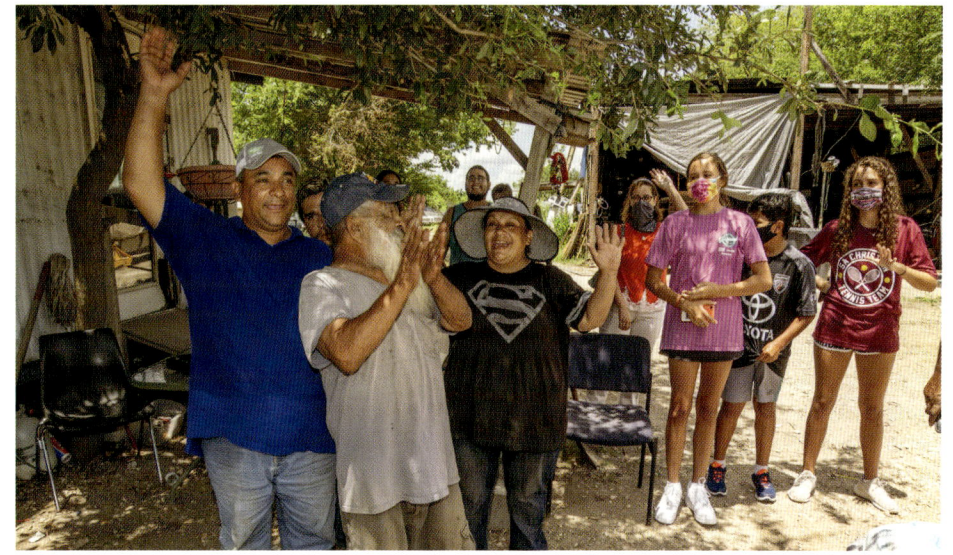

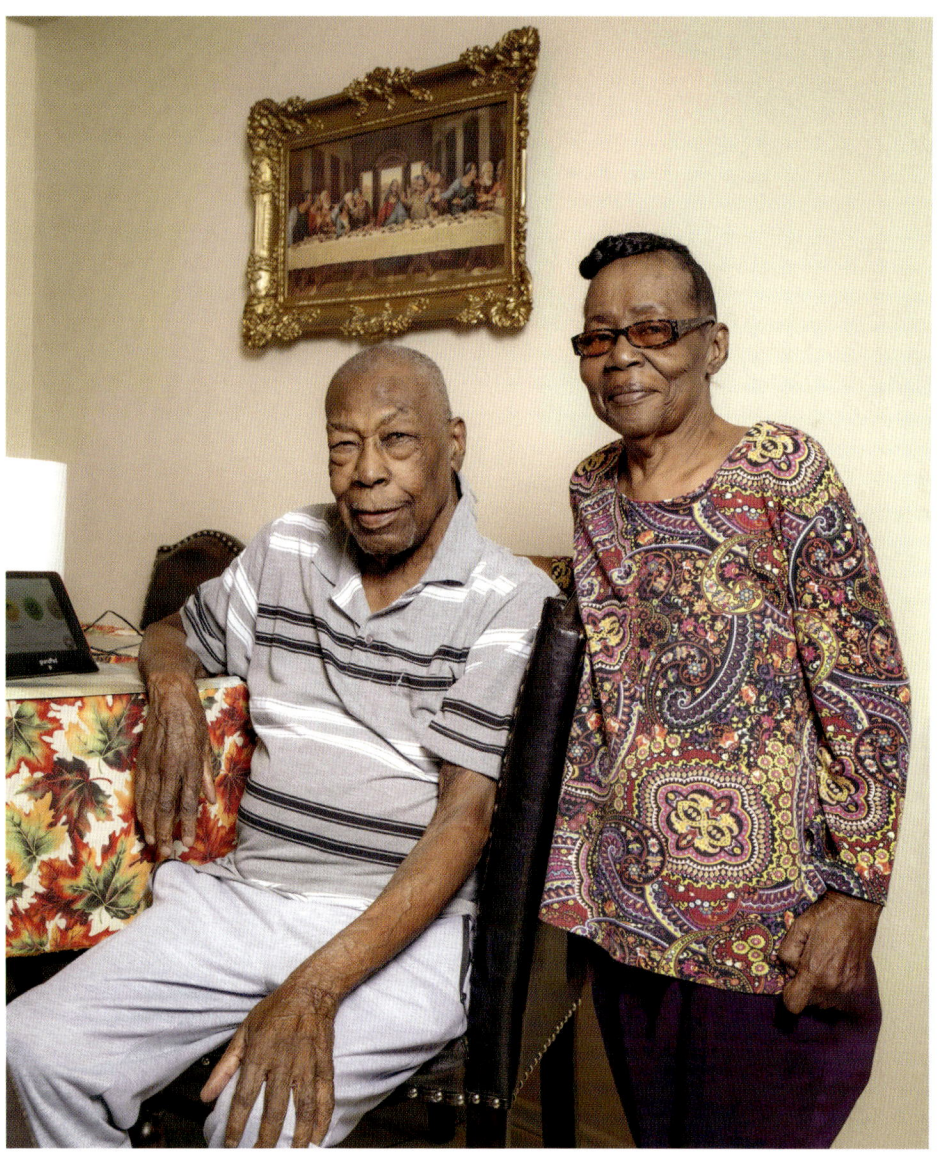

Top: *Nicolas and Family* (2021)
San Antonio, Texas

Bottom: *Bonny Green* (2021)
Houston, Texas

UVALDE

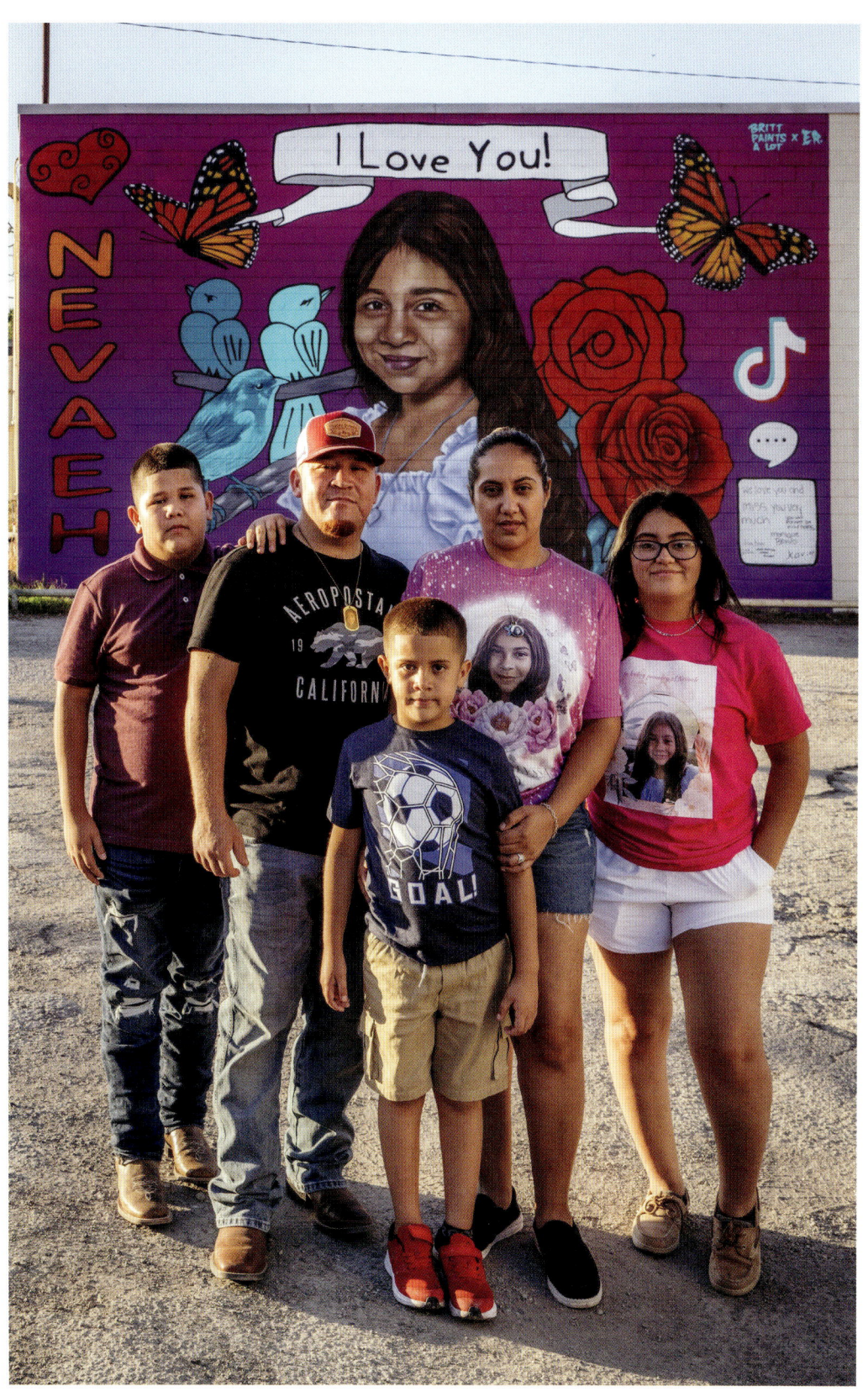

The Family of Nevaeh Bravo: Maria Magdalene Garcia and Juan Julian Bravo, both of Uvalde;
two brothers, Juan Julian Bravo Jr. and Xavier A. Bravo; and sister, Monique Justin Bravo (2022)
Uvalde, Texas

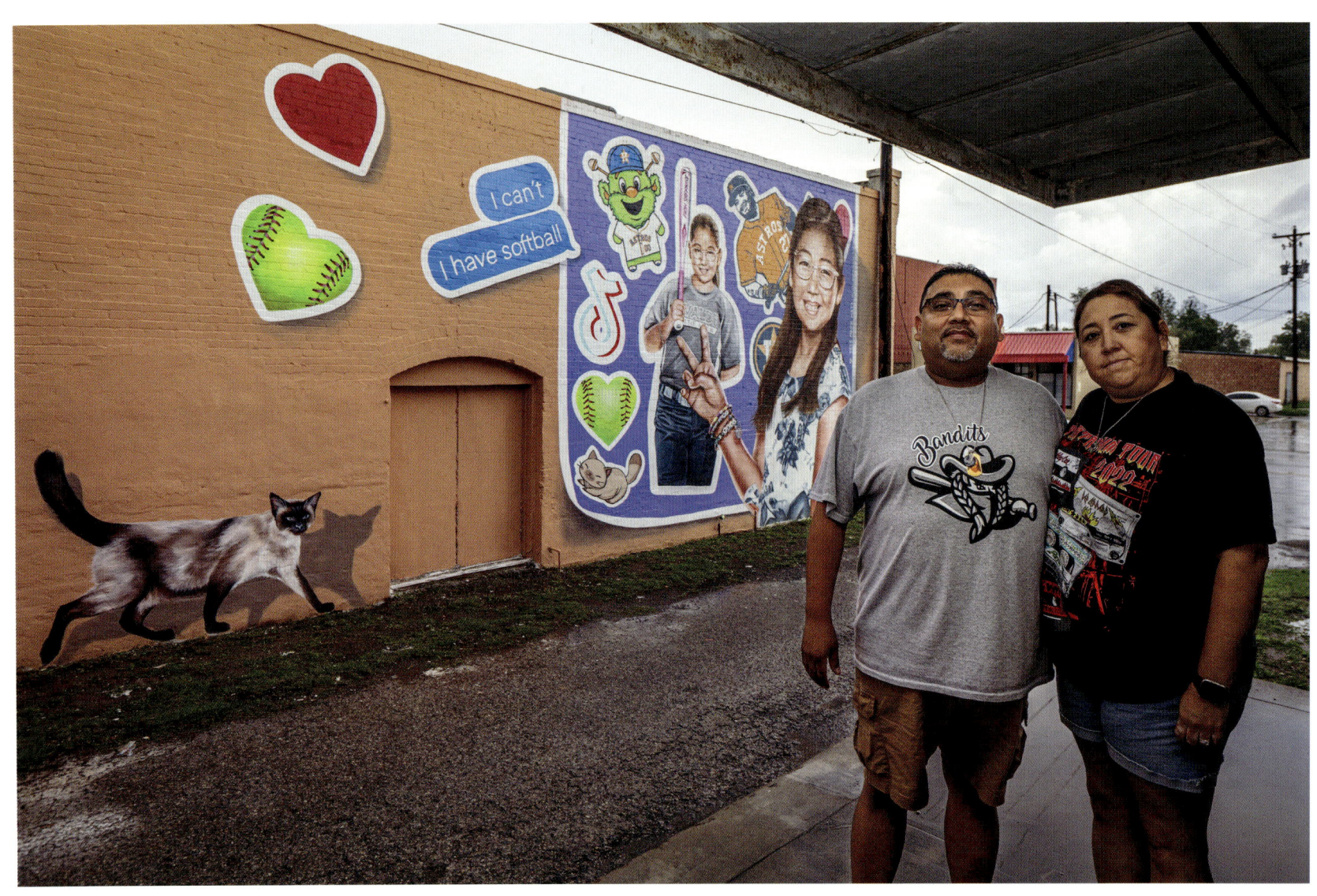

Parents of Tess Mata: Jerry & Veronica Mata (2022)
Uvalde, Texas

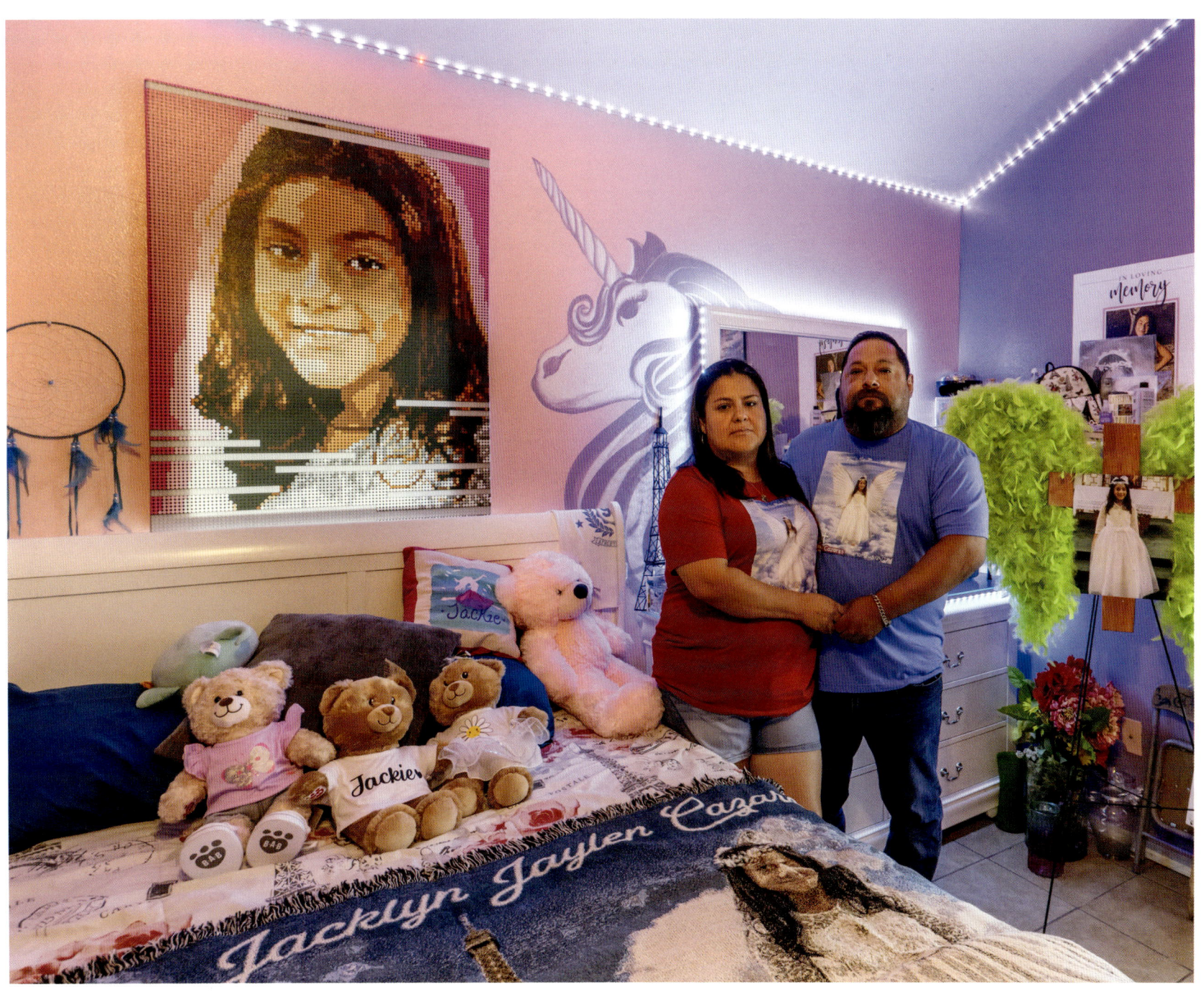

Parents Javier and Gloria Cazares of Jackie Cazaras in her bedroom (2022)
Uvalde, Texas

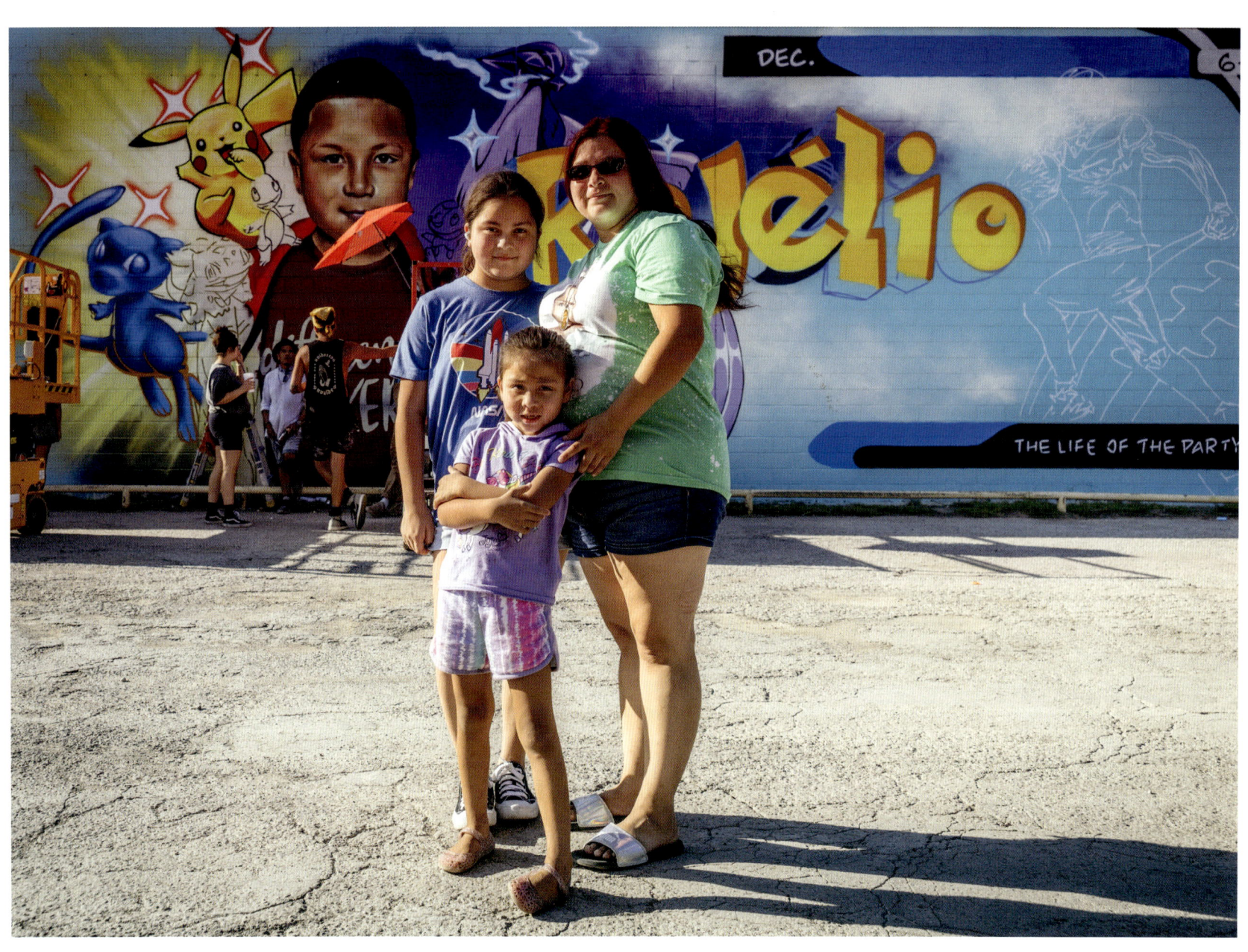

Mother, Evadulia Orta, and sisters, Sara Lee Torres and Mary Fernandez Torres, in front of mural in progress of son Rojelio Torres (2022)
Uvalde, Texas

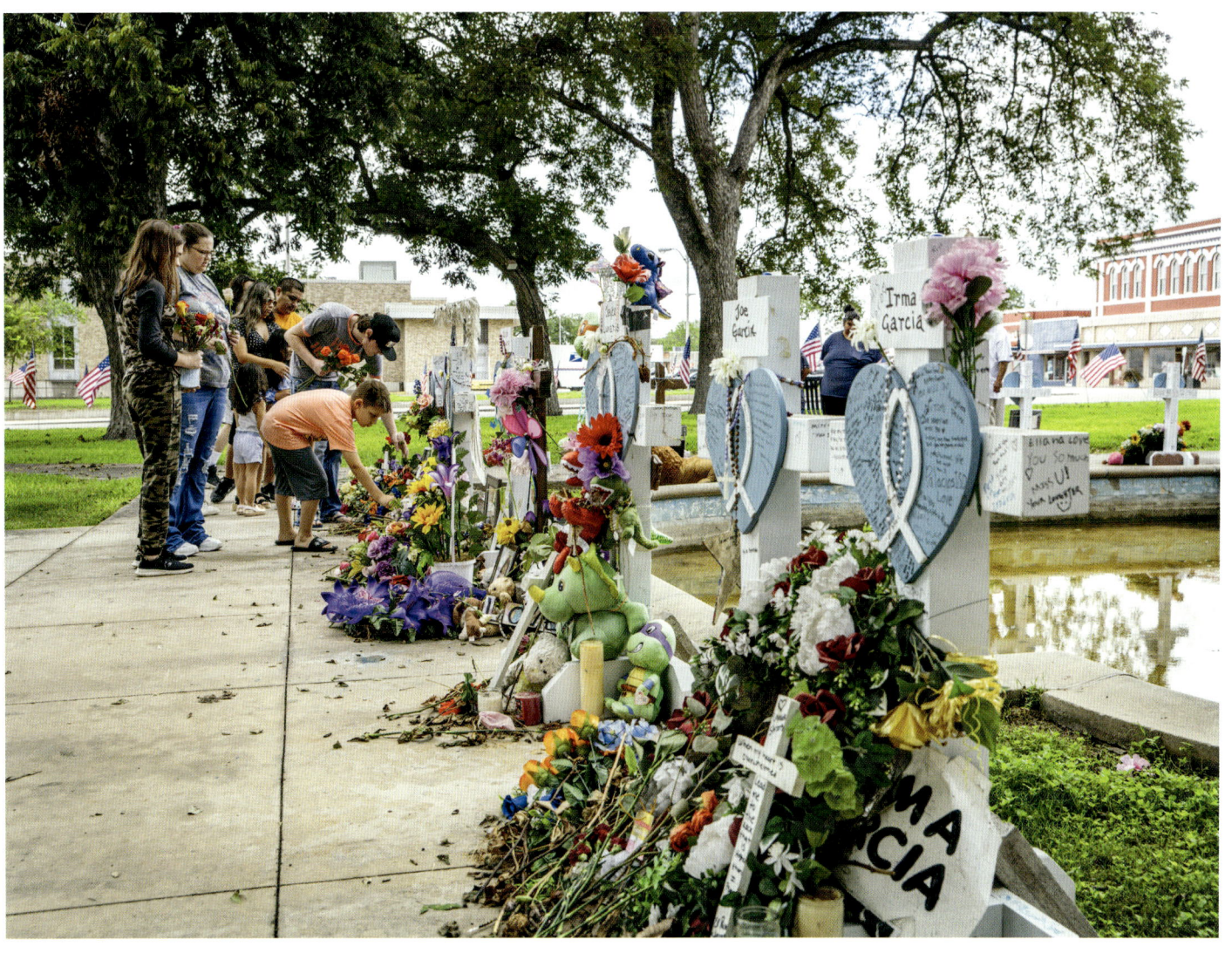

Memorial (2022)
Uvalde, Texas

ARTIST INSIGHTS

by Tomás Ybarra Frausto

Vato

By the early 1980s, renovations, and the creation of a Centro de Artes (Center for the Arts) in the space of the old Farmer's Market now called El Mercado in the west side of downtown became a major destination for tourists and locals. El Mercado transformed into a varied group of shops selling Mexican arts and crafts, clothes, and food carts as well as various restaurants built around fountains and shade trees. Food carts and restaurants were anchored by Mi Tierra, a traditional Mexican restaurant and *panadería* (bakery).

Rendón was in his early photographic career and had already established his habit of walking around spaces where tourists and locals congregated looking for fleeting moments of people engaged in everyday activities. Rendón wanted to capture scenes that could go by unnoticed except for their documentation in photographs.

During one of his frequent visits to El Mercado, Rendón noticed a well-dressed young man zipping around in his low-rider bike. Rendón asked the rider if he could take a picture. "Yes," he answered, "but not with my bike." The young man crouched in his favorite pose that reflected his personality as a proud *vato* (barrio youth). The Vato's self-presentation showed a concern with grooming and clothing reminiscent of the *Pachuco* (Zoot-Suit) period. It included a felt fedora, well-ironed white shirt, with black suspenders, and little chains closing the collar. His accessories included many rings on his fingers, a classy wrist watch, and well-shined lace-up shoes. Looking straight at the viewer, the Vato and his sartorial style project confidence, pride, and self-assurance.

This photograph is from Rendón's early career when he says, "I was still reacting more than planning, when my gaze was wide and my mind open to every possibility."

The Cisco Kid

Rendón always carries his camera when walking, observing, and documenting life in the less traveled streets of San Antonio. One day while leisurely strolling by the Guadalupe Cultural Arts Center in San Antonio's Westside barrio, he stopped when an apparition of an old gentleman with a weathered wrinkled face and hands came into view. The old man was waiting for a bus and agreed to have his picture taken.

Rendón snapped a "street photograph" of the gentleman wearing an improvised, yet carefully considered cowboy outfit. The man's outfit combines a cowboy hat with an armadillo pin on the front brim, a western shirt with two bronco-riding cowboys embroidered above the two shirt pockets. A beige, buckled western belt completes the old man's notion of a cowboy outfit.

Walking with a cane, the elderly man appears proud and aware of self-presentation and making an impression. He is the personification of the Mexican adage *genio y figura hasta la sepultura* (a leopard never changes his spots). One must strive to make a good impression in life until death.

Balloons

As a flâneur, Al Rendón took many photographs while exploring the nooks and crannies of San Antonio, especially the West Side streets around the Guadalupe Arts Center.

On a warm, drizzly 16 de Septiembre, Mexican Independence Day, he photographed the annual Fiestas Patrias Independence Day parade as it passed down Guadalupe Street. The photograph is divided into several planes. In the background, in the upper lefthand corner, the mounted Charros are receding into the distance. In the midplane, a boy with a balloon is standing underneath a school crossing sign. He is standing on the wet concrete with water running down the curbless sidewalk. In the mid-foreground of the photograph a boy in patterned shorts and a dark top is holding hands with his younger sister who is carrying a cluster of balloons. To their right, many parade onlookers are leaning against a building wall to avoid the slight drizzle. One person has an open umbrella, while another gestures with the palm of his left hand.

The dress code for the crowd of parade watchers varies with age; a few women wear dark tops and shorts. The younger boys are in t-shirts, shorts, and Adidas socks; an older man wears jeans and a patterned shirt and an older teenager wears dark pants, with a bandana draped over his undershirt.

This photographic tableau of gesture and movement demonstrates how Rendón engages the viewer's gaze with the optical illusion of a foreground, middleground, and background on the flat surface of a photograph.

Shades of Guadalajara

During a visit to Guadalajara, Mexico, Rendón picked the Guadalajara Food Market as a gathering place where he might encounter a scene worthy of documentation.

As he sauntered around the clothing and textile stalls of the market, he stumbled into a mysterious vision of two people behind a series of Venetian blinds, seeking shade from the blazing sun. Even though the figures are barely visible, you can discern that one is a woman wearing a dress and medium heels, and a man facing her in dress pants and lace-up shoes. With only their shoes visible at the bottom of the Venetian blinds, the woman's arm reaches out to open or further close the blinds.

Are we witnessing a lover's tryst? A conversational meeting of friends? Or two people planning an unknown scenario?

Rendón's photograph shows how photographic images compel us to look and use our imagination to decipher their eloquence.

La Reina

Walking around the streets of Puerto Vallarta, Mexico, Rendón saw a luxury car slowly driving up to a Catholic Church. The driver got out and opened the back door to reveal a young lady in an elegant frothy white gown, wearing full-length, white, opera gloves, with a tiara on her head and carrying a beautiful flower bouquet. To Al, she look like a *Reina* (Queen). La Reina is framed in the opening of the oval door of the car.

The *Quinceañera* fiesta is a rite of passage for Latina young women signaling their passage from adolescence into adulthood and proclaiming that they are ready for marriage and starting a family. These celebrations can be very elaborate, often costing as much as a wedding. They include a church mass and a grand reception with dinner and dancing for family and friends, including eligible young men who connect the Quinceañera to wider social circles of possible boyfriends and perhaps a future husband. In socially conservative Mexican and Mexican-American communities, the Quinceañera fiesta assures that only acceptable young men are in line as future mates and family members of the Quinceañera's family.

Grandma's House

Visual storytelling is a strong point of Rendón's photography. His paternal grandmother lived in Nuevo Laredo, Mexico and he and his father would visit regularly. During one afternoon visit, while his father said goodbye to his mother, Al stepped outside and leaned against his father's car while waiting to drive back to San Antonio. It was early twilight with evening coming on.

Suddenly a little girl appeared walking down the deserted driveway next to Rendón's grandmother's house. She is wearing a white t-shirt and long trousers, and appears to be deep in thought. Al took his camera from the car and took the photograph that has the aura of a story. Perhaps the little girl had been playing with her friends and her mother called her to hurry and come home to supper.

The photograph has an aura of menace. In the mid-foreground we see some empty, coffin-like wooden troughs. Behind the troughs, high up on a wooden post is a gas meter with a little wooden box that says REZIBOZ LUZ (light receiver misspelled). On the right-hand foreground, written on the wooden surface under the darkened window is written MEDIDOR GAZ meaning gas meter.

The driveway is eerily quiet, and the little girl is hurrying home before night descends. Already the shadows are lengthening around the girl. Soon it will be dark, and the creatures of the night and unseen presences will come out. The little girl doesn't want to turn around, she is afraid that someone or something is following her. The child is hurrying home to the warmth of mother and home.

Beach Boom Box

In the 1980s, early in his career having graduated from high school and honing his craft, Rendón spent his Spring Break from working on a trip to the Gulf Coast and the beach at Port Aransas.

Always carrying a camera, Rendón found a spot on the beach, unfolded his umbrella, sat in his beach chair, and watched the world go by. He saw steady streams of girls and other streams of boys, everyone eyeing each other hoping to pair up. Three brawny guys came into view, swinging their arms as they strutted past with hyper-masculine swagger and "macho" self-assurance. The two guys facing the camera wore swimming trunks and the one facing the water wore cut-off blue jeans. The lead guy wore white sneakers and a baseball cap. He was the tallest, most robust, and seemed to show off his muscles in a "muy macho" stance.

What caught Rendón's attention was the shorter fellow looking to the side of the frame, he was carrying a gigantic 1980s boombox. The boombox was almost as big as he was. He played music loudly, hoping to call attention to himself. Rendón captured the trio in a slow motion of walking bodies strutting their stuff.

This early photograph already contains some of the hallmarks of Rendón's evolving genre of street photography, including clarity of image, narrative content, and a focus on ordinary people engaged in daily activities.

Dia De Los Muertos, Azul Barrientos as "La Calavera Catrina"

Azul Barrientos is a notable singer and performance artist. She accompanies herself on a guitar and has a vast repertoire of Mexican and Latin American vernacular music as well as songs anchored in the social movements of the Americas. Barrientos is also a composer, arranger, and jazz musician.

In her concerts, Azul sometimes contextualizes her musical selections with short clips from the Golden Age of Mexican Cinema or from classic North American movies. As an additional element of her performance, Azul wears folkloric costumes themed to the music of each presentation.

For one Día de los Muertos concert Azul wore a full Catrina (skeleton) costume, channeling both the Calavera Catrina (the Skeleton Dandy) made famous by José Guadalupe Posada in his prints, and the fabled Mexican folkloric dresses worn by Frida Kahlo.

Azul changes the plumed hat of Posada's Catrina to a crown of leaves and flowers, supporting a heavily starched Tehuana headdress. She wears a heavily embroidered dress with leaf and flower designs, and wears gold necklaces and earrings. This Calavera is not meant to scare, but to display her elegance.

In her beautiful and elaborate costume, Azul was photographed at an annual event called "Spiritlandia" at La Villita, one of the many festive Día de los Muertos celebrations held throughout the city.

Raúl Salinas

Confined in prison, Salinas wrote the epic poem, "A trip through the Mind Jail" a rumination on the meaning of place in shaping identity, Memories of "La Loma," the barrio in East Austin, Texas where the poet grew up, is a requiem for all Chicano neighborhoods as sites of refuge but also places of spiritual and physical violence.

In prison, the Virgin of Guadalupe tattoo functions like a shield of protection. The strong image of the Virgin of Guadalupe tattooed on the chest of Chicano poet and cultural activist, Raúl Salinas is an indelible site of memories of resistance and affirmation.

 When Raúl Salinas was finally released from prison, he got his college degree, taught at the University of Texas at Austin, opened Resistencia Bookstore, and traveled throughout the country lecturing about the prison experience and reading from his poetic work. He was especially adept at counseling and leading workshops with "at-risk" youth.

The Rendón photograph of Raúl Salinas' full chest image of "La Guadalupana" was done in prison. The aura around the Virgin is not fully inked in on the right side because Salinas was released from the penitentiary at Leavenworth, Kansas before the tattoo was complete.

Halloween

For children, the festivities of Halloween and Día de los Muertos seem like the same celebration, a time to enjoy candy treats and wear scary costumes of skeletons, ghosts, and goblins. Among the most traditional Halloween/ Día de los Muertos celebrations are parades held around the streets of the Alazán Apache Housing Units in the West Side barrio of San Antonio.

People gather to display their original costumes. Many wear masks or have faces painted as *calaveras*. They form parade units and bring homemade instruments like kitchen pots and pans struck with wooden spoons, drums, guitars, and even trumpets. *Matachín* dancers with elaborate feathered headdresses and sequined outfits dance the ancient rituals accompanied by rattles and singling in Spanish and Nahuatl.

The neighbors spectating along the streets are blessed with sage and copal smoke as the dancers hold braziers aloft while winding their way around the many streets of "Los Courts." For some, the parade is a religious pilgrimage, for others it's a collective fiesta celebrating the triumph of life over death. Rendón has many photographs of these yearly rituals. Once as he walked down the alleyways and side streets of the Alazán Courts, he saw a young boy crouching near a trash can. Al approached with his camera. The boy dressed in a simple white tunic and death mask sprang up like a cat, with hands in an attack position and growled ay... ay... ay. Rendón quickly captured the moment as the boy scampered and quietly disappeared into the dark night.

When Rendón developed the image, the boy had posed in front of a wall image of The Virgin of Guadalupe, a perfect visual metaphor for the meaning of Día de los Muertos. The skeleton symbolic of death and the Virgin proclaiming rebirth and regeneration, a potent synthesis of Halloween and Día de los Muertos.

Taco Truck

An example of Rendón's street photography of ordinary folk engaged in ordinary activities, is a photograph taken at the first Rock and Roll Marathon in 2008. As runners passed on their way towards the finish line at the Mission State Park, an elderly couple waved them on with a warm and friendly smile. Rendón's photograph shows the husband inside the food truck giving a military salute, while his wife sitting in front of the truck and smiling broadly, encourages the passing runners.

What caught Rendón's eye was the food truck that was like a visual dictionary of signs, symbols, and visuals reminiscent of the Puro San Antonio way of life. The truck is brightly painted and decorated with an image of the Virgin of Guadalupe enclosed inside a garland of roses with little electric Christmas lights around it. Beneath the Virgin is a sign advertising cold drinks and paletas. An American flag waves on the truck's upper edge with signs for mini-tacos, raspas, nachos, corn cups, and tortas. A large receptacle next to the wife's chair advertises Fiesta with chile pepper, charro hat, and maraca designs. The truck itself with its multiple combinations of visual and written texts depicts a total San Antonio ambiente.

Tía Lupe

In 1986, Kathy Vargas, a well-known San Antonio photographer and head of the Visual Arts Department of the Guadalupe Cultural Arts Center, invited Rendón to participate in a group exhibit commemorating The Virgen of Guadalupe at the Guadalupe Art Gallery.

Venerated throughout the Americas, La Virgen is the patron saint of Mexico. The Virgen's feast day on December 12th is celebrated with ritual Indigenous dances, ceremonies, and special masses. The site of her miraculous apparitions at Mount Tepeyac on the fringe of Mexico City is where a huge Catholic Basilica has been built to accommodate thousands of pilgrims from throughout Mexico and beyond, who yearly converge to bring her gifts and pray for their salvation. The Basilica on the hill of Tepeyac houses the original tilma (Indigenous outer garment) with an impression of the sacred image of the madonna as she appeared to the Indian Juan Diego on the cold winter morning of December 12, 1512.

Speaking in Nahuatl she asked that a temple dedicated to her be erected at the site. Tepeyac is the ancient site sacred to *Tonantzín*, the Pre-Colombian "Earth Mother." Post-conquest, Tonantzín was conflated with the powerful Madonna of Guadalupe, celebrating the Mestizo (Indigenous and Spanish roots of the Mexican people).

In Mexican American communities throughout the United States, the sacred image of Guadalupe is a constant presence in murals, printed sources, and art works in multiple genres. Al Rendón has a series of photographs depicting this miraculous icon.

Rendón's first photograph as an art piece is a touching private moment made public. The image shows his aunt, Tía Lupita in her bedroom as she spreads her hands smoothing her bedspread decorated with a large image of her namesake, La Virgen, Our Lady of Guadalupe.

This photo is significant to Rendón because it documents his Tía who was like a second mother to him. His aunt lived across the street from his family and whenever he was in trouble at home, he would run to her house for refuge. Al could do no wrong in her eyes.

Tía Lupita and Al shared a special bond evident in the reverential quiet feeling captured in this photograph of an indelible moment in time.

Ronald Rocha

As a photographer you never know when an opportunity will present itself for an interesting photograph. One day out of the blue, Rendón's good friend Joe Esparza, who has a restoration shop, called him saying "would you mind coming down here and documenting my artist friend Ronald Rocha who is painting La Virgen on his mother's coffin?"

When Rendón arrived he captured this image of local artist Ronald Rocha as he puts the finishing touches on the casket for his mother's burial. There is a quiet tenderness in Ronald's expression as he quietly works to fulfill his mother's last wish. Preparing to rest in peace, his mother wished to be enfolded in the Virgen's mantle in her journey to the afterworld. Rendón's photograph represents the "void Between life and death."

Flaco Jiménez

This photo of Conjunto great Flaco Jiménez is in the Smithsonian National Portrait Gallery, and it's got an interesting backstory—a combination of equipment failure, on-the-spot inspiration, and determined darkroom work.

He had taken photos of Flaco for his new new album in the Rendón studio for Arhoolie records. It was the first time he had met him, and after the studio session, he decided to catch his performance that night and get some photos of his own.

This was back in 1987. He was working with a film camera, a Nikon, in low light, shooting black and white film.

This particular camera had a mechanical problem. It always worked fine up until just about two thirds end of the roll, and then, without any warning, it sometimes stopped advancing the film. It didn't prevent him from shooting, but any additional shots were double (or triple or whatever) exposures.

He was aware of the problem, and usually he was pretty careful, but his mind was on the challenging lighting conditions and he lost track of his shot count.

By the time he noticed, he had already shot four or five exposures of Flaco on the same frame. But he decided the shots didn't have to be wasted. Because of the low light, it occurred to him that he might be able to salvage something interesting.

So he decided to make one more exposure.

This time, he reframed the shot a bit, so that this last exposure wouldn't precisely overlap the others. He wanted Flaco's face to be outside the boundaries of the earlier exposures, up above them. Then, holding that framing, he waited. And waited.

Finally, Flaco looked his way and he snapped it.

He had the raw material, but it wasn't exactly print-ready. He developed the film, and then he spent a lot of time in the darkroom, dodging and burning different areas of the shot, until he got the print that he wanted. That print—in a wood frame that was hand-carved by his dad—is now in the Smithsonian.

Papá

An intimate, profile headshot of Sr. Enrique Rendón, Al's father, at a table surrounded by woodworking tools. He is totally immersed in carving an image of the Virgin of Guadalupe out of a pliable piece of ash wood.

For forty-three years, Señor Rendón got up at dawn to work at Kelly Air Force Base. After a full day at his job, he would return home to relax by doing what he liked best, carving in wood. He carved Mexican colonial designs on chests, jewelry boxes, tables, and chairs. His sculptured wall pieces were refined and elegant. Mr. Rendón joined an informal circle of other carvers who formed a craftsman's guild to share tools and techniques with time for camaraderie.

Much of Mr. Rendón's work was creating and repairing hand carved furniture. Antique dealers would come to his workshop with furniture that needed repairs and replacements. Perhaps a hand carved leg or a headboard for a bed, he would duplicate the missing carved pieces making the piece of furniture reusable again. Much of his work was for the W.R. Dallas furniture company, a 100-year-old enterprise started in San Antonio that made and sold hand-crafted, western style furniture. For his son Al, Señor Rendón carved elaborate frames that set-off Al's sepia toned colored photographs of San Antonio's people and events. With a defined work ethic, Señor Rendón inspired, understood and supported Al's decision not to go to college, but to follow his heart and seriously pursue photography.

El Curro and Teresa Champion

Scholars often cite San Antonio as the capital of Mexican American culture. The city is recognized for nurturing multiple generations of visual, dramatic, musical, and literary artists in all genres.

San Antonio is famous for many mariachi ensembles and Mexican *baile folklorico* groups. An equally robust tradition of Flamenco music and dance is maintained by guitar virtuoso Willie "El Curro" Champion and his wife, flamenco dancer-singer Teresa Champion. The duo have a dance academy where children and adults have learned the fundamentals of flamenco music and dance.

Teresa and "El Curro" often traveled to Spain, especially to Sevilla and Granada to refresh their repertoire, taking advanced classes from renowned masters of Flamenco music and dance and honing their skills of *canto hondo* (a trance-like deep song) and the traditional and contemporary elements of the many flamenco dance forms.

In Rendón's dual portrait of Willie "El Curro" Champion and his wife Teresa, the couple poses in front of the mirrored wall of their dance academy studio. Reflected in the upper corner of the mirror are many framed photographs of dancers from San Antonio who have gone on to fame in the Flamenco dance world, as well as photographs of Flamenco musicians and dancers from Spain who have come to San Antonio to impart their knowledge of Flamenco traditions. Informally posed, "El Curro" and Teresa Champion appear radiant in the full bloom of life. They look out at the world with a bemused and openly mischievous expression.

Sandra Cisneros

Rendón's informal portrait of Sandra Cisneros shows her taking respite from writing by sitting on the front porch of her house in San Antonio's historic King William District. She is accompanied by her dog Beto and a clay statue of a smaller dog, all watching the world go by.

Sandra Cisneros is a dual citizen of the United States and Mexico, and currently lives in San Miguel de Allende, but she lived in San Antonio for many years. Her works of poetry and fiction are translated into many languages and are part of the contemporary literary canon taught in literature classes worldwide. Rendón's forthright photograph shows a boldly confident modern woman at ease in her role as a consummate literary diva.

David Zamora Casas

Rendón's photograph captures David Zamora Casas in the theatrical environment of his studio. The artist is surrounded by several Day of the Dead calaveras including a Pre-Columbian sculpture of a woman giving birth to a small skull, symbolizing the duality of life and death. The sculpture is placed on a draped table together with a ceramic Catrina.

Under a tower of flowers and holding a large paper rose (flowers remind us of the beauty and brevity of life), Zamora Casas is posed with butterflies fluttering at his throat, in his hair, and other butterflies flying about. Monarch Butterflies make a yearly journey flying from their habitat in Mexico, crossing into the United States to spend time foraging for food and to lay their eggs. The next generations will make it back to their resting habitats in Mexico. The Monarch butterflies are like the thousands of migrants who cross deserts, climb mountains, and forge rivers with the hope of making a better life in the United States.

In his installations and performances, Zamora Casas includes socially concerned themes that reflect a dictum often quoted by his mother: "Tenemos que luchar por lo que es justo y necesario (We must fight for what is just and necessary)."

Jorge Cortez

There are many historic Mexican restaurants in San Antonio, like the humble El Nopal and the elegant Carta Blanca, both now closed. Mi Tierra Restaurant and Panaderia is arguably the most well-known and famous San Antonio eatery throughout the United States.

Many famous people including Hollywood movie stars, nationally recognized musicians, and cultural and sports figures have dined here. It also functions like an eating club for local visual artists, musicians, and literary figures.

Rendón's photograph is of Jorge Cortez, the senior scion of the Cortez restaurant dynasty. Mr. Cortez is always nattily dressed in his signature white hat, white trousers, dress shoes, a blazer, and tie. He is standing in front of one of several murals in the restaurant.

In an oral interview about downtown Mexican-American landmarks, Mr. Cortez recalls the history of Mi Tierra:

"In el Mercado, there were rows of little cafes called Jamaicas, and we had a fruit stand outside our café. Sitting there *en un cajoncito de madera* (on a little wooden box) was like seeing a movie; watching the vendors crossing the street with their carts full of lettuces, potatoes, onions, and all the produce you can imagine. The smells of the Mercado, the aroma of the little Mexican restaurants and cafes like Las Comadres. Also Fred R's Chinese Cafe, the Italian Pizzinis, the Greeks, the whole melting pot of San Antonio meeting there. The cantinas with music blaring out from the juke-box. Las familias, laughing and talking on the wide sidewalks to go make their payments on Saturdays. It was a bustling area of color and sound. "Lo llevo todo en mi corazón."

Today after celebrating its 75th birthday, Mi Tierra at Market Square is open twenty-four hours every day and is always bustling with tourists and locals enjoying Mexican dishes made from family recipes. Mi Tierra has a special ambiente with hanging pinatas, twinkling Christmas tree lights, garlands of *papel picado* (which changes with the season), and hundreds of photographs of loyal customers. Strolling musicians play and sing traditional Mexican folk songs for diners. An in-house photographer captures special occasions like birthdays, holy communions, anniversaries, and other celebrations.

Another unique feature of Mi Tierra is a long Wall of Respect Mural in the restaurant's largest dining area. The mural has portraits of well-known local politicians, businessmen and women, visual artists, musicians, and community activists who contribute to San Antonio's fame as the Cultural Capital of Mexican America. Dining at Mi Tierra is an unforgettable, immersive experience.

Tómas Y Dudley

After retiring from their jobs and living in Manhattan for 20 or so years, Dudley Brooks and Tomás Ybarra-Frausto relocated to San Antonio in 2010. They rented a huge New York style loft on West Commerce Street that they named Casa Cariño. The loft was like a private house museum full of plants, and carefully curated paintings, textiles, and photographs from throughout the Americas. A special component was a major collection of art and literature books shelved on specially made bookcases or stacked in piles in a library area and in the living room area.

Many remember the Friday night seated dinners en casa (at home), Dudley was an excellent cook and Tomás decorated the dining table with candles, flowers, and small art objects from their collections. Guests were a cross-section of San Antonio's literary, arts, and cultural communities. Wine flowed along with spirited conversations.

Rendón's formal portrait shows the compañeros in their living room surrounded by art and artifacts from their collections. Both men wear white-cotton, Cuban and Merida style *guayaberas*. Dudley is seated and wears the traditional four-pocket shirt and Tomás, standing behind Dudley, wears a contemporary version of a pocket-less, ribbon trimmed *guayabera*.

The two compañeros look out at the viewer with the quiet assurance and confidence of a long and lasting friendship. The photograph is enhanced by a lovely carved frame made by Señor Enrique Rendón (Al Rendón's father).

Ángel Rodríguez-Díaz

Born and raised in Puerto Rico and now living and working in San Antonio, visual artist Ángel Rodríguez-Díaz is noted for his oil on canvas photorealist portraits of San Antonio's people, especially members of the local cultural community.

Rodríguez-Díaz makes many preliminary drawings of his portrait subjects posed in his studio with favorite objects they want included in the finished full or half body portrait. After several prolonged sittings, Rodríguez-Díaz unveils the finished oil on canvas portrait that is meticulously painted with panache and an eye for color, composition, and optical pleasure.

Rendón posed Ángel Rodríguez-Díaz in front of one of his self-portraits. The front photograph shows a bemused half-smiling person in a relaxed attitude. The background self-portrait shows Ángel grimacing perhaps suggesting an inner-turmoil.

Late in his career, Ángel Rodríguez-Díaz suffered memory loss and incipient Alzheimer's disease. He passed away in 2023.

WRITER BIOS

Tomás Ybarra Frausto is an independent scholar of Latin American and U.S Latino arts and culture. He was formally the Associate Director of Creativity and Culture at the Rockefeller Foundation. At the Foundation, he developed the Fidecomiso Para La Cultura Mexico – Estado Unidos (the U.S. Mexico Fund for Culture), a bi-national initiative that supported individual artists, humanities scholars, and institutions creating new paradigms for mutual understanding, cooperation, and reciprocal knowledge sharing between the two countries. Prior to joining the Rockefeller Foundation, Dr. Ybarra Frausto was a tenured professor at Stanford University in the Department of Spanish and Portuguese. He also taught at UC San Diego and the University of Washington. He served as chair of the Mexican Museum in San Francisco and the Smithsonian Council, and has written and published extensively on Latin American and U.S. Latino arts and culture. In 1998, Dr. Ybarra Frausto was awarded the Henry Medal by the Smithsonian Institution, and in 2007, the Mexican government bestowed "The Order of the Aztec Eagle" medal upon him, citing his life work in fostering cultural understanding between the United States and Mexico through the National Association of Chicano Studies. In 2010, the National Association of Latino Arts and Culture awarded Dr. Ybarra Frausto a Lifetime Achievement Award for his contributions to the fields of Latino arts and cultures.

Eduardo Díaz is a 40-year veteran of the Latino cultural field. He currently serves as Acting Deputy Director of the National Museum of the American Latino. The Museum supports research, exhibitions, public and educational programs, digital content, publications, and collections about the U.S. Latino experience, and in June 2022, opened the Molina Family Latino Gallery. Díaz is the former Executive Director of the National Hispanic Cultural Center in Albuquerque, and previously served as the City of San Antonio's first Director of Arts and Culture. Díaz has a law degree from University of California, Davis, and bachelor's degree in Latin American Studies from San Diego State University.

Bruce Shackelford is the Texas History Curator for the Witte Museum in San Antonio, Texas. Shackelford has curated dozens of exhibitions dealing with the history of the American west and Texas art for over 24 years. He was the curator for the creation of the Robert J. and Helen C. Kleberg South Texas Heritage Center at the Witte Museum in the historic Centennial Hall on the Witte grounds. During his time at the Witte Shackelford has written two books, *Photography on the South Texas Frontier: Images from the Witte Museum Collection*, and *The Wests of Texas: Cattle Ranching Entrepreneurs*. He has written for a number of other books and publications as well most recently *King Ranch: A Legacy in Art* for Texas A&M University Press.

Bruce Shackelford served as Curator-Director of the Creek Council House National Landmark in the 1970s and 1980s. He then worked as an art dealer until the late 1980s when he returned to the museum world as guest curator at the Witte Museum for the exhibition *Thundering Hooves,* which toured nationally. Shackelford started working on the television series Antiques Roadshow for WGBH Harvard Public Television in the mid 1990s. He has participated on the show for 28 seasons as of summer 2023.

Juan Tejeda is a musician, writer, arts administrator, educator, activist and publisher. In 2016 he retired from Palo Alto College in San Antonio, Texas where he was a professor of Mexican American Studies and Music. From 1980-1998, he was the Xicano Music Program Director for the Guadalupe Cultural Arts Center where among his many duties he founded and directed the internationally renowned Tejano Conjunto Festival en San Antonio which will celebrate its 41st anniversary in 2023. He is the button accordionist for the Conjunto Aztlan; and he and his wife, Anisa Onofre, are the co-owners/publishers of Aztlan Libre Press. He continues to work with the Guadalupe Cultural Arts Center as a consultant and mentor in producing the Tejano Conjunto Festival.